TOZER ON THE HOLY SPIRIT

TOZER FOR TODAY

DEVOTIONAL SERIES

TOZER
ON THE
HOLY
SPIRIT

A 366-DAY DEVOTIONAL

COMPILED BY MARILYNNE E. FOSTER

CHRISTIAN PUBLICATIONS, INC.
CAMP HILL, PENNSYLVANIA

Christian Publications, Inc.
3825 Hartzdale Drive, Camp Hill, PA 17011
www.cpi-horizon.com

Faithful, biblical publishing since 1883

Tozer on the Holy Spirit
ISBN: 0-87509-861-4
LOC Catalog Card Number: 99-080097

00   01   02   03   04   5   4   3   2   1

Unless otherwise indicated,
Scripture taken from the
Holy Bible: King James Version

PREFACE

*A*iden Wilson Tozer as born April 21, 1897, on a small farm among the spiny ridges of Western Pennsylvania. Within a few short years, Tozer, as he preferred to be called, would earn the reputation and title "twentieth-century prophet."

When he was fifteen years old, Tozer's family moved to Akron, Ohio. One afternoon as he walked home from his job at Goodyear, he overheard a street preacher say, "If you don't know how to be saved . . . just call on God." When he got home, he climbed the narrow stairway to the attic where, heeding the preacher's advice, Tozer was launched into a lifelong pursuit of God.

In 1919, without formal education, he was called to pastor a small storefront church in Nutter Fort, West Virginia. That humble beginning thrust him and his wife, Ada, into a forty-four-year ministry with The Christian and Missionary Alliance.

Thirty-one of those years were spent at Chicago's Southside Alliance Church. The congregation, captivated by Tozer's preaching, grew from eighty to 800.

His humor, written and spoken, has been compared to that of Will Rogers—honest and homespun. Congregations could one moment be swept by gales of laughter and the next sit in a holy hush.

But Tozer's forte was his prayer life which often found him walking the aisles of a sanctuary or lying face down on the floor. Tozer biographer James L. Snyder notes that "his preaching as well as his writings were but extensions of his prayer life." An earlier biographer and confidante, David J. Fant, wrote, "He spent more time on his knees than at his desk."

Tozer's final years of pastoral ministry were at Avenue Road Church in Toronto, Canada. On May 12, 1963, his pursuit of God was realized when he died of a heart attack at age 66. In a small cemetery in Akron, Ohio, his tombstone bears this simple epitaph: "A Man of God."

As Tozer once affirmed, "The Holy Spirit makes a difference!"

Our prayer for these pages is that they and He will make a difference in your life.

Please note:

Each passage cited is followed by a code and number which represent the name of the book and the page from which the quote was taken. A list of the reference codes and a Scripture index are provided in the back of the book.

Marilynne E. Foster holds a B.A. in Communication from Azusa Pacific University. The compiler of three other books, she serves in the editing and marketing departments of Christian Publications and is the editor of the Jaffray Collection of Missionary Portraits, now more than twenty-five volumes. The Fosters live in Mechanicsburg, Pennsylvania.

January

WHAT THE LORD MAY EXPECT OF ME

Put off concerning . . . [that] which is corrupt . . . and be renewed in the spirit of your mind.

—Ephesians 4:22-23

𝒥or some of us last year was one in which we did not acquit ourselves very nobly as Christians, considering the infinite power available to us through the indwelling Spirit. . . .

The man of illuminated mind will learn from his mistakes, yes even from his sins. If his heart is trusting and penitent, he can be a better man next year for last year's fault—but let him not return again to folly.

Repentance should be radical and thorough, and the best repentance for a wrong act, as Fenelon said, is not to do it again. . . .

Brother Lawrence expressed the highest moral wisdom when he testified that if he stumbled and fell he turned at once to God and said, "O Lord, this is what You may expect of me if You leave me to myself." He then accepted forgiveness, thanked God and gave himself no further concern about the matter. WOS095-096

"Tell the backslider," says the Lord, "I am married unto him." Was there ever a tenderer message? SAN058

TRUTH MADE PRACTICAL

As Christ was raised up from the dead by the glory of the Father, even so we also should walk in newness of life.

—Romans 6:4

$\mathcal{W}$e who pride ourselves on our orthodoxy . . . have in recent years committed a costly blunder. . . . Our blunder (or shall we frankly say our sin?) has been to neglect the doctrine of the Spirit to a point where we virtually deny Him His place in the Godhead.

This denial has not been by open doctrinal statement, for we have clung closely enough to the biblical position wherever our creedal pronouncements are concerned. Our formal creed is sound; *the breakdown is in our working creed.*

This is not a trifling distinction. A doctrine has practical value only as far as it is prominent in our thoughts and makes a difference in our lives. POM060

> *Truth consists not in correct doctrine, but in correct doctrine* plus the inward enlightenment of the Holy Spirit . . . *Deity indwelling men!* . . . . *No man has experienced rightly the power of Christian belief until he has known this for himself as a living reality.* POM084, 100

THE HOLY SPIRIT: PRESENT OR ABSENT?

And grieve not the holy Spirit of God, whereby ye are sealed unto the day of redemption.

—Ephesians 4:30

$\mathcal{I}$n most Christian churches the Spirit is quite entirely overlooked. Whether He is present or absent makes no real difference to anyone. Brief reference is made to Him in the doxology and the benediction. Further than that He might as well not exist. . . .

Our neglect of the doctrine of the blessed Third Person has had and is having serious consequences. For doctrine is dynamite. It must have emphasis sufficiently sharp to detonate it before its power is released. . . .

The doctrine of the Spirit is buried dynamite. Its power awaits discovery and use by the Church. The power of the Spirit will not be given to any mincing assent to pneumatological truth. The Holy Spirit cares not at all whether we write Him into our creeds in the back of our hymnals; He awaits our *emphasis*. POM060-061

> *[The Holy Spirit] loves us so much that when we insult Him, He is grieved; when we ignore Him, He is grieved; when we resist Him, He is grieved; and when we doubt Him, He is grieved.* COU052

WALK IN THE SPIRIT

*There is therefore now no con-
demnation to them . . . who walk
not after the flesh, but after the
Spirit.*

—Romans 8:1

*T*he idea of the Spirit held by the average church member is so vague as to be nearly nonexistent. When he thinks of the matter at all he is likely to try to imagine a nebulous substance like a wisp of invisible smoke which is said to be present in churches and to hover over good people when they are dying. . . .

Now, how should we think of the Spirit? A full answer might well run to a dozen volumes. We can at best only point to the "gracious unction from above" and hope that the reader's own desire may provide the necessary stimulus to urge him on to know the blessed Third Person for himself.

If I read aright the record of Christian experience through the years, those who most enjoyed the power of the Spirit have had the least to say about Him by way of attempted definition. The Bible saints who walked in the Spirit never tried to explain Him. POM061-062

> *We will never understand the Holy Spirit so long as we terminate our thought upon Him. The Scriptures always lead us on beyond every subjective experience to the person of the Lord Jesus Christ Himself.* HS544

KNOWING BY EXPERIENCE

Wash you, make you clean; put away the evil of your doings from before mine eyes; cease to do evil.

—Isaiah 1:16

$\mathcal{I}$n post-biblical times many who were filled and possessed by the Spirit were by the limitations of their literary gifts prevented from telling us much about Him. They had no gifts for self-analysis but lived from within in uncritical simplicity.

To them the Spirit was One to be loved and fellowshiped the same as the Lord Jesus Himself. They would have been lost completely in any metaphysical discussion of the nature of the Spirit, but they had no trouble in claiming the power of the Spirit for holy living and fruitful service.

This is as it should be.

Personal experience must always be first in real life. . . . Knowledge by acquaintance is always better than mere knowledge by description, and the first does not presuppose the second nor require it. POM062-063

Happy is the man who will not allow himself to be diverted and distracted, but having emptied and cleansed his heart, will stand waiting . . . for Christ to descend, fill and ever remain as the glorious indweller of the soul. SAN037

KNOWING
OR KNOWING
ABOUT?

*I*n religion more than in any other field of human experience a sharp distinction must always be made between *knowing about* and *knowing*. The distinction is the same as between knowing about food and actually eating it. . . . A man can remain spiritually dead while knowing all the historic facts of Christianity.

"This is life eternal, that they might know thee the only true God, and Jesus Christ, whom thou hast sent" (John 17:3). We have but to introduce one extra word into this verse to see how vast is the difference between knowing about and knowing. "This is life eternal, that they might know *about* thee the only true God, and Jesus Christ, whom thou hast sent."

That one word makes all the difference between life and death. . . .

We dare not conclude that because we learn about the Spirit we for that reason actually know Him. Knowing Him comes only by a personal encounter with the Holy Spirit Himself. POM063-064

The Spirit is an imperative necessity. Only the
Eternal Spirit can do eternal deeds. MDP066

WHO IS THE HOLY SPIRIT?

But the Comforter, which is the Holy Ghost, whom the Father will send in my name, he shall teach you all things.

—John 14:26

*H*ow shall we think of the Spirit? The Bible and Christian theology agree to teach that He is a Person, endowed with every quality of personality, such as emotion, intellect and will. He knows, He wills, He loves; He feels affection, antipathy and compassion. He thinks, sees, hears and speaks and performs any act of which personality is capable.

One quality belonging to the Holy Spirit, of great interest and importance to every seeking heart, is penetrability. He can penetrate mind; He can penetrate another spirit, such as the human spirit. He can achieve complete penetration of and actual intermingling with the human spirit. He can invade the human heart and make room for Himself without expelling anything essentially human. The integrity of the human personality remains unimpaired. Only moral evil is forced to withdraw. POM065

> *By nature we are in correspondence with sin; but by union with Christ in His death and resurrection and by the incoming and indwelling of the Holy Spirit we are out of correspondence with it . . . [and] dead alike to its presence and power.* CDL166

TWO SHALL BECOME ONE

A new heart also I will give you, and a new spirit will I put within you . . . and I will give you an heart of flesh.

—Ezekiel 36:26

*H*ow can one personality enter another? The candid reply would be simply that we do not know, but a near approach to an understanding may be made by a simple analogy borrowed from the old devotional writers of several hundred years ago.

We place a piece of iron in a fire and blow up the coals. At first we have two distinct substances, iron and fire. When we insert the iron in the fire we achieve the penetration of the iron and we have not only the iron in the fire but the fire in the iron as well. . . . Two distinct substances . . . have co-mingled and interpenetrated to a point where the two have become one.

In some such manner does the Holy Spirit penetrate our spirits. In the whole experience we remain our very selves. There is no destruction of substance. Each remains a separate being as before; the difference is that now the Spirit penetrates and fills our personalities and we are *experientially one with God.* POM066

The Christian . . . is in correspondence with God. He walks "in newness of life." . . . Indeed, the deeper walk of the Holy Spirit in sanctification quickens every spiritual sense. CDL167

THE HOLY SPIRIT IS GOD

I will put my spirit within you . . . and ye shall keep my judgments, and do them.

—Ezekiel 36:27

*H*ow shall we think of the Holy Spirit? The Bible declares that He is God. Every quality belonging to Almighty God is freely attributed to Him. All that God is, the Spirit is declared to be. The Spirit of God is one with and equal to God just as the spirit of a man is equal to and one with the man. . . .

The historic Church when she formulated her "rule of faith" boldly wrote into her confession her belief in the Godhood of the Holy Ghost. The Apostles' Creed witnesses to faith in the Father and in the Son and in the Holy Ghost and makes no difference between the three. The fathers who composed the Nicene Creed testified in a passage of great beauty to their faith in the deity of the Spirit:

> And I believe in the Holy Ghost, the Lord and Giver of life, who proceedeth from the Father and the Son; who with the Father and the Son together is worshiped and glorified. POM066-067

> *[A]ll that the Son is the Holy Ghost is, and all that the Father is the Holy Ghost is, and the Holy Ghost is in His Church.* HTB020

TRINITY IN UNITY

It is expedient for you that I go away: for if I go not away, the Comforter will not come unto you.

—John 16:7

$\mathcal{A}$ mong the important writings which appeared [in the fourth century] is the Athanasian Creed. . . . It was written as an attempt to state in as few words as possible what the Bible teaches about the nature of God; and this it has done with a comprehensiveness and precision hardly matched anywhere in the literature of the world. Here are a few quotations bearing on the deity of the Holy Ghost:

There is one Person of the Father, another of the Son: and another of the Holy Ghost.

But the Godhead of the Father, of the Son, and of the Holy Ghost, is all one: the Glory equal, the Majesty co-eternal.

And in this Trinity none is afore, or after other: none is greater, or less than another;

But the whole three Persons are co-eternal together: and co-equal. So that in all things, as is aforesaid: the Unity in Trinity, and Trinity in Unity is to be worshiped. POM067-068

The Holy Spirit came to carry the evidence of Christianity from the books of apologetics into the human heart. HTB028-029

THE GODHEAD OF THE SPIRIT

And I will pray the Father, and he shall give you another Comforter . . . even the Spirit of truth.

—John 14:16-17

$\mathcal{I}$n her sacred hymnody the Church has freely acknowledged the Godhead of the Spirit and in her inspired song she has worshiped Him with joyous abandon. Some of our hymns to the Spirit have become so familiar that we tend to miss their true meaning. . . .

In the poetical works of Frederick Faber I have found a hymn to the Holy Spirit which I would rank among the finest ever written . . . :

> Fountain of Love! Thyself true God!
>   Who through eternal days
> From Father and from Son hast flowed
>   In uncreated ways!
>
> I dread Thee, Unbegotten Love!
>   True God! sole Fount of Grace!
> And now before Thy blessed throne
>   My sinful self abase.
>
> O Light! O Love! O very God
>   I dare no longer gaze
> Upon Thy wondrous attributes
>   And their mysterious ways. POM068-069

[T]he Holy Spirit is a Being dwelling in another mode of existence. . . . He nevertheless exists as surely as you exist. HTB011

THE GODHEAD NEVER WORKS SEPARATELY

We will come unto him, and make our abode with him.

—John 14:23

*W*hat we have in the Christian doctrine of the Holy Spirit is Deity present among us. He is not God's messenger only; *He is God.* He is God in contact with His creatures, doing in them and among them a saving and renewing work.

The Persons of the Godhead never work separately. We dare not think of them in such a way as to "divide the substance." Every act of God is done by all three Persons. God is never anywhere present in one Person without the other two. He cannot divide Himself.

Where the Spirit is, there also is the Father and the Son. "We will come unto him, and make our abode with him" (John 14:23). For the accomplishment of some specific work one Person may for the time be more prominent than the others are, but never is He alone. God is altogether present wherever He is present at all.
POM070

> *[Jesus] is the epitome of love, kindliness, geniality, warm attractiveness and sweetness. And that is exactly what the Holy Ghost is, for He is the Spirit of the Father and the Son.* HTB021

UNITY IN WORSHIP IF NOT IN DOCTRINE

When thou saidst, Seek ye my face; my heart said unto thee, Thy face, LORD, will I seek.

—Psalm 27:8

*C*hristianity is rarely found pure. Apart from Christ and His inspired apostles probably no believer or company of believers in the history of the world has ever held the truth in total purity.

One great saint believed that the truth is so vast and mighty that no one is capable of taking it all in, and that it requires the whole company of ransomed souls properly to reflect the whole body of revealed truth. . . .

The Spirit always says the same thing to whomsoever He speaks and altogether without regard to passing doctrinal emphases or theological vogues. He flashes the beauty of Christ upon the wondering heart, and the awed spirit receives it with a minimum of interference. BAM076-077

> *No single doctrinal principle is important enough to displace the Lord Jesus Christ Himself as the one name that alone should dominate His Church. . . . It is not union but unity that God wants, and that is a matter of life and love.* CTBC, Vol. 5/155

A BUSH WITH NO FIRE!

True worshippers shall worship the Father in spirit and in truth: for the Father seeketh such to worship him.

—John 4:23

*W*hatever direction the theological wind may set there are two things of which we may be certain: One is that God will not leave Himself without a witness. . . . Saving truth will never be completely hidden from the sight of men. The poor in spirit, the penitent, will always find Christ close at hand ready to save them.

The other is that the Holy Spirit is the true conservator of orthodoxy and will invariably say the same thing to meek and trusting souls. Illuminated hearts are sure to agree at the point where the light falls.

Our only real danger is that we may grieve the blessed Spirit into silence and so be left to the mercy of our intellects. . . . We'll have the bush, pruned and trimmed and properly cultivated, but in the bush there will be no fire. BAM078-079

> *Mere wisdom . . . [makes] us hard and cold, but wisdom set on fire with love and energized by power [through the Holy Spirit] will enable us to bless the world.* HS496

KNEEL, ADORE AND OBEY

I am the way, the truth, and the life: no man cometh unto the Father, but by me.... If ye love me, keep my commandments.

—John 14:6, 15

*T*ruth is forever the same, but modes and emphases and interpretations vary. It is a cheering thought that Christ can adapt Himself to any race or age or people. He will give life and light to any man or woman anywhere in the world regardless of doctrinal emphasis or prevailing religious customs, provided that man or woman takes Him as He is and trusts Him without reservation.

The Spirit never bears witness to an argument about Christ, but He never fails to witness to a proclamation of Christ crucified, dead and buried, and now ascended to the right hand of the Majesty on high.

The conclusion of the matter is that we should not assume that we have all the truth and that we are mistaken in nothing. Rather we should kneel in adoration before the pierced feet of Him who is the Truth and honor Him by humble obedience to His words. BAM079

> *The first [principle and condition of divine guidance] is a surrendered spirit. Next, there must be a readiness to obey. He will not give us light unless we mean to follow it.* WCC77

SEEING THINGS AS THEY ARE

And John bare record, saying, I saw the Spirit descending from heaven like a dove, and it abode upon him.

—John 1:32

*J*ohn the Baptist possessed . . . the right kind of vision, a true spiritual discernment. He could see things as they were.

The Holy Spirit came like a dove, descended like a dove, putting down His pink feet and disappearing into the heart of the Son of God.

I wonder out of all those crowds who saw the Holy Ghost come?

Only John the Baptist. I do not think anyone else had the kind of vision that was necessary to see Him. . . .

John the Baptist was a man of vision in the midst of men who had no vision. He knew where he was in his times. The drift of the hour or the trend of the times in religion would never carry him away. CES132-133

> *To serve the present age,*
> *My calling to fulfill—*
> *Oh, may it all my powers engage*
> *To do my Master's will.* HCL358

DYING TO LIVE

> *Know ye not, that to whom ye yield yourselves servants to obey, his servants ye are to whom ye obey....?*
>
> —Romans 6:16

$\mathcal{F}$or all God's good will toward us He is unable to grant us our heart's desires till all our desires have been reduced to one. When we have dealt with our carnal ambitions; when we have trodden upon the lion and adder of the flesh, have trampled the dragon of self-love under our feet and have truly reckoned ourselves to have died unto sin, then and only then can God raise us to newness of life and fill us with His blessed Holy Spirit.

It is easy to learn the doctrine of personal revival and victorious living; it is quite another thing to take our cross and plod on to the dark and bitter hill of self-renunciation. Here many are called and few are chosen. BAM010

> *The meaning of self-denial is not an infliction of personal torment nor penance, but it is simply the giving up of the very principle of living for ourselves. It is completely changing the direction of our being and will, so that no longer in any sense do we act with reference to how anything will affect us, but our one thought is how it will affect God or others.* WL128

ANOTHER NATURE

And you ... hath he reconciled in the body of his flesh through death, to present you holy and unblameable and unreproveable.

—Colossians 1:21-22

$\mathcal{F}$or the moral unlikeness between man and God the Bible has a word, alienation, and the Holy Spirit presents a frightful picture of this alienation as it works itself out in human character.

Fallen human nature is precisely opposite to the nature of God as revealed in Jesus Christ. Because there is no moral likeness there is no communion, hence the sense of physical distance, the feeling that God is far away in space. . . .

The new birth makes us partakers of the divine nature. There the work of undoing the dissimilarity between us and God begins. From there it progresses by the sanctifying operation of the Holy Spirit till God is satisfied. BAM121-122

> *The only remedy for human nature is to destroy it and receive instead the divine nature. God does not improve man. He crucifies the natural life with Christ and creates the new man in Christ Jesus.* DHE/October013

PRACTICE THE PRESENCE

I have set the LORD always before me: because he is at my right hand, I shall not be moved.

—Psalm 16:8

*T*he scriptural way to see things is to set the Lord always before us, put Christ in the center of our vision, and if Satan is lurking around he will appear on the margin only and be seen as but a shadow on the edge of the brightness. It is always wrong to reverse this—to set Satan in the focus of our vision and push God out to the margin. Nothing but tragedy can come of such inversion.

The best way to keep the enemy out is to keep Christ in. The sheep need not be terrified by the wolf; they have but to stay close to the shepherd. . . .

The instructed Christian . . . will practice the presence of God and never allow himself to become devil-conscious. BAM043

> *Brother Lawrence . . . wouldn't pick up a straw from the ground but for the love of God. When he was dying . . . [h]e said, ". . . When I die I won't change my occupation. I have just been worshiping God for 40 years on earth, and when I get to heaven I'll just keep right on doing what I am doing."* COU116

I AM THE SUM OF MY THOUGHTS

Casting down imaginations ... and bringing into captivity every thought to the obedience of Christ.

—2 Corinthians 10:5

*A*nyone who wishes to check on his true spiritual condition may do so by noting what his voluntary thoughts have been over the last hours or days. What has he thought about when free to think of what he pleased? Toward what has his inner heart turned when it was free to turn where it would?

When the bird of thought was let go did it fly out like the raven to settle upon floating carcasses or did it like the dove circle and return again to the ark of God? Such a test is easy to run, and if we are honest with ourselves we can discover not only what we are but what we are going to become.

We'll soon be the sum of our voluntary thoughts. BAM046-047

> *It is possible to have our whole life so possessed by the Holy Spirit that our very thoughts and intuitions will come to us in quietness and simplicity, with the consciousness that they have been touched by His thoughts and illumined by His light, that we are walking continually with our Father, and receiving constantly the testimony that we please God.* CTBC, Vol. 2/093

THE HABIT
OF HOLY
THOUGHT

The carnal mind is enmity against God: for it is not subject to the law of God, neither indeed can be.

—Romans 8:7

*E*very normal person can determine what he will think about. Of course the troubled or tempted man may find his thoughts somewhat difficult to control and even while he is concentrating upon a worthy object, wild and fugitive thoughts may play over his mind like heat lightning on a summer evening. These are likely to be more bothersome than harmful and in the long run do not make much difference one way or another.

The best way to control our thoughts is to offer the mind to God in complete surrender. The Holy Spirit will accept it and take control of it immediately. Then it will be relatively easy to think on spiritual things, especially if we train our thought by long periods of daily prayer. Long practice in the art of mental prayer (that is, talking to God inwardly as we work or [relax]) will help to form the habit of holy thought. BAM047

> *This is what the Holy Spirit brings to us, the vision of the Lord, power to see divine things as God sees them. . . . The Spirit also thinks in us by giving us divine instincts, intuitions and enablements.* HS571-572

WORMY FRUIT?

For promotion cometh neither from the east, nor from the west, nor from the south. But God is the judge.

—Psalm 75:6-7

*G*od may allow His servant to succeed when He has disciplined him to a point where he does not need to succeed to be happy. The man who is elated by success and cast down by failure is still a carnal man. At best his fruit will have a worm in it.

God will allow His servant to succeed when he has learned that success does not make him dearer to God nor more valuable in the total scheme of things. We cannot buy God's favor with crowds or converts or new missionaries sent out or Bibles distributed. All these things can be accomplished without the help of the Holy Spirit. . . .

Our great honor lies in being just what Jesus was and is. . . . What greater glory could come to any man? BAM059

> *Oh, to be like Thee! blessed Redeemer,*
> *This is my constant longing and prayer.*
> *Gladly I'll forfeit all of earth's treasures,*
> *Jesus, Thy perfect likeness to wear.*
>
> *Oh, to be like Thee! Oh, to be like Thee,*
> *Blessed Redeemer, pure as Thou art!*
> *Come in Thy sweetness, come in Thy fullness;*
> *Stamp Thine own image deep on my heart.* HCL231

LIGHT
WITHOUT
SIGHT

The god of this world hath blinded the minds of them which believe not, lest the light . . . should shine unto them.

—2 Corinthians 4:4

$\mathcal{S}$atan has no fear of the light as long as he can keep his victims sightless. The uncomprehending mind is unaffected by truth. The intellect of the hearer may grasp saving knowledge while yet the heart makes no moral response to it.

A classic example of this is seen in the story of Benjamin Franklin and George Whitefield. . . . Whitefield talked with Franklin personally about his need of Christ and promised to pray for him. Years later Franklin wrote rather sadly that the evangelist's prayers must not have done any good, for he was still unconverted.

No one could doubt the intellectual brilliance of Franklin and certainly Whitefield preached the whole truth; yet nothing came of it. Why? The only answer is that Franklin had light without sight. He never saw the Light of the World. . . . The gospel is light but only the Spirit can give sight. BAM062-063

True faith is not believing in words merely, even divine words, but believing ON the Lord Jesus Christ. CTBC, Vol. 1/079

PURITY OF TRUTH DETERMINED BY MORALS

Finally, brethren, whatsoever things are true . . . think on these things.

—Philippians 4:8

*T*he light has shone upon men and nations, and (God be praised) it has shone with sufficient clarity to enable millions to travel home in its glow; but no believer, however pure his heart or however obedient his life, has ever been able to receive it as it shines from the Throne unmodified by his own mental stuff.

As a lump of clay when grasped by the human hand remains clay but cannot escape the imprint of the hand, so the truth of God when grasped by the human mind remains truth but bears upon it the image of the mind that grasps it.

Truth cannot enter a passive mind. It must be received into the mind by an active mental response, and the act of receiving it tends to alter it to a greater or less degree. . . .

Of course I refer here to theological and religious truth. How pure this truth is in any place at any given time is revealed by the moral standards of those who hold the truth. . . . Spiritual truth (by which I mean the disclosures of the Holy Spirit to the human spirit) is always the same. BAM076-077

> *Wherever the Holy Spirit still comes, He will always be found witnessing to Jesus and honoring the Son of God.* HS488

NOTHING TO BE ASHAMED OF

> *Wash me thoroughly from mine iniquity, and cleanse me from my sin. . . . Create in me a clean heart, O God.*
>
> —Psalm 51:2, 10

$\mathcal{L}$et me venture an opinion here. Jesus was in harmony with nature in this world and I am of the opinion that the deeper our own Christian commitment becomes the more likely we will find ourselves in tune and in harmony with the natural world around us.

Some people have always scoffed at the habits of St. Francis as though he probably was not in his right mind. I have come to believe that he was so completely yielded to God, so completely and fully taken up with the Presence of the Holy Ghost that all of nature was friendly to him. . . .

Brethren, I am not ashamed of his world—I am only ashamed of man's sin. If you could take all of the sin out of this world, suddenly extract it, there would be nothing in all the world to be ashamed of and nothing to be afraid of. CES075-076

The heart of the Holy Spirit is intensely concerned in preserving us from every stain and blemish and bringing us into the very highest possibilities of the will of God. HS037

GOD'S MIND IN HUMAN WORDS

All scripture is given by inspiration of God, and is profitable for doctrine, for reproof, for correction, for instruction in righteousness.

—2 Timothy 3:16

The Bible will never be a living Book to us until we are convinced that God is articulate in His universe. To jump from a dead, impersonal world to a dogmatic Bible is too much for most people. They may admit that they should accept the Bible as the Word of God, and they may try to think of it as such, but they find it impossible to believe that the words there on the page are actually for them. . . .

The facts are that God is not silent, has never been silent. It is the nature of God to speak. The second Person of the Holy Trinity is called the Word. The Bible is the inevitable outcome of God's continuous speech. It is the infallible declaration of His mind for us put into our familiar human words. POG074-075

The Spirit guides us by the Scriptures, by their general principles and teachings and by bringing to us special passages from the Word, either impressing them on our hearts through the law of mental suggestion or by various ways fitted to emphasize a passage as a divine message to our hearts. ISS042

NOT HERE TO FOOL AROUND

And when he is come, he will re-prove the world of sin, and of righteousness, and of judgement.

—John 16:8

$\mathcal{T}$he Holy Spirit, whom Jesus also called the Spirit of Truth, has not come into this world to fool around. He will be found wherever the Lord's people meet, and in confirming the Word and the Person of Jesus Christ, He will demand moral action!

It is for that reason that when a man goes to a gospel meeting he never knows when the last shred of excuse will be stripped from his naked, trembling conscience forever. Men may joke and play—even about sacred and spiritual matters—but the Spirit of God is in dead earnest!

God is still speaking in this lost world and one of His voices is the presence of the Holy Spirit, convicting a lost human race of such weighty matters as sin, righteousness and judgment. While the Holy Spirit continues in His ministries, we know that this lost world is not yet a forsaken world. EFE025-026

The very fact that the Holy Spirit has left the love and joy of heaven and made His residence for nearly 2,000 years in this uncongenial world, places His sacrifice alongside that of Jesus Christ in His incarnation and redemption. WCC019

THE MOST SIGNIFICANT VOICE

To day if ye will hear his voice, harden not your hearts, as in the provocation.

—Hebrews 3:15

$\mathcal{G}$od is speaking to mankind with more than one voice, but it must be said that the clearest, most distinct and most easily distinguished voice is that of the Holy Spirit. The call and reproof and conviction by the Holy Spirit give grave and serious meaning to all other voices calling men home.

If it were not for the presence of the Holy Spirit speaking through the consciences of men and women, no other voice would have any significance. For the Holy Spirit, the divine Comforter, came to confirm Christ's words and Christ's work and Christ's person. EFE026

> *The Holy Spirit . . . lived in the human Christ for three and a half years, the Spirit who wept in His tears, suffered in His agonies, spoke in His words of wisdom and love, took the little children in His arms, healed the sick and raised the dead.* HS069

> *The Holy Spirit is God's purifying messenger to us, bringing the water and the fire that will make us white as snow. Let us trust Him, let us obey Him, let us receive Him.* CTAB042

A SILENT, HOLY, ELOQUENT WITNESS

While Peter yet spake these words, the Holy Ghost fell on all them which heard the word.

—Acts 10:44

$\mathcal{T}$he Holy Spirit is . . . among us to confirm to the consciences of men the works of Jesus.

There [is] no denying that in His earthly ministry, Jesus was a mighty worker of miracles. He did raise the dead. He did cleanse the leper. He did turn the water into wine. He did feed the multitude with a few pieces of bread.

The Pharisees did not try to deny the miracles He wrought. They could not deny them. . . . You cannot deny a fact that stands and stares you in the face—a fact that you can touch and feel and push around and investigate! The Pharisees simply said: "He does his work in the power of the devil."

The Holy Spirit came that He might confirm and verify the divine quality of those mighty works of Jesus and prove Him indeed to be the very God who had made the world and who could make it do what He pleased for it to do. EFE028

Let us bear in mind . . . that the Holy Spirit identifies Himself with the Lord Jesus and that the coming of the Comforter is just the coming of Jesus Himself to the heart. WCC007

A
LIVING
HISTORY

Ye are manifestly declared to
be the epistle of Christ . . . writ-
ten not with ink, but with the
Spirit of the living God.

—2 Corinthians 3:3

$\mathcal{I}$n our world there is still the holy witness of the Spirit, who in all things speaks for this Man who sits on the throne. . . .

The Holy Spirit is here now to convince the world, and however we treat the warning of the Holy Spirit is exactly how we treat Jesus Christ Himself.

If faith must depend upon a man knowing enough of the historical evidences to arrive at a scholarly belief in the deity of Jesus, then there could only be a relatively few people saved.

But I do not have to be a scholar, a logician or a lawyer to arrive at belief in the deity of the Lord Jesus Christ, for the Holy Spirit has taken the deity of Christ out of the hands of the scholars and put it in the consciences of men.

The Spirit of God came to lift it out of the history books and write it on the fleshy tablets of the human heart. EFE030-031

The Holy Spirit is called the Spirit of Christ . . .
because He brings to us the presence of Jesus and
enables us to realize our oneness with Him. WS107

GOD— THE FIXED POINT

And God said unto Moses, I AM THAT I AM: and he said, Thus shalt thou say unto the children of Israel, I AM hath sent me unto you.

—Exodus 3:14

A satisfactory spiritual life will begin with a complete change in relation between God and the sinner; not a judicial change merely, but a conscious and experienced change affecting the sinner's whole nature.

The atonement in Jesus blood makes such a change judicially possible and the working of the Holy Spirit makes it emotionally satisfying. . . .

In determining relationships we must begin somewhere. There must be somewhere a fixed center against which everything else is measured, where the law of relativity does not enter and we can say "IS" and make no allowances. Such a center is God.

When God would make His name known to mankind He could find no better word than "I AM." When He speaks in the first person He says, "I AM"; when we speak *of* Him we say, "He is"; when we speak *to* Him we say, "Thou art." Everyone and everything else measures from that fixed point. "I am that I am," says God, "I change not." POG092

Our greatest need is to make room for God, [the I AM]. HS167

February

IF JESUS HAD TO DIE

For God so loved the world, that he gave his only begotten Son, that whosoever believeth in him should not perish, but have everlasting life.

—John 3:16

*T*he Holy Spirit is still among us with transforming power for that one who hears the gospel message and really believes it. . . . He still converts. He still regenerates. He still transforms. . . .

It is tragic that we try to hide from Him in the caves and dens of the earth, among the trees of the garden. It is tragic that men and women keep their hearts so hard that they cannot feel, and so deaf that they cannot hear.

There are many who are hearing the Voice of God, but they insist that the "way" should be made easier for them.

Oh, listen! If hell is what God says it is, if sin is what God says it is, if Jesus Christ had to die to save the sinner—is it asking too much for you to let people know that you are turning from sin? EFE036-037

Out of all God's creatures, only the soul has a capacity large enough for [God] to empty . . . the whole ground of his being into it. This He does in the act of giving birth to Himself spiritually in the soul. BME129

GOD'S KIND OF LOVE

He that loveth me shall be loved of my Father, and I will love him, and will manifest myself to him.

—John 14:21

$\mathcal{G}$od, being Himself God, an uncreated being, deriving from no one, owing nothing to anybody, must necessarily be the fountain of all the love there is! That is why I say that as our God, He must love Himself forever with pure and perfect love.

This kind of love, God's love, holy and blameless—this is the love which the three Persons of the Godhead feel and hold for one another. The Father to the Son; the Son to the Father; the Father and Son to the Spirit; the Spirit to the Father and Son—the divine Trinity in perfect and blameless and proper love; loving one another with a holy, poured out devotion! The Trinity's three fountains, eternal, infinite, pouring without measure into each other from the bottomless, boundless, shoreless sea of perfect love and bliss. . . .

God being who and what He is, is Himself the only being that He can love directly. Everything else and everyone else that God loves, He loves for His own sake. EFE012-013

God loved us because of something in Himself, and so if Christ is dwelling is us, we will love because of the Christ within us. HS470

HE GIVES
. . . AND
KEEPS

For the wages of sin is death;
but the gift of God is eternal life
through Jesus Christ our Lord.

—Romans 6:23

*A*s humans, we are aware that if we give something away, we give it up for the time it is away from us. But God lends without giving anything up. God gives you life but He is still the life He gives you so He loses nothing by giving it to you.

So with everything else. God is power, but when He gives you power He does not give His power away. He gives wisdom, but He does not lose it when He gives it. He gives grace, but He does not part with His grace. He keeps it while He gives it because it is Himself that He gives.

So it is with everything—wisdom, being, power, holiness and every quality God bestows upon men. God is constantly giving of Himself to us, because God is life!

Life is sacred. . . . There is a great truth involved here for human beings—for eternal life can best be described as having God in the soul! EFE041

> *Salvation is a stream of grace that [flows] to*
> *men from the foundation of the Father's love. We*
> *have done nothing to deserve it. . . . It is the gift of*
> *God's love.* CTBC, Vol. 6/080

THE VOICE WITHIN

I will hear what God the LORD will speak: for he will speak peace unto his people, and to his saints.

—Psalm 85:8

I once slipped into a noonday service in New York City and I heard something I will never be able to forget.

A minister speaking that day said: "We assume that if a man has heard the Christian gospel he has been enlightened. But that is a false assumption. Just to have heard a man preach truth from the Bible does not necessarily mean that you have been enlightened."

God's voice must speak from within to bring enlightenment. It must be the Spirit of God speaking soundlessly within. . . .

I believe that God has related these somehow: the voice of conviction in the conscience and the Holy Spirit, the point of contact, witnessing within man's being. A person has not been illuminated until that voice begins to sound within him.

Men and women need to be told that it may be fatal to silence the inner voice. It is always perilous to resist the conscience within; but it may be fatal to silence that voice, to continue to ignore that speaking voice within! EFE066-067

> *[W]hen we fail to hear His voice, it is not because He is not speaking so much as that we are not listening.* JAS014

DEPRAVITY
IS NO
EXCUSE

I delight to do thy will, O my God: yea, thy law is within my heart.

—Psalm 40:8

*B*ecause of the treachery of the human soul, it is possible to hide behind the fact that all have sinned. There is a kind of universal reaction which becomes an acceptable philosophy; that "if this is what is wrong with everybody, then nobody need worry about it."

Therefore, when I say that man is a moral wanderer, away from God and still hiding, I do not want you to hide behind that and take comfort in it. I want you to know that it is a very personal thing and that the Holy Spirit never meant to give anyone a sense of comfort in universal depravity.

Actually, the Holy Spirit is saying throughout the Scriptures: "Thou art the man!"

God is calling us with many, many voices, but there is no doubt that He entreats mankind most perfectly in the revealed Word of God. EFE098

> *May Jesus enter into us and clear out and cast away all hindrances of soul and body, to the end that we may be one with him here upon earth and there in heaven. So help us, God.* BME047

GOD'S WORD IS POWERFUL

For the word of God is quick, and powerful . . . and is a discerner of the thoughts and intents of the heart.

—Hebrews 4:12

God Almighty does not bellow to the wide universe and have it come back as an empty echo through His holy ears. He has told us that His word going forth from His mouth does not ever return void and without results. God's word is always powerful and it needs no one to run around apologizing for it and thinking up clever ways to defend it.

The gospel ship, the ark of God, is not a ghost ship floating idly on the sea. [It is] fully manned with a faithful crew, the winds of the Holy Spirit in her sail, passengers who are . . . free men and women, bound for a free port in a holy land!

Throughout this troubled old world, God has His saints and He knows them. They are washed in His blood, born of His Spirit. They are begotten of the Word of Truth, saved by the miracle of redemption. He will call them all home when the time comes. EFE106-107

What comforts me is the thought that we are being shaped here below into stones for the heavenly temple—that to be made like Him is the object of our earthly existence. JAS055

A MYSTICAL BIRTH

Except a man be born of water and of the Spirit, he cannot enter into the kingdom of God.

—John 3:5

*T*he invisible birth of which John speaks is an act of God. John is talking about something beyond the physical birth that we know. The senses can touch the physical birth. When we were born into this world, those around us could see and feel and hold and weigh us. They could wash and clothe and feed us.

But this invisible, mysterious birth of which John speaks has nothing to do with the flesh. It is of heaven. This birth is of the Spirit—a birth of another kind, a mystical birth. . . .

If Jesus our Lord had talked merely about people being born physically into the world, He would never have been heard, and His teachings would not have been preserved in print. Physical birth is too common—everyone is born. But these people experienced a birth not of the body but of the heart. They were born not into time but into eternity. They were born not of earth but of heaven. They had an inward birth, a spiritual birth, a mysterious birth, a mystical birth! FBR005-006

> *God is in all things as being, as activity, as power. God gives birth in the soul alone, for though every creature bears God's mark, the soul is the natural image of God.* BME013

RELIGION, YES— HOLY SPIRIT, NO

I fear, lest by any means, as the serpent beguiled Eve . . . so your minds should be corrupted from the simplicity that is in Christ.

—2 Corinthians 11:3

*E*vangelical Christianity is gasping for breath. We happen to have entered a period when it is popular to sing about tears and prayers and believing. You can get a religious phrase kicked around almost anywhere—even right in the middle of a worldly program dedicated to the flesh and the devil.

Old Mammon, with two silver dollars for eyes, sits at the top of it, lying about the quality of the products. . . . In the middle of it, someone trained in a studio to sound religious will say with an unctuous voice, "Now, our hymn for the week!" So they break in, and the band goes twinkle, twankle, twinkle, twankle, and they sing something that the devil must blush to hear.

They call that religion, and I will concede that religion it is. It is not Christianity, and it is not the Holy Spirit. It is not New Testament and it is not redemption. It is simply making capital out of religion. FBR012

For any man to presume to represent the Son of God . . . without the anointing of the Holy Spirit, is the most daring presumption. HS074

ON HIS TERMS

But as many as received him, to them gave he power to become the sons of God, even to them that believe on his name.

—John 1:12

$\mathcal{I}$ ... believe ... that if someone should come along who could make himself heard to thousands instead of to a few hundred, someone with as much oil as intellect and as much power as penetration, we could yet save evangelical Christianity from the dead-end street where it finds itself. I warn you: do not for one second let the crowds, the bustle of religious activity, the surge of religious thinking fool you into supposing that there is a vast amount of spirituality. It is not so.

That is why the meaning of the word *received* is so important here. "As many as received him"—actively and aggressively took Him. This means a determined exercise of the will. It means to not deny any condition that the Lord lays down. That is something quite different from what we are hearing. They did not come to the Lord and try to make terms, but they came to the Lord and actively took Him on His terms. FBR012-013

A sanctified life is a life conformed to the Scriptures in every particular. It commences with our hearts; it next reaches to our ears, and then it is accomplished in our feet. CTBC, Vol. 2/025

FUEL FOR THE FIRE

And when they had prayed, the place was shaken where they were assembled together; and they were all filled with the Holy Ghost.

—Acts 4:31

A church can go on holding the creed and the truth for generations and grow old. New people can follow and receive that same code and also grow old. Then some revivalist comes in and fires his guns and gets everybody stirred, and prayer moves God down on the scene and revival comes to that church.

People who thought they were saved get saved. People who had only believed in a code now believe in Christ. And what has really happened? It is simply New Testament Christianity having its place. It is not any deluxe edition of Christianity; it is what Christianity should have been from the beginning. . . .

[T]he Holy Spirit will not come on a church where there is no biblical body of truth. The Holy Spirit never comes into a vacuum, but where the Word of God is, there is fuel, and the fire falls and burns up the sacrifice. FBR027-029

> *His Word is not mere intellectual light, but spiritual life and celestial fire. . . . [R]ead it with burning hearts and glowing love as the love letter of His affection and the mirror of His face.* CTBC, Vol. 4/347

THE KNOWING

The Spirit itself beareth witness with our spirit, that we are the children of God.

—Romans 8:16

$\mathcal{I}$ know what Charles Wesley meant when he wrote, "His Spirit answers to the blood,/ And tells me I am born of God!" No one had to come and tell me what he meant. "Those who are willing to do my will," said Jesus in effect, "shall have a revelation in their own hearts. They shall have an inward illumination that tells them they are children of God."

If a sinner goes to the altar and a worker with a marked New Testament argues him into the kingdom, the devil will meet him two blocks down the street and argue him out of it again. But if he has an inward illumination—that witness within—because the Spirit answers to the blood, you cannot argue with such a man. . . . He will say, "But I *know!*"

A man like that is not bigoted or arrogant; he is just sure. . . . This is normal Christianity. That is the way we should be. If anyone chooses to do God's will, he will find out. He will know.

FBR030-031

> *If you are a friend to God, God will be an everlasting friend to you. Nothing shall separate you from His love.* DTC080

INWARD BLINDNESS

But God be thanked, that ye were the servants of sin, but ye have obeyed from the heart that form of doctrine which was delivered you.

—Romans 6:17

I once read a book about the inner spiritual life by a man who was not a Christian at all. He was a sharp intellectual. . . . He examined spiritual people from the outside, but nothing ever reached him. And that is possible!

You cannot argue around this. You can read your Bible . . . and if you are honest you will admit that it is either obedience or inward blindness. You can repeat Romans word for word and still be blind inwardly. You can quote all the Psalms and still be blind inwardly. You can know the doctrine of justification by faith . . . and be blind inwardly. It is not the body of truth that enlightens; it is the Spirit of truth who enlightens.

If you are willing to obey the Lord Jesus, He will illuminate your spirit. He will inwardly enlighten you. The truth you have known intellectually will now be known spiritually. Power will begin to flow up and out, and you will find yourself changed, marvelously changed. FBR032

God works for a wholly blessed end, namely, Himself: to bring the soul and all her powers into that end, into Himself. BME016

FAITH—
THE HIGHEST
KIND OF REASON

For by grace are ye saved through faith; and that not of yourselves: it is the gift of God: not of works, lest any man should boast.

—Ephesians 2:8-9

*I*n our day, we send reason ahead on its little short legs and faith never follows. Nobody marvels, because the whole business can be explained. I have always claimed that a believing Christian is a miracle, and at the precise moment that you can fully explain him, you have a Christian no longer!

I have read the efforts of William James to psychologize the wonders of God's workings in the human life and experience. But the genuine child of God is someone who cannot be explained by human reasoning.

In this relationship with Jesus Christ through the new birth, something takes place by the ministry of the Spirit of God which psychology cannot explain. This is why I must contend that faith is the highest kind of reason after all, for faith goes straight into the presence of God. FBR040

The reason that faith is so important an element in every true life is simply because it links our nothingness with God Himself. CTBC, Vol. 3/146

No Twilight Zone

He that believeth not the Son shall not see life; but the wrath of God abideth on him.

—John 3:36

$\mathcal{S}$ome teachers have tried to enshroud Jesus in a pink fog of sentimentality. But there is really no excuse for misunderstanding Him. He drew the line as taut as a violin string. He said, "He that is not with me is against me; and he that gathereth not with me scattereth abroad" (Matthew 12:30). . . .

At that great day when He judges mankind, Jesus says He "shall separate them one from another, as a shepherd divideth his sheep from the goats." The one group "shall go away into everlasting punishment: but the righteous into life eternal" (25:32, 46). Those statements leave no twilight zone, no in-between.

Consider the benefits promised to the true disciples. Jesus said, "And ye shall know the truth, and the truth shall make you free" (John 8:32). No one can know truth except the one who obeys truth. . . . Truth is in the text, but it takes the text plus the Holy Spirit to bring truth to a human soul. FBR063-064

God has solemnly told us in His Word that there is no other name under heaven given among men whereby we must be saved. Only Jesus can save.

MM056

"REAL" TRUTH

If ye continue in my word, then are ye my disciples indeed; and ye shall know the truth, and the truth shall make you free.

—John 8:31-32

*T*ruth must be understood by inward illumination. Then we know the truth. Until that time, we do not know it. . . .

I heard through missionaries of a boy overseas who had memorized Jesus' entire Sermon on the Mount. He did it in such record time and with such apparently little effort that someone called him in to find out how he had done it.

"Well," said the boy, "I would memorize a verse and then trust God to help me put it into practice. Then I would memorize the next verse and say, 'Lord, help me to live this one, too.' . . ."

That boy had truth on his side. He did not consider truth to be something objective, simply to be filed in the mind as knowledge. Rather, truth to him was also subjective—to be acted on.

Truth becomes real to us within our beings by obedience and faith. FBR064-065

> *Before we can truly obey Him, we must fully receive Him and be so united with Him that His interests are ours and His will is just the expression of our inmost being.* NJ100

ENJOYING THE BENEFITS

Blessed is every one that feareth the LORD; that walketh in his ways.... Happy shalt thou be, and it shall be well with thee.

—Psalm 128:1-2

*O*ur contacts with civilization make our clothes dirty, greasy, sometimes spotted. The dirt is not only on our clothes; soon it is actually *in* them. We can shake the garment, argue with it, talk to it, read Shakespeare to it. . . . Still it is soiled and dirty. The dirt must be loosed. The garment must be set free from its soil. . . .

The only solution that will loose us from our sins is the blood of Jesus Christ. He loved us and freed us—washed us—from our sins in His own blood. Education, refinement—nothing else worked. But when Jesus' blood did its work, we were free!

"Ye shall know the truth," Jesus said, "and the truth shall make you free" (John 8:32). . . . But there must be a moral commitment. If there is not, there is no understanding. If there is no understanding, there is no cleansing.

Are you obeying the truth as it is revealed by the Spirit of God? Are you enjoying the benefits of freedom in Jesus Christ? Are you one of His *true* disciples? FBR066-067

> *Happiness is nothing but that inward sweet delight, which will arise from the harmonious agreement between our wills and the will of God.*
> JAS147

THE WORD AND THE SPIRIT

Of his own will begat he us with the word of truth, that we should be a kind of firstfruits of his creatures.

—James 1:18

$\mathcal{S}$ome people wish they could have lived in Jesus' day so they could have heard His voice and His teaching. They forget there were thousands who heard Jesus but who had no idea what He was talking about. They forget that His own disciples had to wait for the Holy Spirit at Pentecost to know what He had been telling them.

"If only I had heard Jesus," you may have said. No, you are better off now. You have the Light that lights every person. You have the voice of the inner conscience.

Some are sorry they never heard Dwight L. Moody or Albert B. Simpson in person. But I remind you that even if we could have [heard] the apostle Paul on magnetic tape . . . his speech could do no more for us than the Holy Spirit can do with the Bible and the human conscience. . . .

We have heard the voice of the Light within the heart. . . . The Church needs to listen to the inner voice and do something about its message! FBR076-077

> *There are two extremes. The Word without the Spirit is dry and dead, but the Spirit without the Word is incomplete.* HS489

EXCHANGING ONE SIN FOR ANOTHER

Present your bodies a living sacrifice, holy, acceptable unto God, which is your reasonable service.

—Romans 12:1

$\mathcal{T}$he offering and the sacrifice and the sanctifying energies of the Holy Spirit are indeed sufficient to prepare the soul for communion with God. This the Bible declares and this ten thousand times ten thousand witnesses confirm.

The big danger is that we assume that we have been delivered from our sins when we have in reality only exchanged one kind of sin for another. This is the peril that lies in wait for everyone. It need not discourage us nor turn us back, but it should make us watchful.

We must, for instance, be careful that our repentance is not simply a change of location. Whereas we once sinned in the far country among the swineherds, we are now chumming with religious persons, considerably cleaner and much more respectable in appearance, to be sure, but no nearer to true heart purity than we were before. BAM081-082

In the deeper experience of a sanctified heart, there must be another conviction, not of sin, but of sinfulness, before the soul is ready to receive the Holy Spirit and the abiding presence of the Lord.

CTBC, Vol. 3/049

MIDWIVES IN THE HENHOUSE

Which were born, not of blood, nor of the will of the flesh, nor of the will of man, but of God.

—John 1:13

I was once a farm boy. I learned that when it came time for eggs to hatch, we did well not to help the process along. The chick that had been helped in its birth could be spotted every time. It was weak, and it walked with a stagger.

But that is what we do with the penitents who want to get right with God. Well-meaning people kneel down with the seeking sinners, find a Bible text and pray away until they see a little sign of life. Then, like eager midwives in the henhouse, they pull the penitents from their shells, dry them off, write down their names as converts—and later wonder why they do not develop.

But when the Holy Spirit brings penitents to the new birth, they bounce out into the world healthy and howling. Their sins are forgiven; their burdens have been lifted! FBR082

> *The will in man is the point of contact which God acts upon us, and, like the helm and the engine of the vessel, it is the directing and impelling power of life. . . . They greatly err who look for its sphere in the emotions. Its seat is in the will. A clear, calm, inflexible choice is the mightiest element in the life of faith.* SI215

RESPONDING TO THE VOICE

That which I see not teach thou me: if I have done iniquity, I will do no more.

—Job 34:32

$\mathcal{I}$t can be fatal to silence the inner voice, the voice of human conscience. Some silence it, for instance, when that voice speaks in outraged protest at the human habit of lying. It may plead eloquently against the habit of dishonesty, or take a person to task for jealousy or for some other sin.

It is always perilous to resist conscience, to ignore the inner voice. Let the Lord talk to your inner spirit, to your innermost being. Within you is a conscience that cannot lean on anybody, that cannot share the blame with anybody—a conscience that singles you out, isolates you and says, "You are the man!" "You are the woman!" It is the voice that makes you want to lower your head and tiptoe away while no one is watching.

I am grateful for the human conscience. If there was no conscience and no voice of God in the world, we would all become beasts in very short order. . . . If that voice is speaking to you—that inner preacher who does not preach to a crowd but only to the lone individual soul—respond! FBR082-083

The chief thing is not to listen to yourself, but silently to listen to God. JAS171

GETTING ALONE WITH GOD

In returning and rest shall ye be saved; in quietness and in confidence shall be your strength.

—Isaiah 30:15

There are some things that you and I will never learn when others are present. I believe in church and I love the fellowship of the assembly. There is much we can learn when we come together on Sundays and sit among the saints. But there are certain things that you and I will never learn in the presence of other people.

Unquestionably, part of our failure today is religious activity that is not preceded by aloneness, by inactivity. I mean getting alone with God and waiting in silence and quietness until we are charged with God's Spirit. Then, when we act, our activity really amounts to something because we have been prepared by God for it. FBR130

> *You do not need to seek Him here or there, He is no further off than the door of your heart. There He stands lingering, waiting for whoever is ready to open and let Him in. You do not need to call to Him in the distance. He is waiting much more impatiently than you, for you to open to Him. He is longing for you a thousand times more urgently than you are for Him. It is instantaneous: the opening and the entering.* BME034

INACTIVITY— THE HIGHEST ACTIVITY

Wait on the LORD: be of good courage, and he shall strengthen thine heart: wait, I say, on the LORD.

—Psalm 27:14

*T*here is an inactivity that, paradoxically, is the highest possible activity. There can be a suspension of the activity of the body, as when our Lord told His disciples to "tarry ye in the city of Jerusalem, until ye be endued with power from on high" (Luke 24:49). They waited. And the Holy Spirit came on them in power.

In the Old Testament, to wait on God meant coming before His presence with expectation and waiting there with physical and mental inactivity.

"Cease thy thinking, troubled Christian," one of the old poets wrote. There is a place where the mind quits trying to figure out its own way and throws itself wide open to God. And the shining glory of God comes down into the waiting life and imparts an activity.

Do you understand what I mean when I say that we can go to God with an activity that is inactive? We go to God with a heart that is not acting in the flesh or in the natural—trying to do something. We go to God in an attitude of waiting. FBR131-132

Hearing, I am receptive; seeing, I am active. Yet our bliss does not consist in being active but in being receptive to God. BME018

SEEING THE INVISIBLE

But God hath revealed them unto us by his Spirit: for the Spirit searcheth all things, yea, the deep things of God.

—1 Corinthians 2:10

*W*e must press on in the Holy Spirit. If we do not see beyond the visible, if we cannot touch that which is intangible, if we cannot hear that which is inaudible, if we cannot know that which is beyond knowing, then I have serious doubts about the validity of our Christian experience.

The Bible tells us: "Eye hath not seen, nor ear heard, neither have entered into the heart of man, the things which God hath prepared for them that love him" (1 Corinthians 2:9).

That is why Paul goes on to remind us that God has revealed these mysteries to us by the Holy Spirit. If we would only stop trying to make the Holy Spirit our servant and begin to live in Him as the fish lives in the sea, we would enter into the riches of glory about which we know nothing now. FBR152-153

What I am trying to describe here is the sacred gift of seeing, the ability to peer beyond the veil and gaze with astonished wonder upon the beauties and mysteries of things holy and eternal. BAM094-095

Whoever will listen will hear the speaking Heaven.
POG073

LONGING FOR HIGHER GROUND

As the hart panteth after the water brooks, so panteth my soul after thee, O God.

—Psalm 42:1

*T*oo many want the Holy Spirit in order that they may have the gift of healing. Others want Him for the gift of tongues. Still others seek Him so that their testimony may become effective. All of these things, I will grant, are a part of the total pattern of the New Testament. But it is impossible for us to make God our servant. Let us never pray that we may be filled with the Spirit of God for secondary purposes.

God wants to fill us with His Spirit in order that we should know Him first of all and be absorbed in Him. We should enter into the fullness of the Spirit so that God's Son may be glorified in us.

I try to bathe my soul in the writings and the hymns of the devoted saints of God. . . . I wonder why we ever stoop to read or sing or quote anything but that which is elevated and divine, noble and inspiring. FBR153-154

> *When the Holy Spirit comes, He lifts our minds*
> *to new ideals and gives us conceptions of things so*
> *much in advance of our present experiences that*
> *we long for higher ground.* WCC096

WHO
IS
PRAYING?

Likewise the Spirit also helpeth our infirmities: for we know not what we should pray for as we ought.

—Romans 8:26

$\mathcal{T}$he spiritual quality of a prayer is determined not by its intensity but by its origin. In evaluating prayer we should inquire who is doing the praying—our determined hearts or the Holy Spirit? If the prayer originates with the Holy Spirit, then the wrestling can be beautiful and wonderful; but if we are the victims of our own overheated desires, our praying can be as carnal as any other act.

Two examples are given in the Old Testament, Jacob and the prophets of Baal. Jacob's wrestling was a real exercise, and at first it was not Jacob's doing. . . . The wrestling [became] of divine origin, and the blessed results are known to every Bible student.

The other example does not turn out so well. The prophets of Baal wrestled also, much more violently than Jacob, but they wrestled in the flesh. Their writhings were born of ignorance and superstition and got them nowhere. . . . They were wrong in spite of their zealous praying. . . . Only the Spirit can pray effectively. TWP016-017

> *This is the spirit of prayer—sincere, humble, believing, submissive. Other prayer than this the Bible does not require—God will not accept.* DTC155

BREATHLESS ADORATION

There is no God like thee . . . which . . . shewest mercy unto thy servants, that walk before thee with all their hearts.

—2 Chronicles 6:14

The theory [of impromptu service planning] is that if the meeting is unplanned the Holy Spirit will work freely, and that would be true if all the worshipers were reverent and Spirit-filled. But mostly there is neither order nor Spirit, just a routine prayer that is, except for minor variations, the same week after week, and a few songs that were never much to start with and have long ago lost all significance by meaningless repetition.

In the majority of our meetings there is scarcely a trace of reverent thought, no recognition of the unity of the body, little sense of the divine Presence, no moment of stillness, no solemnity, no wonder, no holy fear. . . .

The whole Christian family stands desperately in need of a restoration of penitence, humility and tears. May God send them soon. GTM005-006

We would do well to follow our old-fashioned forbears who knew what it was to kneel in breathless, wondering adoration in the presence of God. JMI043

THE HOLY SPIRIT IN CREATION

And God said, Let us make man in our image, after our likeness.

—Genesis 1:26

*G*od is creative. He has not relinquished His place as Creator, even though the specific work of forming the first heaven and earth has long been completed.

The Holy Spirit as one of the blessed Godhead is also creative. He is forever bringing new things into being, forever giving out and setting in motion, forever making "all things new." Wherever He is at work, the effects will be creative rather than conservative, though we should know that He also conserves whatever He creates. To create and not conserve would be to waste the creative act. But the whole psychology of the Spirit is toward the creation of new things rather than toward the cautious preservation of what has been created.

It should be said that the Holy Spirit always creates in accord with His character as very God of very God. He stamps whatever He does with the mark of eternity. It has upon it the quality of everlastingness—the dignity and holiness of the Deity set it apart. TWP036

> *Christ makes the difference between death and life, always and everywhere. He is the Prince of Life, and whatever He touches lives.* TET060

THE
HABITATION
OF GOD

For where two or three are gathered together in my name, there am I in the midst of them.

—Matthew 18:20

*A*ccording to the Scriptures the Church is the habitation of God through the Spirit, and as such is the most important organism beneath the sun. She is not one more good institution along with the home, the state and the school; she is the most vital of all institutions—the only one that can claim a heavenly origin.

The cynic may inquire which church we mean, and may remind us that the Christian Church is so divided that it is impossible to tell which is the true one, even if such a one exists. . . .

Being inside the Church we are probably as well aware of her faults as any person on the outside could possibly be. And we believe in her nevertheless wherever she manifests herself in a world of darkness and unbelief.

The Church is found wherever the Holy Spirit has drawn together a few persons who trust Christ for their salvation, worship God in spirit and have no dealings with the world and the flesh. GTM024-025

The Church was never intended to be a natural and intellectual organization, but a supernatural instrumentality wholly dependent upon the power of God. ISS029

A HARD
BUT GLORIOUS
WAY

If any man will come after me, let
him deny himself, and take up his
cross daily, and follow me.

—Luke 9:23

*T*o enter [into the deeper] life, seekers must be ready to accept without question the New Testament as the one final authority on spiritual matters. They must be willing to make Christ the one supreme Lord and ruler in their lives. They must surrender their whole being to the destructive power of the cross, to die not only to their sins but to their righteousness as well as to everything in which they formerly prided themselves.

If this should seem like a heavy sacrifice for anyone to make, let it be remembered that Christ is Lord and can make any demands upon us that He chooses, even to the point of requiring that we deny ourselves and bear the cross daily.

The mighty anointing of the Holy Spirit that follows will restore to the soul infinitely more than has been taken away. It is a hard way, but a glorious one. Those who have known the sweetness of it will never complain about what they have lost. They will be too well pleased with what they have gained. TWP120-121

> *The one misery of man is self-will, the one secret*
> *of blessedness is the conquest over our own wills.*
> *To yield [it] up to God is rest and peace.* JAS147

March

CELLS OF THE SAME BODY

God that made the world and all things therein, seeing that he is Lord of heaven and earth, dwelleth not in temples made with hands.

—Acts 17:24

*C*hurch members may by necessity be scattered over the surface of the earth and separated . . . but in every true member of the Church is the homing instinct and the longing of the sheep for the fold and the Shepherd.

Give a few real Christians half a chance and they will get together and organize and plan regular meetings for prayer and worship. . . . [T]hey will hear the Scriptures expounded, break bread together in one form or another according to their light, and try as far as possible to spread the saving gospel to the lost world.

Such groups are cells in the Body of Christ, and each one is a true Church, a real part of the greater Church. It is in and through these cells that the Spirit does His work on earth. Whoever scorns the local church scorns the Body of Christ.
GTM025-026

The Holy Spirit's presence with the Church is better than the continued physical presence of the Lord Jesus would have been. For . . . it is an internal and not an external presence . . . [and] equally accessible to all God's people. CTBC, Vol. 4/499

FREE FROM THE FLESH

For the law of the Spirit of life in Christ Jesus hath made me free from the law of sin and death.

—Romans 8:2

*W*hen the Holy Spirit is ignored or rejected, religious people are forced either to do their own creating or to fossilize completely. A few churches accept fossilization as the will of God and settle down to the work of preserving their past—as if it needed preserving. Others seek to appear modern, and imitate the current activities of the world with the mistaken idea that they are being creative. And after a fashion they are, but the creatures of the creative skill are sure to be toys and trifles, mere imitations of the world and altogether lacking in the qualities of eternity—holiness and spiritual dignity. The hallmark of the Holy Spirit is not there. . . .

It is hard to imagine a more painful disillusionment than to come to the judgment seat of Christ and find that all our earthly lives we had been striving after the flesh and never permitting the creative Holy Spirit to work in us that which was pleasing in His sight. TWP036-037

There is a way of release from [the] tyranny [of the flesh]. It is by the cross of Jesus. . . . That ends the bondage of the flesh. The power to live free from it comes from the Holy Ghost. TET058

SILENCE—
AN UNUTTERABLE
BEATITUDE

While he thus spake, there came a cloud, and overshadowed them. . . . And there came a voice out of the cloud, saying, This is my beloved Son: hear him.

—Luke 9:34-35

Not all silence is spiritual. Some Christians are silent because they have nothing to say; others are silent because what they have to say cannot be uttered by mortal tongues. We . . . will confine our remarks to the latter.

Where the Holy Spirit is permitted to exercise His full sway in a redeemed heart, the progression is likely to be as follows: First, voluble praise, in speech or prayer or witness. Then, when the crescendo rises beyond the ability of studied speech to express, comes song. When song breaks down under the weight of glory, then comes silence where the soul, held in deep fascination, feels itself blessed with an unutterable beatitude.

At the risk of being written off as an extremist or a borderline fanatic, we offer it as our mature opinion that more spiritual progress can be made in one short moment of speechless silence in the awesome Presence of God than in years of mere study. . . . The exposure may be brief, but the results are permanent. TWP041-042

Very few of us know the secret of bathing our souls in silence. It was a secret our Lord Jesus Christ knew very well. . . . We never really come to know ourselves because we cannot keep quiet long enough. UNKNOWN

THE CHRIST QUESTION

What shall I do then with Jesus which is called Christ?

—Matthew 27:22

"*Where* is Jesus now?" asks the world, and the Christian answers, "At the right hand of God." He died but He is not dead. He rose again as He said He would. . . . Better than all, His Spirit now reveals to the Christian heart not a dead Christ but a living one. This we are sent to declare with all the bold dogmatism of those who know, who have been there and experienced it beyond the possibility of a doubt.

The gospel is the official proclamation that Christ died for us and is risen again, with the added announcement that everyone who will believe, and as a result of that belief will cast in his lot with Christ in full and final committal, shall be saved eternally.

He . . . will not be popular and . . . he will be called to stand where Jesus stood before the world: to be admired by many, loved by a few and rejected at last by the majority of men. He must be willing to pay this price; or let him go his way; Christ has nothing more to say to him now. GTM040-041

*The question for every man is the Christ question.
. . . The turning point of every life is its direct relationship to the Lord Jesus Christ.* CTBC, Vol. 5/420

A RELIGION
LIKE NO
OTHER

Neither is there salvation in any other: for there is none other name under heaven given among men, whereby we must be saved.

—Acts 4:12

*T*here are in the Christian religion three major elements: spiritual life, moral practice and community organization, and these all spring out of and follow New Testament doctrine; or more correctly, the first must and the others should. . . .

Life comes mysteriously to the soul that believes the truth. "He that heareth my word, and believeth on him that sent me, hath everlasting life, and shall not come into condemnation; but is passed from death unto life" (John 5:24). And again, "He that beliveth on me, as the scripture hath said, out of his belly shall flow rivers of living water. (But this spake he of the Spirit, which they that believe on him should receive)" (7:38-39).

The message of the cross offers eternal life and the blessedness of the Holy Spirit indwelling the soul. These distinguish Christianity from every other religion; and it is significant that these distinguishing marks are of such a nature as to be wholly above and beyond the reach of man. GTM044-045

> *Christianity tells humanity, "You have destroyed yourself, but in Me is your help." It is a supernatural religion . . . the indwelling of the living God in human life.* CTBC, Vol. 4/186

THE INSTANT OBLIGATION

Though he were a Son, yet learned he obedience by the things which he suffered.

—Hebrews 5:8

*T*he life of God in the soul of a man is wholly independent of the social status of that man. In the early church the Spirit leaped across all artificial lines that separate men from each other and made of all believers a spiritual brotherhood. Jew and Gentile, rich and poor, Greek and barbarian were all baptized into one body, of which Christ was and is the Head.

Along with the gift of eternal life, the entrance of the Holy Spirit into the believer's heart and the induction of the newborn soul into the Body of Christ comes instant obligation to obey the teachings of the New Testament.

These teachings are so plain and so detailed that it is difficult to understand how they could appear different to persons living under different political systems or on different cultural levels. That they have so appeared cannot be denied; but always the reasons lie in the imperfect state of the believers composing the different groups. GTM045-046

> *Since I am God's temple, I am not to serve my own ends with my body, but the cause of Jesus Christ as His devoted disciple. . . . Do I regard His temple, my body, as more mine than His?*
> PRL68

THE SPIRIT'S CALL

For ... we have many members in one body, and all members have not the same office.

—Romans 12:4

*W*hile there is only one way to become a true preacher, unfortunately there are many doors into the pulpit. One is to be endowed with what is sometimes called a "good pulpit presence." Many a tall Absalom whose commanding presence and sonorous voice mark him as a natural leader of men is attempting to speak for God when he has not been sent by God. His call is from the people instead of from the Spirit and the results cannot but be disastrous.

Others have become ministers from a genuine but altogether human love for mankind. These have a strong sense of social obligation which they feel they can best discharge by entering the ministry.

Of all wrong reasons for becoming a preacher this would seem to be the most laudatory, but it is nevertheless not a spiritually valid reason, for it overlooks the sovereign right of the Holy Spirit to call whom He will. GTM088

> *The church that is man-managed instead of God-governed is doomed to failure. A ministry that is college-trained but not Spirit-filled works no miracles. . . . Things will get no better until we get back to the realized presence and power of the Holy Spirit.* PRL037

CALLED TO BE A VOICE

Then flew one of the seraphims unto me, having a live coal in his hand . . . and he laid it upon my mouth.

—Isaiah 6:6-7

$\mathcal{M}$ost surely the Church has a service of compassion to render to the world, but her motives are not humanitarian. They are higher than this by as much as the new creation is higher than the old. It is inherent in the Christian spirit that the followers of Christ should wish to minister to the bodies as well as the souls of men. But the call to give God's prophetic message to the world is something apart.

The call to witness and serve comes to every Christian; the call to be a Voice to mankind comes only to the man who has the Spirit's gift and special enabling. We need not fewer men to show mercy, but we need more men who can hear the words of God and translate them into human speech. GTM088-089

It is not enough that we are willing and eager to work for God, but the work itself must be of God. . . . This is one of the deepest deaths that Christians are often called to die. Indeed, our work is unacceptable to God and useless to ourselves and others until it first has been bathed in the blood of Calvary and touched with the sign of crucifixion. It must cease to be our work and thus become His and His alone. CTBC, Vol. 2/359

CALLED TO BE GOOD, NOT GREAT

A good man out of the good treasure of the heart bringeth forth good things.

—Matthew 12:35

*E*very pastor knows . . . the plain people who have nothing to recommend them but their deep devotion to their Lord and the fruit of the Spirit which they all unconsciously display. Without these the churches . . . could not carry on.

These are the first to come forward when there is work to be done and the last to go home when there is prayer to be made. They are not known beyond the borders of their own parish because there is nothing dramatic in faithfulness or newsworthy in goodness, but their presence is a benediction wherever they go.

They have no greatness to draw to them the admiring eyes of carnal men but are content to be good men and full of the Holy Spirit. . . .

When they die they leave behind them a fragrance of Christ that lingers long after the cheap celebrities of the day are forgotten. . . .

It remains only to be said that not all men can be great, but all men are called to be good by the blood of the Lamb and the power of the Holy Spirit. GTM100, 102

Come unto God, unite yourself to God, and the doing power you have is infinite! JAS275

THE HOLY SPIRIT IS INDISPENSABLE

Repent, and be baptized every one . . . and ye shall receive the gift of the Holy Ghost.

—Acts 2:38

*T*he continued neglect of the Holy Spirit by evangelical Christians is too evident to deny and impossible to justify.

Evangelical Christianity is Trinitarian: "Praise Father, Son and Holy Ghost" is sung in almost every church every Sunday of the year; and whether the singer realizes it or not he is acknowledging that the Holy Spirit is God indeed with equal claim to be worshiped along with the Father and the Son. Yet after this claim is sung at or near the beginning of the service little or nothing is heard of the Spirit again until the benediction. . . .

[T]here can be no doubt that there is a huge disparity between the place given to the Spirit in the Holy Scriptures and the place He occupies in popular evangelical Christianity. In the Scriptures the Holy Spirit is necessary. GTM108, 110

> *David Brainerd once compared a man without the power of the Spirit trying to do spiritual work to a workman without fingers attempting to do manual labor. The figure is striking but it does not overstate the facts. The Holy Spirit is not a luxury. . . . The Spirit is an imperative necessity. Only the Eternal Spirit can do eternal deeds.* MDP066

IF CHRIST, THEN US

God anointed Jesus of Nazareth with the Holy Ghost and with power: who went about doing good . . . for God was with him.

—Acts 10:38

*A*ccording to the Scriptures everything God did in creation and redemption He did by His Spirit. The Spirit was found brooding over the world at the moment God called it into being. His presence there was necessary.

The life-giving work of the Spirit is seen throughout the entire Bible; and it is precisely because He is the Lord and giver of life that the mystery of the Incarnation could occur. "The Holy Ghost shall come upon thee, and the power of the Highest shall overshadow thee: therefore also that holy thing which shall be born of thee shall be called the Son of God" (Luke 1:35).

It is highly significant that our Lord, though He was very God of very God, did not work until He had been anointed with the Holy Spirit (Acts 10:38). The Son did His work of love as a Spirit-anointed Man; His power derived from the Spirit of power. GTM110-111

How little some Christians accomplish for God! . . . Get filled with the Spirit, and you will neither be idle or unfruitful. CTBC, Vol. 6/311

ONLY ONE SOURCE OF POWER

Every man's work shall be made manifest . . . and the fire shall try every man's work of what sort it is.

—1 Corinthians 3:13

*T*he only power God recognizes in His Church is the power of His Spirit whereas the only power actually recognized today by the majority of evangelicals is the power of man. God does His work by the operation of the Spirit, while Christian leaders attempt to do theirs by the power of trained and devoted intellect. Bright personality has taken the place of the divine afflatus.

Everything that men do in their own strength and by means of their own abilities is done for time alone; the quality of eternity is not in it. Only what is done through the Eternal Spirit will abide eternally; all else is wood, hay, stubble.

It is a solemn thought that some of us who fancy ourselves to be important evangelical leaders may find at last we have been but busy harvesters of stubble. GTM111-112

> *[Jesus] has left us the same power which He possessed. He has bequeathed to the Church the very Holy Spirit that lived and worked in Him. Let us accept this mighty gift. Let us believe in Him and His all-sufficiency. Let us receive Him and give Him room.* HS314

HUMILITY— EVIDENCE OF GODLINESS

Not unto us, O LORD, not unto us, but unto thy name give glory, for thy mercy, and for thy truth's sake.

—Psalm 115:1

Someone wrote to the godly Macarius of Optino that his spiritual counsel had been helpful. "This cannot be," Macarius wrote in reply. "Only the mistakes are mine. All good advice is the advice of the Spirit of God, His advice that I happened to have heard rightly and to have passed on without distorting it."

There is an excellent lesson here that we must not allow to go unregarded. It is the sweet humility of the man of God. "Only the mistakes are mine." He was fully convinced that his own efforts could result only in mistakes, and that any good that came of his advice must be the work of the Holy Spirit operating within him.

Apparently this was more than a sudden impulse of self-depreciation, which the proudest of men may at times feel—it was rather a settled conviction with him, a conviction that gave direction to his enter life. TWP063

The spirit of humility is conclusive evidence of vital godliness. It enters into the essence of religion. Here the new nature eminently discovers itself. The humble spirit is that childlike, Christlike temper, which is exclusively the effect of the almighty power of God upon the heart. DTC130

THE HOLY SPIRIT IS HERE

And when the day of Pentecost was fully come, they were all with one accord in one place.

—Acts 2:1

*P*entecost did not come and go—Pentecost came and stayed. Chronologically the day may be found on the historic calendar; dynamically it remains with us in all its fullness of power.

Today is the day of Pentecost. With the blessed Holy Spirit there is no Yesterday or Tomorrow—there is only the everlasting Now. And since He is altogether God, enjoying all the attributes of the Godhead, there is with Him no Elsewhere; He inhabits an eternal Here. His center is Everywhere; His bound is Nowhere. It is impossible to leave His presence, though it is possible to have Him withdraw the manifestation of that presence.

Our insensibility to the presence of the Spirit is one of the greatest losses that our unbelief and preoccupation have cost us. We have made Him a tenet of our creed, we have enclosed Him in a religious word, but we have known Him little in personal experience. TWP091

> *When the Holy Spirit comes into our [lives] He does something. He accomplishes something. He is more than a sentiment, a feeling, a fancy. He is an infinite force that . . . enables us to accomplish all for which we were called as the disciples of Christ.* CTBC, Vol. 4/518

WE NEED A REVIVAL!

*Will thou not revive us again:
that thy people may rejoice in
thee?*

—Psalm 85:6

*W*e need a revival! We need a revival of consecration to death, a revival of happy abandonment to the will of God that will laugh at sacrifice and count it a privilege to bear the cross through the heat and burden of the day.

We are too much influenced by the world and too little controlled by the Spirit. We of the deeper life persuasion are not immune to the temptations of ease and we are in grave danger of becoming a generation of pleasure lovers. . . .

May God raise up a people who will consult their pleasures less and the great need more. I know of one successful layman who refuses again and again to take perfectly legitimate pleasure trips because he cannot bring himself to leave his class of adolescent Sunday school boys. May God multiply such men and women among us till the reproach of Egypt is rolled away and man's confidence in us restored. GTM159-160

A sanctified life is a life conformed to the Scriptures in every particular. It communes with our hearts; it next reaches our ears, and then it is accomplished in our feet. CTBC, Vol. 2/025

EXPECT . . . RECEIVE

*And blessed is she that be-
lieved: for there shall be a per-
formance of those things which
were told her from the Lord.*

—Luke 1:45

*E*xpectation has always been present in the Church in the times of her greatest power. When she believed, she expected, and her Lord never disappointed her. . . .

Every great movement of God in history, every unusual advance in the Church, every revival, has been preceded by a sense of keen anticipation. Expectation accompanied the operations of the Spirit always. His bestowals hardly surprised His people because they were gazing expectantly toward the risen Lord and looking confidently for His word to be fulfilled. His blessings accorded with their expectations. . . .

We need today a fresh spirit of anticipation that springs out of the promises of God. We must declare war on the mood of nonexpectation and come together with childlike faith. Only then can we know again the beauty and wonder of the Lord's presence among us. GTM168, 170

> *We are to do all things to the glory of God (1 Corin-
> thians 10:31). This includes our pleasures. . . . The
> only question is, what is God's will for us in each
> matter? We are never to abandon our God-given
> common sense in the victorious life.* PRL309

ONE THING NEEDFUL

Blessed are the poor in spirit: for theirs is the kingdom of heaven.

—Matthew 5:3

The truly humble man does not expect to find virtue in himself, and when he finds none he is not disappointed. He knows that any good deed he may do is the result of God's working in him. . . .

When this belief becomes so much a part of a man that it operates as a kind of unconscious reflex he is released from the burden of trying to live up to his own opinion of himself. . . . The emphasis of his life shifts from self to Christ, where it should have been in the first place, and he is thus set free to serve his generation by the will of God without the thousand hindrances he knew before.

Should such a man fail God in any way he will be sorry and repent, but he will not spend his days castigating himself for his failure. He will say with Brother Lawrence: "I shall never do otherwise if You leave me to myself; it is You who must hinder my falling and mend what is amiss," and after that "give himself no further uneasiness about it." GTM173-174

In the character of a Christian, humility is the one thing needful. Where this is wanting, all is wanting. DTC134

SINNING WITH SILENCE

*A*t this hour in world history the state of religion is such that the Church is in grave danger of losing this priceless treasure [wisdom]. Her gold is being turned to copper and her diamonds to glass. . . .

Even among those who make a great noise about believing the Bible, that Bible has virtually no practical influence left. Fiction, films, fun, frolic, religious entertainment, Hollywood ideals, big business techniques and cheap, worldly philosophies now overrun the sanctuary. The grieved Holy Spirit broods over the chaos but no light breaks forth. "Revivals" come without rousing the hostility of organized sin and pass without raising the moral level of the community or purifying the lives of professing Christians. Why?

Could it be that too many of God's true children . . . are sinning against God by guilty silence? When those whose eyes are opened by the touch of Christ become vocal and active God may begin to fight again on the side of truth. GTM179-180

> *There are moral situations where it is immoral to say nothing and basely immoral to do nothing.*
> GTM177

BECOMING WHAT WE LOVE

Simon, son of Jonas, lovest thou me? He saith unto him, Yea, Lord; thou knowest that I love thee.

—John 21:16

We are becoming what we love. We are to a large degree the sum of our loves and we will of moral necessity grow into the image of what we love most; for love is among other things a creative affinity; it changes and molds and shapes and transforms. It is without doubt the most powerful agent affecting human nature next to the direct action of the Holy Spirit of God within the soul.

What we love is therefore not a small matter to be lightly shrugged off; rather it is of present, critical and everlasting importance. It is prophetic of our future. It tells us what we shall be, and so predicts accurately our eternal destiny.

Loving wrong objects is fatal to spiritual growth; it twists and deforms the life and makes impossible the appearing of the image of Christ in the soul. It is only as we love right objects that we become right, and only as we go on loving them that we continue to experience a slow but continuous transmutation toward the objects of our purified affection. GTM196-197

> *How shall we become lovely? By loving Him who is ever lovely.* JAS076

OLD CROSS . . .
OLD POWER

I am crucified with Christ: nevertheless I live; yet not I, but Christ liveth in me.

—Galatians 2:20

*G*od offers life, but not an improved old life. The life He offers is life out of death. It stands always on the far side of the cross. . . .

What does this mean to the individual, the condemned man who would find life in Christ Jesus? How can this theology be translated into life?

Simply, he must repent and believe. He must forsake his sins and then go on to forsake himself. Let him cover nothing, defend nothing, excuse nothing. Let him not seek to make terms with God, but let him bow his head before the stroke of God's stern displeasure and acknowledge himself worthy to die.

Having done this, let him gaze with simple trust upon the risen Savior, and from Him will come life and rebirth and cleansing and power.

The cross that ended the earthly life of Jesus now puts an end to the sinner; and the power that raised Christ from the dead now raises him to a new life along with Christ. OCN004

There will be nothing in heaven that does not have the mark of the cross upon it. UNKNOWN

No Contest

Submit yourselves therefore to God. Resist the devil, and he will flee from you.

—James 4:7

*T*ruth is a glorious but hard mistress. She never consults, bargains or compromises. She cries from the top of the high places, "Receive my instruction, and not silver; and knowledge rather than choice gold" (Proverbs 8:10). After that, every man is on his own. He may accept or refuse. . . .

Were this an unfallen world the path of truth would be a smooth and easy one. Had the nature of man not suffered a huge moral dislocation there would be no discord between the way of God and the way of man.

I assume that in heaven the angels live through a thousand serene millenniums without feeling the slightest discord between their desires and the will of God. But not so among men on earth. Here . . . the flesh lusts against the Spirit and the Spirit against the flesh, and these are contrary one to the other.

In that contest there can be only one outcome. We must surrender and God must have His way. OCN008-009

> *[T]here is a moment in every life when we meet God, and by a supreme surrender enter into His sovereign will and His perfect peace.* CTBC, Vol. 6/102

OUTPOURINGS AND MORE OUTPOURINGS

If we walk in the light, as he is in the light, we have fellowship one with another.

—1 John 1:7

$\mathcal{G}$od desires to advance His work among men by frequent outpourings of the Spirit upon His people as they need them and are prepared to receive them. . . .

The Bible . . . encourages us to expect "showers of blessing" and "floods upon the dry ground." It was impossible for the outpouring which came at Pentecost to affect persons who were not present or congregations not yet in existence.

The Bible does not sponsor [the] chilling doctrine of once-for-all blessing. It is obvious that the spiritual benefits of Pentecost must be prolonged beyond the lifetimes of the persons who were the first to receive them. . . .

In brief, the teaching of the New Testament is that the outpouring at Pentecost was the historic beginning of an era which was to be characterized by a continuous outpouring of the Holy Spirit. PTP049-051

> *The Holy Ghost comes with the light of truth in one hand, so to speak, and the blood of Christ in the other.* What the light reveals, the blood cleanses. CDL106

FEELING VERSUS FAITH

Now faith is the substance of things hoped for, the evidence of things not seen.

—Hebrews 11:1

*I*f God wills to pour out His Spirit upon us, why do not more Christians and more churches receive an experience of power like that of the early Church? That some have so received is joyfully admitted, but why is the number so few? When the provision is so broad and the promise so sure, what doth hinder us? . . .

One obstacle to the reception of power is a widespread fear of our emotions wherever they touch the religious life. . . .

This anti-emotionalism . . . is an unwarranted inference, not a scriptural doctrine, and is in violent opposition to psychology and common sense. Where in the Bible are feeling and faith said to be at odds?

The fact is that *faith engenders feeling.* . . . We can have feeling without faith, it is true, but we can never have faith without feeling. Faith as a cold, unemotional light is wholly unknown in the Scriptures. The faith of those Bible heroes listed in the Book of Hebrews invariably aroused emotion and led to positive action in the direction of their faith. PTP052-054

[I]f we love Him, He can make us supremely happy. JAS076

THE HOLY SPIRIT IS GRACIOUS

And the Holy Ghost descended in a bodily shape like a dove upon him.

—Luke 3:22

*A*nother hindrance [to receiving power from the Holy Spirit] is fear of fanaticism. Instinctive revulsion from fleshly excesses and foolish undisciplined conduct on the part of some who profess lofty spiritual attainments has closed the door to a life of power for many of God's true children. . . .

They have made the mistake of putting all teaching concerning the Holy Spirit in the same category, and consequently will have nothing to do with any of it. This is as much to be regretted as it is easy to understand.

Such victims must be taught that the Holy Spirit is the Spirit of Jesus, and is as gracious and beautiful as the Saviour Himself. Paul's words should be kept in mind, "For God hath not given us the spirit of fear; but of power, and of love, and of a sound mind" (2 Timothy 1:7).

The Holy Spirit is the *cure* for fanaticism, not the cause of it.

PTP054-055

The heart in which the Holy Spirit lives will always be characterized by gentleness, lowliness, quietness, meekness and forbearance. HS007

FAITH LEADS TO OBEDIENCE

If ye love me, keep my commandments.

—John 14:15

*A*nother thing which clearly hinders believers from enjoying the power of the Holy Spirit . . . is the habit of instructing seekers to "take it by faith" when they become concerned with their need of the fullness of the Holy Spirit.

Now, it is a fact written all over the New Testament that the benefits of atonement are to be received by faith. This is basic in redemptive theology, and any departure from it is fatal to true Christian experience. Paul teaches emphatically that the Spirit is received through faith, and rebukes anyone who would teach otherwise. So it would seem, on the surface of it, to be sound procedure to instruct a seeker to "take it by faith." . . .

The trouble seems to be with our conception of faith. Faith, as Paul saw it, was a living, flaming thing leading to surrender and obedience to the commandments of Christ. . . . Many persons, convinced of their need of power, but unwilling to go through the painful struggle of death to the old life, turn with relief to this "take it by faith" doctrine as a way out of their difficulty. PTP055-057

> *[T]o live in the Spirit is to live with God—hearing Him, and knowing Him, and loving Him, and delighting to do His will.* JAS134

THE EVIDENCE OF POWER

But we have this treasure in earthen vessels, that the excellency of the power may be of God, and not of us.

—2 Corinthians 4:7

A sharp contrast is observable between Spirit-filled Christians of St. Paul's time and many who claim to be filled with the Spirit today. Paul's converts received the Spirit by faith to be sure, *but they actually received Him*: thousands now go through the motion of taking Him by faith, and believe they do so take Him, but show by their continued feebleness that they do not know Him in real power. . . .

And unless they see it differently later and decide to go through the hard way, they are fated to spend the rest of their lives in secret disappointment.

Let it be remembered that no one ever received the Holy Spirit's power without knowing it. He always announces Himself to the inner consciousness. God will pour out His Spirit upon us in answer to simple faith, but real faith will be accompanied by deep poverty of spirit and mighty heart yearnings. PTP056-057

The essential condition of the baptism of the Holy Spirit is to yield everything to God, even the things that in themselves may be harmless. Why? For no other reason than to prove our will is wholly laid down and that God is all in all. CTBC, Vol. 2/244

UNITY PRECEDES BLESSING

And it shall come to pass in the last days, saith God, I will pour out of my Spirit upon all flesh.

—Acts 2:17

$\mathcal{G}$od always works where His people meet His conditions, but only when and as they do. . . .

The first condition is oneness of mind among the persons who are seeking the visitation. "Behold, how good and how pleasant it is for brethren to dwell together in unity! It is like the precious ointment upon the head, that ran down upon the beard, even Aaron's beard: that went down to the skirts of his garments; as the dew of Hermon, and as the dew that descended upon the mountains of Zion: for there the LORD commanded the blessing, even life for evermore" (Psalm 133:1-3).

Here the unity precedes the blessing, and so it is throughout the Bible. An individual may seek and obtain great spiritual help from God; and that is one thing. For a *company* of people to unite to seek a new visitation from God for the entire group is quite another thing, and is a spiritual labor greatly superior to the first.

PTP059-060

What a joyful experience it is for us in this church age to be part of a congregation drawn together by the desire to know God's presence, to sense His nearness. TRA106

THE SPIRIT IS HIMSELF GOD

Whither shall I go from thy spirit? . . . There shall thy hand lead me, and thy right hand shall hold me.

—Psalm 139:7, 10

Satan has hindered us all he could by raising conflicting opinions about the Spirit, by making Him a topic for hot and uncharitable debate between Christians. . . .

It would help us if we could remember that the Spirit is Himself God, the very nature of the Godhead subsisting in a form that can impart itself to our consciousness. We know only as much of the other Persons of the Trinity as He reveals to us.

It is His light upon the face of Christ, which enables us to know Him. It is His light within us, which enables us to understand the Scriptures. Without Him the Word of truth is only darkness.

The Spirit is sent to be our Friend, to guide us over the long way home. He is Christ's own Self come to live with us, allowing Him to fulfill His word, "Surely I am with you always," even while He sits at the right hand of the Majesty in the heavens. TWP091-092

[W]e are not filled with an influence; we are not filled with a sensation; we are not filled with a set of ideas and truth; we are not filled with a blessing, but we are filled with a Person . . . and its very essence is the indwelling life of Christ Himself. WCC122-123

TO
WANT
NO MORE

Acquaint now thyself with him, and be at peace: thereby good shall come unto thee.

—Job 22:21

*T*o know God, this is eternal life; this is the purpose for which we are and were created. The destruction of our God-awareness was the master blow struck by Satan in the dark day of our transgression.

To give God back to us was the chief work of Christ in redemption. To impart Himself to us in personal experience is the first purpose of God in salvation. To bring acute God-awareness is the best help the Spirit brings in sanctification. All other steps in grace lead up to this.

Were we allowed but one request, we might gain at a stroke all things else by praying one all-embracing prayer:

Thyself, Lord! Give me Thyself and I can want no more.

WTA071

> *To be able to look into God's face, and know with the knowledge of faith that there is nothing between the soul and Him, is to experience the fullest peace the soul can know. Whatever else pardon may be, it is above all things admission into full fellowship with God.* JAS062

PROBLEMS! PROBLEMS!

Beloved, let us love one another: for love is of God; and every one that loveth is born of God, and knoweth God.

—1 John 4:7

$\mathcal{W}$hat . . . is the conclusion of the matter? That problems are the price of progress, that friction is the concomitant of motion, that a live and expanding church will have a certain quota of difficulties as a result of its life and activity. A Spirit-filled church will invite the anger of the enemy.

How then shall we deal with our problems? First, expect them so you will not be taken off guard. Second, realize that every live body of Christians has its troubles, from Christ and His apostles to the present day, so yours are not unique. Third, pour in copious amounts of love, the best lubricant in the world. Love will reduce friction to a minimum and keep the whole body working smoothly and without injury to its parts.

Where does this love come from? The love of God bursts forth from the Holy Spirit in our hearts. TWP113

> *The same bond which unites believers to Christ, binds them to each other. . . . Those who love Christ, love those who are like Him and those who are beloved by Him. . . . There is unity of design, a common interest in the objects of their pursuits.* DTC167-168

POWER IN ACTION

Not by might, nor by power, but by my spirit, saith the LORD of hosts.

—Zechariah 4:6

The greatest event in history was the coming of Jesus Christ into the world to live and to die for mankind. The next greatest event was the going forth of the Church to embody the life of Christ and to spread the knowledge of His salvation throughout the earth.

It was not an easy task which the Church faced. . . . To carry on the work of a man who was known to have died . . . to persuade others that this man had risen again from the dead and that He was the Son of God and Saviour: this mission was, in the nature of it, doomed to failure from the start. Who would credit such a fantastic story? . . .

That the Church did not . . . perish was due entirely to the miraculous element within her. That element was supplied by the Holy Spirit who came at Pentecost to empower her for her task. PTP007-008

> *[T]he same God who led Israel with pillar of cloud and fire, who spoke at Pentecost through the tongues of flame, who opened Peter's prison doors, is waiting to work the greater wonders of His grace for us.* CTBC, Vol. 2/187-188

April

GOD IS THE DEEPER LIFE

Let him that glorieth glory in this, that he understandeth and knoweth me, that I am the LORD.

—Jeremiah 9:24

*T*he deeper life has . . . been called the "victorious life," but I do not like that term. It appears to me that it focuses attention exclusively upon one feature of the Christian life, that of personal victory over sin, when actually this is just one aspect of the deeper life—an important one, to be sure, but only one.

That life in the Spirit that is denoted by the term "deeper life" is far wider and richer than mere victory over sin, however vital that victory may be. It also includes the thought of the indwelling of Christ, acute God-consciousness, rapturous worship, separation from the world, the joyous surrender of everything to God, internal union with the Trinity, the practice of the presence of God, the communion of saints and prayer without ceasing. TWP120

[N]o one seems to want to know and love God for Himself! God is the deeper life! Jesus Christ Himself is the deeper life. . . . This means that there is less of me and more of God—thus my spiritual life deepens, and I am strengthened in the knowledge of His will. ITB017

FIRE
IN THE
BUSH

*But truly I am full of power by
the spirit of the LORD, and of
judgment, and of might, to declare . . . to Israel his sin.*

—Micah 3:8

*T*he greatest proof of our weakness these days is that there is
no longer anything terrible or mysterious about us. . . . We now
have little that cannot be accounted for by psychology and statistics.

In that early Church they met together on Solomon's porch,
and so great was the sense of God's presence that "durst no man
join himself to them" (Acts 5:13). The world saw fire in that
bush and stood back in fear; but no one is afraid of ashes.

Today they . . . even slap the professed bride of Christ on the
back and get coarsely familiar. If we ever again impress un-
saved men with a wholesome fear of the supernatural we must
have once more the dignity of the Holy Spirit; we must know
again that awe-inspiring mystery which comes upon men and
churches when they are full of the power of God. PTP011

> *The Holy Spirit is pure, for He is the Holy
> Spirit. He is wise, for He is the Spirit of wisdom.
> He is true, for He is the Spirit of truth. He is like
> Jesus, for He is the Spirit of Christ. He is like the
> Father, for He is the Spirit of the Father. He
> wants to be Lord of your life.* COU075

GETTING RID OF THE HANDLES

There is joy in the presence of the angels of God over one sinner that repenteth.

—Luke 15:10

$\mathcal{I}$n the things-which-God-cannot-do category is this: *God cannot do our repenting for us.* In our efforts to magnify grace we have so preached the truth as to convey the impression that repentance is a work of God. This is a grave mistake. . . . God has commanded all men to repent. It is a work which only they can do. It is morally impossible for one person to repent for another. Even Christ could not do this. He could die for us, but He cannot do our repenting for us.

God in His mercy may "incline" us to repent and by His inworking Spirit assist us to repent; but before we can be saved we must of our own free will repent toward God and believe in Jesus Christ. . . .

Repentance involves moral reformation. The wrong practices are on man's part, and only man can correct them. Lying, for instance, is an act of man, and one for which he must accept full responsibility. When he repents he will quit lying. God will not quit for him; he will quit for himself. PTP017-018

Anyplace where a person sins, he puts handles on his soul for Satan to grasp. Repentance gets rid of the handles. UNKNOWN

THE FRUIT OF OBEDIENCE

But be ye doers of the word, and not hearers only, deceiving your own selves.

—James 1:22

$\mathcal{L}$ook at the fruits of obedience as described in the New Testament: The house of the obedient man is builded upon a rock (Matthew 7:24).

He shall be loved by the Father and shall have the manifestation of the Father and the Son, who will come unto him and make their abode with him (John 14:21, 23).

He shall abide in the love of Christ (15:10). . . . He is set free from sin and made a servant of righteousness (Romans 6:17-18). The Holy Spirit is given to him (Acts 5:32).

He is delivered from self-deception and blessed in his deeds (James 1:22-25). His faith is perfected (2:22).

He is confirmed in his assurance toward God and given confidence in prayer, so that what he asks is given to him (1 John 3:18-22). . . .

What does all this add up to? . . . Just that the power of God is at our disposal, waiting for us to call it into action by meeting the conditions which are plainly laid down. PTP028-029

We . . . have a power within us to do what we are commanded to do. What is it we lack? The power? No; the will. JAS084

YOU CAN HAVE WHAT YOU WANT

I am come that they might have life, and that they might have it more abundantly.

—John 10:10

*T*here are two kinds of lives . . . : the fallow and the plowed. . . .

The man of fallow life is contented with himself and the fruit he once bore. He does not want to be disturbed. He smiles in tolerant superiority at revivals, fastings, self-searchings. . . . He is steady, "faithful," always in his accustomed place. . . . But he is fruitless. The curse of such a life is that it is fixed. . . . *To be* has taken the place of *to become*. . . .

The plowed life is the life that has, in the act of repentance, thrown down the protecting fences and sent the plow of confession into the soul. The urge of the Spirit, the pressure of circumstances and the distress of fruitless living have combined thoroughly to humble the heart.

Such a life has put away defense, and has forsaken the safety of death for the peril of life. PTP032-033

God gives us what we want. If you want a little of His grace, you may get it. If you want to be halfhearted, you may. But if you want to be wholly His and have all His fullness, His great heart is just longing to find room and vent for His love. CTBC, Vol. 4/297

BREATHING OUT AND BREATHING IN

The fear of the LORD is to hate evil: pride, and arrogancy, and the evil way, and the froward mouth, do I hate.

—Proverbs 8:13

Our attachment to the Person of Christ must exclude all that is contrary to Christ. These are the days when we are trying to be 100 percent positive. But the Scripture says of Jesus, "Thou lovest righteousness, and hatest wickedness" (Psalm 45:7). . . . If He had to hate in order to love, so do you and I.

To be 100 percent positive would be as fatal as to inhale steadily all your life without exhaling. You can't do that. . . .

When the Church inhales the Holy Spirit she must exhale everything that is contrary to Him.

I don't believe any man can love until he's able to hate. . . . I don't think he can love righteousness unless he hates sin; for the Scripture leaves us with the belief that in order to accept there are some things you must reject. In order to affirm there are things you have to deny; in order to say *yes* you have to be able to say *no*. TCC008-009

Jesus, breathe Thy Spirit on me,
Teach me how to breathe Thee in,
Help me pour into Thy bosom
All my life of self and sin. HCL251

THE CROSS ON THE HILL—AND IN MY HEART

And they that are Christ's have crucified the flesh with the affections and lusts.

—Galatians 5:24

*O*ne time a young man came to an old saint . . . and said to him, "Father, what does it mean to be crucified?" The old man thought for a moment and said, "Well, to be crucified means three things. First, the man who is crucified is facing only one direction." I like that—facing only one direction . . . and that is the direction of God and Christ and the Holy Ghost . . . the direction of sanctification and the direction of the Spirit-filled life.

And the old man scratched his scraggly gray hair and said, "One thing more, son, about a man on a cross—he's not going back." The fellow going out to die on the cross doesn't say to his wife, "Good-bye, honey. I'll be back shortly after five."

When you go out to die on the cross you bid good-bye— you're not going back! . . . Get a man converted who knows that if he joins Jesus Christ he's finished, . . . he's not going back—then you have a real Christian indeed. TCC012-013

In every Christian's heart there is a cross and a throne, and the Christian is on the throne till he puts himself on the cross. ROR066

WORSHIPER FIRST, WORKER SECOND

Thou shalt worship the Lord thy God, and him only shalt thou serve.

—Matthew 4:10

I think that God has given me a little bit of a spirit of a crusader and I am crusading where I can that Christians of all denominations and shades of theological thought might be restored again to our original purpose.

We're here to be worshipers first and workers only second. We take a convert and immediately make a worker out of him. God never meant it to be so. God meant that a convert should learn to be a worshiper, and after that he can learn to be a worker.

Jesus said, "Go ye into all the world, and preach the gospel" (Mark 16:15). Peter wanted to go at once, but Christ said, "Don't go yet. Wait until you are endued with power." (See Luke 24:49.)

Power for service? Yes, but that's only half of it; maybe that's only one-tenth of it. The other nine-tenths are that the Holy Ghost may restore to us again the spirit of worship. Out of enraptured, admiring, adoring, worshiping souls, then, God does His work. The work done by a worshiper will have eternity in it. WMJ010

What [God] asks from us is worship. . . . The homage He claims is the devotion of our hearts.

CTBC, Vol. 4/010

WORSHIP AND WORK IN THE SPIRIT

God is a Spirit: and they that worship him must worship him in spirit and in truth.

—John 4:24

*O*nly the Holy Spirit can enable a fallen man to worship God acceptably. As far as that's concerned, only the Holy Spirit can pray acceptably; only the Holy Spirit can do anything acceptably. My brethren, I don't know your position about the gifts of the Spirit, but I believe that all the gifts of the Spirit not only ought to be but have been present in His Church all down the centuries. . . .

You cannot account for Augustine and Chrysostom and Luther and Charnock and Wesley and Finney except they were men gifted by the Holy Ghost.

I believe that the Holy Spirit distributes His gifts severally as He will. . . . The Church has been propagated by the Holy Spirit, so we can only worship in the Spirit, we can only pray in the Spirit, and we can only preach effectively in the Spirit, and what we do must be done by the power of the Spirit. WMJ014-015

We do not need many gifts but one. . . . The Holy spirit is wisdom, power, holiness, faith, love . . . all comprehended in the one living Presence that comes to abide in the heart that is yielded wholly to Him. CTBC, Vol. 4/332

THE ART OF WORSHIP

Give unto the LORD the glory due unto his name; worship the LORD in the beauty of holiness.

—Psalm 29:2

*W*orship is the missing jewel in modern evangelicalism. We're organized; we work; we have our agendas. We have almost everything, but there's one thing that the churches, even the gospel churches, do not have: that is the ability to worship. We are not cultivating the art of worship. It's the one shining gem that is lost to the modern church, and I believe that we ought to search for this until we find it.

I think I ought to talk a little more about what worship is and what it would be like if it were in the church. Well, it's an attitude, a state of mind, a sustained act, subject to degrees of perfection and intensity. As soon as He sends the Spirit of His Son into our hearts we say "Abba" and we're worshiping. That's one thing. But it's quite another thing to be worshipers in the full New Testament sense of the word and up to our possibilities. WMJ020

> *God wants us to worship Him. He doesn't need us, for He couldn't be a self-sufficient God and need anything or anybody, but He wants us. When Adam sinned it was not he who cried, "God, where art Thou?" It was God who cried, "Adam, where art thou?"* QTB199

ADMIRE HIM!

Delight thyself also in the LORD; and he shall give thee the desires of thine heart.

—Psalm 37:4

Admiration . . . is appreciation of the excellency of God. Man is better qualified to appreciate God than any other creature because he was made in His image and is the only creature who was. This admiration for God grows and grows until it fills the heart with wonder and delight.

"In our astonished reverence we confess Thine uncreated loveliness," said the hymn writer. "In our astonished reverence."

The God of the modern evangelical rarely astonishes anybody. He manages to stay pretty much within the constitution. Never breaks over our bylaws. He's a very well-behaved God and very denominational and very much one of us, and we ask Him to help us when we're in trouble and look to Him to watch over us when we're asleep. The God of the modern evangelical isn't a God I could have much respect for. But when the Holy Ghost shows us God as He is we admire Him to the point of wonder and delight. WMJ022-023

> *O Lord, You're beautiful,*
> *Your face is all I seek,*
> *And when Your eyes are on this child,*
> *Your grace abounds to me.*

How Artistic and Musical God Is!

... teaching and admonishing one another in psalms and hymns and spiritual songs, singing with grace in your hearts to the Lord.

—Colossians 3:16

I remember as a young Christian when I got my first awful, wonderful, entrancing vision of God. I was in West Virginia in the woods sitting on a log reading the Scriptures. . . .

I got up and wandered away to have prayer by myself. I had been reading one of the driest passages imaginable from the Scriptures where Israel came out of Egypt and God arranged them into . . . a diamond-shaped moving city with a flame of fire in the middle giving light.

Suddenly it broke over me; God is a geometrician, He's an artist! When He laid out that city He laid it out skillfully . . . and it suddenly swept over me like a wave of the sea: how beautiful God is and how artistic and how poetic and how musical, and I worshiped God there under that tree all by myself. You know after that I began to love the old hymns and I have been a lover of the great hymns ever since. WMJ023-024

> *Holy Father, Holy Son, Holy Spirit—*
> *Three we name Thee;*
> *Though in essence only one,*
> *Undivided God we claim Thee,*
> *And adoring bend the knee*
> *While we sing our praise to Thee.* HCL006

AM I REALLY CONVERTED?

As the body without the spirit is dead, so faith without works is dead also.

—James 2:26

I believe in the deeper Christian life and experience—oh yes! But I believe we are mistaken when we try to add the deeper life to an imperfect salvation, obtained imperfectly by an imperfect concept of the whole thing.

Under the working of the Spirit of God through such men as Finney and Wesley, no one would ever dare to rise in a meeting and say, "I am a Christian" if he had not surrendered his whole being to God and had taken Jesus Christ as his Lord. . . .

Today, we let them say they are saved no matter how imperfect and incomplete the transaction, with the proviso that the deeper Christian life can be tacked on at some time in the future.

Can it be that we really think that we do not owe Jesus Christ our obedience?

We have owed Him obedience ever since the second we cried out to Him for salvation, and if we do not give Him . . . obedience, I have reason to wonder if we are really converted! ICH013

> *I am satisfied that when a man believes on Jesus Christ he must believe on the whole Lord Jesus Christ—not making any reservation!* ICH007

GOD'S BOOK— FRESH AS THE DEW

Ye received the word of God . . . not as the word of men, but as it is in truth, the word of God.

—1 Thessalonians 2:13

*T*here isn't anything dated in the Book of God. When I go to my Bible, I find dates but no dating. I mean that I find the sense and the feeling that everything here belongs to me. . . .

When the Holy Spirit wrote the epistles, through Peter and Paul and the rest, He wrote them and addressed them to certain people and then made them so universally applicable that every Christian who reads them today in any part of the world, in any language or dialect, forgets that they were written to someone else and says, "This was addressed to me. The Holy Spirit had me in mind. This is not antiquated and dated. This is the living Truth for me—now!" . . .

Brethren, this is why . . . the Word of the Lord God is as fresh as every new sunrise, as sweet and graciously fresh as the dew on the grass the morning after the clear night—because it is God's Word to man! ICH027-028

> *God has given us the Book, brother, and the Book comes first. If it can't be shown in the Book, then I don't want anyone coming to me all aquiver and trying to tell me anything. The Book—you must give me the Word!* COU114

IT'S TIME TO STAND UP!

Ye are the salt of the earth: but if the salt have lost his savour, wherewith shall it be salted?

—Matthew 5:13

$\mathcal{M}$any Christians spend a lot of time and energy in making excuses, because they have never broken through into a real offensive for God by the unlimited power of the Holy Spirit!

The world has nothing that we want—for we are believers in a faith that is as well authenticated as any solid fact of life. The truths we believe and the links in the chain of evidence are clear and rational.

I contend that the church has a right to rejoice and that this is no time in the world's history for Christian believers to settle for a defensive holding action! ICH030

> We Christians must stop apologizing for our moral position and start making our voices heard, exposing sin as the enemy of the human race and setting forth righteousness and true holiness as the only worthy pursuits for moral beings.
>
> I have no doubt that historians will conclude that we of the twentieth century had intelligence enough to create a great civilization but not the moral wisdom to preserve it. TTPI, Book 1/113

A SOUND, THEN A VOICE, THEN A WORD

> *He that dwelleth in the secret place of the most High shall abide under the shadow of the Almighty.*
>
> —Psalm 91:1

*I*t is important that we get still to wait on God. And it is best that we get alone, preferably with our Bible outspread before us. Then if we will we may draw near to God and begin to hear Him speak to us in our hearts.

I think for the average person the progression will be something like this: First a sound as of a Presence walking in the garden. Then a voice, more intelligible, but still far from clear.

Then the happy moment when the Spirit begins to illuminate the Scriptures, and that which had been only a sound, or at best a voice, now becomes an intelligible word, warm and intimate and clear as the word of a dear friend.

Then will come life and light, and best of all, ability to see and rest in and embrace Jesus Christ as Savior and Lord and All. POG074

> *O God and Father, I repent of my sinful preoccupation with visible things. The world has been too much with me. Thou hast been here and I knew it not. I have been blind to Thy presence. Open my eyes that I may behold Thee in and around me. For Christ's sake. Amen.* POG064

THE NEW BIRTH— UNEXPLAINABLE

Therefore if any man be in Christ, he is a new creature: old things are passed away; behold, all things are become new.

—2 Corinthians 5:17

I insist that the new birth was provided in the love and grace and wisdom of God in order to draw a sharp line between those who acquire Christianity by any other method and those who have experienced regenesis. . . .

[S]ome professing Christians are still trying to find natural and reasonable explanations for that which God has said He would do miraculously by His Spirit.

Let me warn you that if you are a Christian believer and you have found a psychologist who can explain to you exactly what happened to you in the matter of your faith, you have been unfrocked! . . . The honest psychologist can only stand off respectfully and say, "Behold the works of the Lord."

He never can explain it! ICH035-036

The humblest Christian is called to live a miracle, a life that is a moral and spiritual life with such intensity and such purity that no human being can do it—only Jesus Christ can do it. TTPI, Book 2/060

[T]he . . . genuine child of God is someone who cannot be explained by human reasoning. TTPI, Book 3/047

NOT WASTE BUT GLORY

My soul longeth, yea, even fainteth for the courts of the LORD: my heart and my flesh crieth out for the living God.

—Psalm 84:2

*I*n our private prayers and in our public services we are forever asking God to do things that He either has already done or cannot do because of our unbelief. We plead for Him to speak when He has already spoken and is at that very moment speaking. We ask Him to come when He is already present and waiting for us to recognize Him. We beg the Holy Spirit to fill us while all the time we are preventing Him by our doubts.

Of course the Christian can hope for no manifestation of God while he lives in a state of disobedience. Let a man refuse to obey God on some clear point, let him set his will stubbornly to resist any commandment of Christ, and the rest of his religious activities will be wasted. . . . "To obey is better than sacrifice." (1 Samuel 15:22) I need only add that all this tragic waste is unnecessary. The believing Christian will relish every moment in church and will profit by it. The instructed, obedient Christian will yield to God as the clay to the potter, and the result will be not waste but glory everlasting. BAM102

> *Speak, Thy servant heareth,*
> *Be not silent, Lord;*
> *Waits my soul upon Thee*
> *For the quickening word.* HCL205

PRUNING COMES BEFORE FRUIT

Yield yourselves unto God, as those that are alive from the dead, and your members as instruments of righteousness unto God.

—Romans 6:13

I want to emphasize the manner in which the apostles were Spirit-led. They were not known as men of rash and impulsive moods, constantly changing decisions and judgments. Led by the Spirit of God, they wanted always to do what God wanted them to do. As a result, the things that God wanted them to do always seemed to fit perfectly into the total scheme of redemption and the whole will of God in the New Testament!

This allows me to say that Peter was of little use to God until he got the victory over being whimsical and temperamental and impulsive. . . .

But when Peter was filled with the Holy Spirit and received a divine vision and began to suffer for Jesus' sake, he got leveled down and became the great apostle, second only to Paul in the New Testament. But God had to take those lightning charges out of Peter and stabilize him in the harness where he would work effectively and fruitfully for the Lord. ICH047

We must recognize the true character of our self-life. . . . We must consent to its destruction . . . and lay it at the feet of God in willing sacrifice.
HS031

HOLINESS IS NOT AN OPTION!

As he which hath called you is holy, so be ye holy in all manner of conversation; because it is written, Be ye holy; for I am holy.

—1 Peter 1:15-16

*Y*ou cannot study the Bible diligently and earnestly without being struck by an obvious fact—the whole matter of personal holiness is highly important to God!

Neither do you have to give long study to the attitudes of modern Christian believers to discern that by and large we consider the expression of true Christian holiness to be just a matter of personal option: "I have looked it over and considered it, but I don't buy it!"

I have always liked the word *exhort* better than *command* so I remind you that Peter has given every Christian a forceful exhortation to holiness of life and conversation. He clearly bases this exhortation on two great facts—first, the character of God, and second, the command of God. ICH061-062

> *[In the New Testament] the emphasis is not upon happiness but upon holiness. God is more concerned with the state of people's hearts than with the state of their feelings.* OGM049

A
WORSHIPING
PEOPLE

Give unto the LORD the glory due unto his name: ... come before him: worship the LORD in the beauty of holiness.

—1 Chronicles 16:29

$\mathcal{W}$e are brought to God and to faith and to salvation that we might worship and adore Him. We do not come to God that we might be automatic Christians, cookie-cutter Christians, Christians stamped out with a die.

God has provided His salvation that we might be, individually and personally, vibrant children of God, loving God with all our hearts and worshiping Him in the beauty of holiness.

This does not mean, and I am not saying, that we must all worship alike. The Holy Spirit does not operate by anyone's preconceived idea or formula. But this I know: when the Holy Spirit of God comes among us with His anointing, we become a worshiping people. WHT014

> *Worship means to "express in some appropriate manner" what you feel. Now, expressing in some appropriate manner doesn't mean that we always express it in the same way all the time. And it doesn't mean that you will always express your worship in the same manner. But it does mean that it will be expressed in some manner.* QTB197

THE FINAL TEST OF LOVE

He that loveth me not keepeth not my sayings: and the word which ye hear is not mine, but the Father's which sent me.

—John 14:24

There is something basically wrong with our Christianity and our spirituality if we can carelessly presume that if we do not like a biblical doctrine and choose not to "buy" it, there is no harm done.

Commandments which we have received from our Lord or from the apostles cannot be overlooked or ignored by earnest and committed Christians. God has never instructed us that we should weigh His desires for us and His commandments to us in the balances of our own judgment and then decide what we want to do about them.

A professing Christian may say, "I have found a place of real Christian freedom; these things just don't apply to me."

Of course you can walk out on it! God has given every one of us the power to make our own choices. ICH062-063

> *The final test of love is obedience. Not sweet emotions, not willingness to sacrifice, not zeal, but obedience to the commandments of Christ. Our Lord drew a line plain and tight for everyone to see.* TIC166

WORSHIP—
A SPIRIT-GIVEN
RESPONSE

O worship the LORD in the beauty of holiness: fear before him, all the earth.

—Psalm 96:9

$\mathscr{H}$ ow thankful we should be to discover that it is God's desire to lead every willing heart into depths and heights of divine knowledge and communion. As soon as God sends the Spirit of His Son into our hearts we say "Abba"—and we are worshiping, but probably not in the full New Testament sense of the word.

God desires to take us deeper into Himself. We will have much to learn in the school of the Spirit. He wants to lead us on in our love for Him who first loved us.

He wants to cultivate within us the adoration and admiration of which He is worthy. He wants to reveal to each of us the blessed element of spiritual fascination in true worship. He wants to teach us the wonder of being filled with moral excitement in our worship, entranced with the knowledge of who God is. He wants us to be astonished at the inconceivable elevation and magnitude and splendor of Almighty God!

There can be no human substitute for this kind of worship and for this kind of Spirit-given response to the God who is our Creator and Redeemer and Lord. WHT026

The man who has not been humbled in the presence of God will never be a worshiper of God at all. QTB197

A DISTURBING VERSE

Follow peace with all men, and holiness, without which no man shall see the Lord.

—Hebrews 12:14

*T*he word *holy* is used to describe the character of angels, the nature of heaven and the character of God. It is written that angels are holy and those angels who gaze down upon the scenes of mankind are called the watchers and holy ones.

It is said that heaven is a holy place where no unclean thing can enter in.

God Himself is described by the adjective *holy*—Holy Ghost, Holy Lord and Holy Lord God Almighty. These words are used of God throughout the Bible, showing that the highest adjective that can be ascribed to God, the highest attribute that can be ascribed to God is that of holiness, and, in a relative sense, even the angels in heaven partake of the holiness of God.

We note in the Bible, too, that the absence of holiness is given as a reason for not seeing God. . . . This text does have a meaning and it ought to disturb us until we have discovered what it means and how we may meet its conditions. ICH064-065

The divine antidote for the satanic poison of sin is holiness. . . . Holiness is an attribute of God and a requirement of the people of God. CDL059

APRIL 24

TRUE HOLINESS IS POSITIVE

It shall be called The way of holiness; the unclean shall not pass over it.

—Isaiah 35:8

*W*hat does this word *holiness* really mean? Is it a negative kind of piety from which so many people have shied away? No, of course not!

Holiness in the Bible means moral wholeness—a positive quality which actually includes kindness, mercy, purity, moral blamelessness and godliness. It is always to be thought of in a positive, white intensity of degree. Whenever it is written that God is holy it means that God is kind, merciful, pure and blameless in a white, holy intensity of degree.

When used of men, it does not mean absolute holiness as it does of God, but it is still the positive intensity of the degree of holiness—and not negative.

This is why true Bible holiness is positive—a holy man can be trusted. A holy man can be tested. ICH065-066

[The Holy Spirit] is an infinite force that makes our life powerful, and enables us to accomplish all for which we are called as the disciples of Christ. It is power over sin, power over self, power over the world . . . power to be, to do. CTBC Vol. 4/518-519

HOLINESS— SOMETHING BEYOND

According as he hath chosen us . . . that we should be holy and without blame before him in love.

—Ephesians 1:4

*G*enuine holiness can be put into the place of testing without fear. Whenever there is a breakdown of holiness, that is proof there never was any real degree of holiness in the first place.

Personally, I truly have been affected in my heart by reading the testimonies and commentaries of humble men of God whom I consider to be among the great souls of Christian Church history.

I have learned from them that the word and idea of holiness as originally used in the Hebrew did not have first of all the moral connotation. It did not mean that God first of all was pure, for that was taken for granted!

The original root of the word *holy* was of something beyond, something strange and mysterious and awe-inspiring. When we consider the holiness of God we talk about something heavenly, full of awe, mysterious and fear-inspiring. Now, this is supreme when it relates to God, but it is also marked in men of God and deepens as men become more like God. ICH066-067

Holiness is not a condition wrought in us. It is simply the Holy One in us ruling, filling. SK007

NO
COPYRIGHT
ON HOLINESS

*And the Lord make you to in-
crease and abound in love . . . to
the end he may stablish your
hearts unblameable in holiness.*

—1 Thessalonians 3:12-13

True holiness is a sense of awareness of the other world, a mysterious quality and difference that has come to rest upon some. . . . Now, if a man should have that sense and not be morally right, then I would say that he is experiencing a counterfeit of the devil.

Whenever Satan has reason to fear a truth very gravely, he produces a counterfeit. He will try to put that truth in such a bad light that the very persons who are most eager to obey it are frightened away from it. Satan is very sly and very experienced . . . and . . . pawns his parody off as the real thing and soon frightens away the serious-minded saints.

I regret to say that some who have called themselves by a kind of copyrighted name of holiness have allowed the doctrine to harden into a formula which has become a hindrance to repentance, for this doctrine has been invoked to cover up frivolity and covetousness, pride and worldliness. ICH067

> *The Spirit cannot fill whom He cannot separate,
> and whom He cannot fill, He cannot make holy,
> and whom He cannot make holy, He cannot
> make happy!* ITB031

WALKING
IN
HOLY WAYS

*Sanctify yourselves therefore,
and be ye holy: for I am the
LORD your God.*

—Leviticus 20:7

*M*en of God have reminded us in the Word that God does ask us and expect us to be holy men and women of God, because we are the children of God, who is holy.

The doctrine of holiness may have been badly and often wounded—but the provision of God by His pure and gentle and loving Spirit is still the positive answer for those who hunger and thirst for a life and spirit well-pleasing to God.

When a good man with this special quality and mysterious Presence is morally right and walking in all the holy ways of God and carries upon himself without even knowing it the fragrance of a kingdom that is supreme above the kingdoms of this world, I am ready to accept that as being of God and from God! ICH068

[H]oliness depends upon contact with God. Anything that breaks or impairs this vital contact, however slight it may be, interrupts our communion with Christ and brings defeat instead of victory into our lives. CDL180

An Obligation to Adore

O come, let us worship and bow down: let us kneel before the LORD our maker. For he is our God.

—Psalm 95:6-7

*I*f the Holy Spirit should come again upon us as in earlier times, visiting church congregations with the sweet but fiery breath of Pentecost, we would be greater Christians and holier souls. . . .

Men and women continue to try to persuade themselves that there are many forms and ways that seem right in worship. But God in His revelation has told us that He is spirit and those who worship Him must worship Him in spirit and in truth. God takes the matter of worship out of the hands of men and puts it in the hands of the Holy Spirit.

It is impossible for any of us to worship God without the impartation of the Holy Spirit. It is the operation of the Spirit of God within us that enables us to worship God acceptably through that Person we call Jesus Christ, who is Himself God. So worship originates with God and comes back to us and is reflected from us, as a mirror. God accepts no other kind of worship. WHT044-045

> *[God] is the Being whom we are under the greatest obligations to adore, because He is supremely adorable; a Being whom we are under the greatest obligations to love, because He is infinitely lovely.* DTC086

IN SPIRIT AND IN TRUTH

Now we know that God heareth not sinners: but if any man be a worshipper of God, and doeth his will, him he heareth.

—John 9:31

*W*e need to double our efforts to tell the world that God is Spirit and those who worship Him must worship Him in spirit and in truth.

It must be by the Holy Spirit and truth. We cannot worship in the spirit alone, for the spirit without truth is helpless.

We cannot worship in truth alone, for that would be theology without fire.

Worship must be in spirit and in truth!

It must be the truth of God and the Spirit of God. When a person, yielding to God and believing the truth of God, is filled with the Spirit of God, even his faintest whisper will be worship.
WHT045-046

> *I can offer no worship wholly pleasing to God if I know that I am harboring elements in my life that are displeasing to Him. I cannot truly and joyfully worship God on Sunday and not worship Him on Monday. . . . I repeat my view of worship*—no worship is wholly pleasing to God until there is nothing in me displeasing to God. WHT124-125

May

AS HOLY
AS I WANT
TO BE

I dwell in the high and holy place . . . to revive the spirit of the humble, and to revive the heart of the contrite ones.

—Isaiah 57:15

$\mathcal{A}$mong revival-minded Christians I have heard the saying, "Revivals are born after midnight."

This is one of those proverbs which, while not quite literally true, yet points to something very true.

If we understand the saying to mean that God does not hear our prayer for revival made in the daytime, it is of course not true. If we take it to mean that prayer offered when we are tired and worn-out has greater power than prayer made when we are rested and refreshed, again it is not true. . . .

Yet there is considerable truth in the idea that revivals are born after midnight, for revivals . . . come only to those who want them badly enough. It may be said without qualification that every man is as holy and as full of the Spirit as he wants to be. BAM007-008

> *Spirit of God, descend upon my heart;*
> *Wean it from earth, through all its pulses move;*
> *Stoop to my weakness, mighty as Thou art,*
> *And make me love Thee as I ought to love.* HCL137

THE FRUIT OF LOVING OBEDIENCE

And the L̶o̶r̶d̶ thy God will circumcise thine heart ... to love the L̶o̶r̶d̶ thy God with all thine heart, and with all thy soul.

—Deuteronomy 30:6

*O*bedience is both the evidence and the definition of our love for Christ and the condition for receiving the Holy Spirit. We demonstrate our love not simply in an intellectual comprehension of Christ's teachings but by applying them to our lives.

A young married man once called on me expressing a desire to be filled with the Spirit. Prompted by the Spirit, I said, "Go and do the next thing God tells you to do!" He left my study hurt that I had not taken more time with him.

For several weeks I did not see the fellow. When he called again, I knew by looking that God had fulfilled the desire of his heart. He confided that at the time he had called on me, he and his wife were estranged. The "next thing God told [him] to do" was to go to the city where his wife was staying and be reconciled to her. He obeyed the voice of God, and his obedience resulted in the indwelling of the Holy Counselor. As one preacher put it, "Obedience is always followed by blessing!" JJJ336

> *God being who He is must have obedience from His creatures. Man being who he is must render that obedience.* ROR143

A SENSE OF THE PRESENCE

When he came down from the mount . . . Moses wist not that the skin of his face shone while he talked with him.

—Exodus 34:29

I have met a few of God's saints who appeared to have this holy brightness upon them, but they did not know it because of their humility and gentleness of spirit. I do not hesitate to confess that my fellowship with them has meant more to me than all of the teaching I have ever received.

I do stand deeply indebted to every Bible teacher I have had through the years, but they did little but instruct my head. The brethren I have known who had this strange and mysterious quality and awareness of God's Person and Presence instructed my heart.

Do we understand what a gracious thing it is to be able to say of a man, a brother in the Lord, "He is truly a man of God"? He doesn't have to tell us that, but he lives quietly and confidently day by day with the sense of this mysterious, awe-inspiring Presence that . . . means more than all the glib tongues in the world!

ICH072-073

> *Nothing is necessary for you in maintaining a triumphant Christian life but just to . . . put yourself in where the power is. Come unto God, unite yourself to God, and the doing power you have is infinite!—and none the less yours because it is His.* JAS275

WHAT'S HAPPENED TO MORALITY?

Having a form of godliness, but denying the power thereof: from such turn away.

—2 Timothy 3:5

The question being discussed by many these days—why religion is increasing and morality slipping, all at the same time—finds its answer in . . . the error of religious intellectualism. Men have a form of godliness but deny the power thereof.

The text alone will not elevate the moral life. To become morally effective, the truth must be accompanied by a mystic element, the very element supplied by the Spirit of truth. The Holy Spirit will not be banished to a footnote without taking terrible vengeance against His banishers. . . .

The mysterious presence of the Spirit is vitally necessary if we are to avoid the pitfalls of religion. As the fiery pillar led Israel through the wilderness, os the Spirit of truth must lead us all our journey through. One text alone could improve things mightily for us if we would but obey it: "Trust in the LORD with all thine heart; and lean not unto thine own understanding" (Proverbs 3:5). WTA097-098

Evangelical obedience expresses not merely the form, but the power of godliness. . . . God neither requires nor will accept obedience which does not spontaneously flow from supreme love to Himself. DTC199

HUMILITY INVADED BY THE PRESENCE

By humility and the fear of the LORD are riches, and honour, and life.

—Proverbs 22:4

$\mathcal{B}$ring your life into line morally so that God can make it holy; then bring your spiritual life into line that God may settle upon you with the Holy Ghost—with that quality of the Wonderful and the Mysterious and the Divine.

You do not cultivate it and you do not even know it, but it is there and it is this quality of humility invaded by the Presence of God which the church of our day lacks. Oh, that we might yearn for the knowledge and Presence of God in our lives from moment to moment, so that without human cultivation and without toilsome seeking there would come upon us this enduement that gives meaning to our witness! It is a sweet and radiant fragrance and I suggest that in some of our churches it may be strongly sensed and felt. ICH073-074

O God, let Thy glory be revealed once more to men: through me if it please Thee, or without me or apart from me, it matters not. Restore Thy Church to the place of moral beauty that becomes her as the Bride of Christ: through me, or apart from me; only let this prayer be answered. O God, honor whom Thou wilt. Let me be used or overlooked or ignored or forgotten. KDL066

GOD'S PRESENCE— WONDERFULLY REAL

Blessed are they which do hunger and thirst after righteousness: for they shall be filled.

—Matthew 5:6

*T*here are qualities in God that can never be explained to the intellect and can only be known by the heart, the innermost being. That is why I say that I do believe in feeling.

I believe in what the old writers called religious affection—and we have so little of it because we have not laid the groundwork for it. The groundwork is repentance and obedience and separation and holy living!

I am confident that whenever this groundwork is laid, there will come to us this sense of the other-worldly Presence of God and it will become wonderfully, wonderfully real. ICH075

> *The deeper life is a continual discovery of how fully Jesus satisfies the deep yearnings of our hearts.*
>
> *Do we long to be holy? The indwelling Christ offers Himself to us as our holiness!*
>
> *Do we long to know our Father, God? Christ is the Revealer of the Father!*
>
> *Do we long for power that enables a fruitful ministry? Christ, by His Holy Spirit, is that power!* JJJ048

THE MYSTERIOUS PRESENCE

My presence shall go with thee, and I will give thee rest.

—Exodus 33:14

$\mathcal{S}$erious, honest persons have turned away from the whole idea of holiness because of those who have claimed it and then lived selfish and conceited lives.

But, brethren, we are still under the holy authority of the apostolic command. Men of God have reminded us in the Word that God does ask us and expect us to be holy men and women of God, because we are the children of God, who is holy. The doctrine of holiness may have been badly and often wounded—but the provision of God by His pure and gentle and loving Spirit is still the positive answer for those who hunger and thirst for a life and spirit well-pleasing to God.

When a good man with this special quality and mysterious Presence is morally right and walking in all the holy ways of God and carries upon himself without even knowing it the fragrance of a kingdom that is supreme above the kingdoms of this world, I am ready to accept that as being of God and from God! ICH067-068

This is the true divine order: first, reconciliation, then holiness. . . . [I]t is required of those who have been redeemed at such cost and brought into this place of privilege, that they should be holy even as He is holy. CTBC, Vol. 1/199

THE TRUE ESSENCE OF FAITH

Now we have received . . . the spirit which is of God; that we might know the things that are freely given to us of God.

—1 Corinthians 2:12

$\mathcal{T}$he witness of the Spirit is a sacred inner thing which cannot be explained. It is altogether personal and cannot be passed from one to another. . . . [T]he outward ear cannot hear what it says. Much less can the worldly onlooker know what is taking place.

The Spirit whispers its mysterious Presence to the heart, and the heart knows without knowing *how* it knows. Just as we know we are alive by unmediated knowledge and without recourse to proof, so we know we are alive in the Holy Spirit. . . . The witness is in the hidden regions of the spirit, too deep for proof, where external evidence is invalid and "signs" are of no use.

When all is said, it may easily be that the great difference between professing Christians (the *important* difference in this day) is . . . between those who have reduced Christianity to an intellectual formula and those who believe that the true essence of our faith lies in the supernatural workings of the Spirit in a region of the soul not accessible to mere reason. WTA089-090

> *Show me a man who makes the law of God the rule, and the glory of God the end of his conduct . . . and I will show you one whose heart has been sanctified by the Spirit of grace.* DTC207

ATTITUDE IS EVERYTHING

Let us therefore follow after the things which make for peace, and things wherewith one may edify another.

—Romans 14:19

I think God looks beyond the situation to the spirit and attitude. I think He is more concerned with how we react to abuse and mistreatment than to the fact that we have been abused by someone.

Some of us have had experiences of being "told off " most eloquently by people with a very descriptive flow of language; but the eloquence is lost completely insofar as God is concerned.

If you are His child taking some abuse or persecution for His sake, His great concern is the attitude that you will show in return.

Will you reveal a stubborn spirit intent upon revenge? If you resist the Spirit of God asking you to demonstrate the love and grace of Jesus Christ, your Savior, you can be sure of one thing: God will resist you! ICH111

> *He who does not seek and find God everywhere, and in everything, finds Him nowhere and in nothing. And he who is not at the Lord's service in everything, is at His service in nothing.* JAS179

THE HOUR TO BE SERIOUS

> *Wherefore gird up the loins of your mind, be sober, and hope to the end.*
>
> —1 Peter 1:13

$\mathcal{T}$he spirit of the prophet is always subject to the prophet. When the Spirit of God moves into a man's heart, He will never make a fool out of him. He will make the man happy but He will never make him silly.

He may make him sad with the woe and the weight of the world's grief but He will never let him become a gloomy cynic. The Holy Spirit will make him warm-hearted and responsive but He will never cause him to do things of which he will be ashamed later.

Peter was not promoting or predicting a cold and lifeless and formal spirituality in the Christian Church when he advised believers to gird up the loins of their minds and be sober. He was saying to the early Christians as he hopes to say to us now: "Brethren, if ever there was an hour when we needed to be serious about our Christian faith, this is the hour!" ICH135

> *There is nothing so delightful as this consciousness of the very life and heart of Christ within us, the trust that springs spontaneously within our breast, the prayer that prays itself, and the song that sings its joyous triumph even when all around is dark and strange.* CTBC, Vol. 6/164

STUDY,
THEN
DO

This book of the law shall not depart out of thy mouth; but thou shalt meditate therein ... to do ... all that is written therein.

—Joshua 1:8

*T*he great American evangelist, Charles Finney, went so far as to declare bluntly that it is sinful to teach the Bible without moral application. He asked what good is accomplished merely to study a course in the Bible to find out what it says, if there is to be no obligation to do anything as a result of what has been learned?

There can be a right and a wrong emphasis in conducting Bible classes. I am convinced that some Bible classes are nothing more than a means whereby men become even more settled in their religious prejudices.

Only when we have moral application are we in the Bible method! When we give ourselves seriously to Bible study, we discover the Holy Spirit's method. "This is what God did, and this is what God did. Therefore, this is what you ought to do!" That is always the Bible way. ICH137

> *Let's practice the art of Bible meditation. . . . Let us open our Bibles, spread them out on a chair and meditate on the Word of God. It will open itself to us, and the Spirit of God will come and brood over it. . . . Put away the questions and answers and the filling in of blank lines . . . and in faith say, "Father, here I am. Begin to teach me!"* COU137

THE DISCIPLINE OF RIGHT THINKING

Be sober, be vigilant; because your adversary the devil, as a roaring lion, walketh about, seeking whom he may devour.

—1 Peter 5:8

*T*he Holy Spirit knows us well and enforces the exhortation to gird up our minds, to pull up our spiritual standards, to eliminate carelessness in word and thought and deed, and in activities and interest!

Now, let us think of what Peter must have had in mind when he added the words, "be sober," to the discipline of right thinking.

Sobriety is that human attitude of mind when calm reason is in control. The mind is balanced and cool and the feelings are subject to reason and this statement is proof enough for me that the Holy Spirit will never urge believers into any kind of spiritual experience that violates and dethrones reason.

All of us are aware of instances where men and women have taken part in unreasonable and unseemly acts and then excused them on the grounds that they were moved by the Spirit.

Frankly, I must doubt that! I doubt that the Holy Ghost ever moves to dethrone reason in any man's mind. ICH146

Wherever the Holy Spirit . . . comes, He will always be found witnessing to Jesus and honoring the Son of God. HS488

OVERFLOWING WORSHIP

Know ye not that ye are the temple of God, and that the Spirit of God dwelleth in you?

—1 Corinthians 3:16

*T*here is another kind of divine working that may occur without our being aware of it, or at least without our recognizing it for what it is. This is that wondrous operation of God known in theology as *prevenient grace*. It may be simple "conviction," or a strange longing which nothing can satisfy, or a powerful aspiration after eternal values, or a feeling of disgust for sin and a desire to be delivered from its repulsive coils. These strange workings within are the stirrings of the Holy Spirit but are rarely identified as such by the soul that is undergoing the experience.

But there are two acts of God within the life of the seeking man that are never done without his knowledge. One is the miracle of the new birth and the other is the anointing of the Holy Spirit. . . .

The workings of God in the hearts of redeemed men always overflow into observable conduct. Certain moral changes will take place immediately in the life of the new convert. A moral revolution without will accompany the spiritual revolution that has occurred within. WTA088-089

> *Try your heart by your practice, and your practice by your heart.* DTC211

EMOTIONS UNDER CONTROL

And be not drunk with wine, wherein is excess; but be filled with the Spirit.

—Ephesians 5:18

*P*eter and Paul . . . join in urging us to practice and display the loftiest fruits of the Spirit of God with the Spirit Himself in control of our emotions and our affections, our worship and our praise. Yes, brothers, the Spirit will make the believing child of God generous but He will never make him foolish! He will make him happy but He will never make him silly! The Spirit will warm the inner life of the Christian's being but he will never lead him to do the things that would cause him to hang his head in shame afterward.

I say, "Thank God" for the kind of enduring joy which comes to the believer whose emotional life is in the keeping of the Spirit. I stand with the dear child of God whose reason is sanctified and who refuses to be swept from his mooring in the Word of God either by the latest popular vogue in religious fad or the ascendence of the most recent sensational personality in gospel circles. ICH148-149

> *Even the Holy Spirit does not take away our mental poise or expect us to surrender our common sense and will or yield ourselves to any hypnotic influence.* WCC102

TOO BUSY TO BE GLOOMY

Who are kept by the power of God through faith unto salvation. . . . Wherein ye greatly rejoice.

—1 Peter 1:5-6

$\mathcal{T}$he life of the normal, believing child of God can never become a life of gloom and pessimism. In every age we will have some people whose concept of Christianity is a kind of gloomy resignation to the inevitable. But it is the Holy Spirit who has promised the ability for the Christian to rejoice in God's promises day by day. . . .

Peter states it as a paradox: the obedient Christian greatly rejoices even in the midst of great heaviness, trials and suffering. God's people know that things here are not all they ought to be, but they are not spending any time in worrying about it. They are too busy rejoicing in the gracious prospect of all that will take place when God fulfills all of His promises to His redeemed children! ICH158-159

> *Whatever else trouble is in the world for, it is here for this good purpose: to develop strength. . . . Every day we are blessed with new opportunities for the development of strength of soul.* JAS071

> *What harm can happen to him who knows that God does everything, and who loves beforehand everything that God does?* JAS070

CHANGE MAY BE STRANGE

How shall we, that are dead to sin, live any longer therein?

—Romans 6:2

*W*e must admit that the true Christian is a rather strange person in the eye of the unbeliever. I use the adjective *true* in regard to the Christian not only to point out the necessity for the new birth but to indicate, also, the Christian who is living according to his new birth. I speak here of a transformed life pleasing to God, for if you want to be a Christian, you must agree to a very much different life.

The life of obedience to Jesus Christ means living moment by moment in the Spirit of God and it will be so different from your former life that you will often be considered strange. . . . The true Christian may seem a strange person indeed to those who make their observations only from the point of view of this present world, which is alienated from God and His gracious plan of salvation.

Consider now this glorious contradiction. . . . The Christian is dead and yet he lives forever. He died to himself and yet he lives in Christ. The reason he lives is because of the death of another. ICH159-160

> *If we truly want to follow God, we must seek to be other-worldly. . . . Every man must choose his world.* POG052

A HABITATION OF THE SPIRIT

That the righteousness of the law might be fulfilled in us, who walk not after the flesh, but after the Spirit.

—Romans 8:4

*T*he true Christian fears God with a trembling reverence and yet he is not afraid of God at all. He draws nigh to God with full assurance of faith and victory and yet at the same time is trembling with holy awe and fear.

To fear and yet draw near—this is the attitude of faith and love and yet the holy contradiction classifies him as a fanatic, too!

Today, as in all the centuries, true Christians are an enigma to the world, a thorn in the flesh of Adam, a puzzle to angels, the delight of God and a habitation of the Holy Spirit.

Our fellowship ought to take in all of the true children of God, regardless of who and where and what, if they are washed in the blood, born of the Spirit, walking with God the Father, begotten unto a living hope through the resurrection of Jesus Christ and rejoicing in the salvation to be revealed! ICH164-165

As we become occupied with Christ and abide in His fellowship, His glorious likeness is reproduced in us, and we stand before the world, not only living epistles but living likenesses, of our blessed Lord. HS432

UNKNOWN GRACES

When men are cast down, then thou shalt say, There is lifting up; and he shall save the humble person.

—Job 22:29

"No one was ever filled with the Holy Spirit without knowing it. The Holy Spirit always announces Himself to the human consciousness." What . . . [is] the nature of this "announcement"? Of what does it consist? How may we recognize it? Is it some kind of physical evidence, or what? . . .

There is such a thing as the secret workings of the Spirit in the soul of man, for a time unknown and unsuspected by the individual. In fact, most of the fruits of the Spirit are unsuspected by the man in whom they are found.

The most loving, most patient, most compassionate soul is unlikely to be aware of these graces. . . . Others will discover the operations of the Spirit within him long before he will and will thank God for his sweet Christian character while he may at the same time be walking in great humility before God, mourning the absence of the very graces that others know he possesses.

WTA087-088

There is an inseparable connection between a holy heart and a holy life. A holy life can no more proceed from an unholy heart, than a pure stream can flow from an impure fountain. DTC206

HALFWAY TO THE PEAK

Choose you this day whom ye will serve . . . as for me and my house, we will serve the LORD.

—Joshua 24:15

*T*he word mediocre comes from two Latin words and literally means "halfway to the peak." This makes it an apt description of the progress of many Christians. They are halfway up to the peak. . . . They are morally above the hardened sinner but they are spiritually beneath the shining saint. . . .

Do we really think that this halfway Christian life is the best that Christ offers—the best that we can know? In the face of what Christ offers us, how can we settle for so little? Think of all that He offers us by His blood and by His Spirit, by His sacrificial death on the cross, by His resurrection from the dead, by His ascension to the right hand of the Father, by His sending forth of the Holy Ghost! ITB043-044

> *O Jesus, come and dwell in me,*
> *Walk in my steps each day,*
> *Live in my life, love in my love,*
> *And speak in all I say;*
> *Think in my thoughts, let all my acts*
> *Thy very actions be,*
> *So shall it be no longer I,*
> *But Christ that lives in me.* CTBC, Vol. 2/052

THE INTERCHANGE OF LOVE

There is one God; and there is none other but he: and to love him with all the heart, and with all the understanding, and with all the soul.

—Mark 12:32-33

*H*aving been made in His image, we have within us the capacity to know God and the instinct that we should worship Him. The very moment that the Spirit of God has quickened us to His life in regeneration, our whole being senses its kinship to God and leaps up in joyous recognition!

That response within our beings, a response to forgiveness and pardon and regeneration, signals the miracle of the heavenly birth—without which we cannot see the kingdom of God.

Yes, God desires and is pleased to communicate with us through the avenues of our minds, our wills and our emotions. The continuous and unembarrassed interchange of love and thought between God and the souls of redeemed men and women is the throbbing heart of the New Testament religion.

WHT025

> *The one who is caught by [love] is bound by the strongest of all bonds—and yet it is a pleasant burden. . . . Nothing makes you so much God's, nor God so much yours, as this sweet bond. The one who has found this way will seek no other.*
>
> BME036

GOD HIMSELF— NOTHING MORE

I saw also the Lord sitting upon a throne, high and lifted up, and his train filled the temple.

—Isaiah 6:1

*B*rethren, when we finally have our meeting with God, it has to be alone in the depths of our being. We will be alone even if we are surrounded by a crowd. God has to cut every maverick out of the herd and brand him all alone. It isn't something that God can do for us en masse.

If it takes a crowd to get you converted, you have not been converted! If it takes a crowd to get you through the fullness of the Holy Ghost, you are going to be disappointed.

I know that people do not want to be alone with God, but if your longing heart ever finds the living water, it will be alone. We humans want to help each other and that is good insofar as we can, but God wants us to press through to His Presence where there is no natural or artificial help. . . .

He asks that we come with a naked intent unto God. We must want God Himself—and nothing more! ITB106

> *The love of God is paramount to every other principle . . . every desire subservient to that of promoting his glory.* DTC072

THE
SILENT
DOVE

And, lo, the heavens were opened unto him, and he saw the Spirit of God descending like a dove, and lighting upon him.

—Matthew 3:16

$\mathcal{G}$od waits for your faith and your love, and He doesn't ask whose interpretation of Scripture you have accepted. The New Testament tells of believers who met and prayed together, the strong taking the burdens of the weak, and all praying for those who had fallen. The place was shaken, and they were all filled with the Holy Ghost.

"Pay no attention to that," we have been told by "interpreters." "That is not for us." So it has been ruled out by interpretation and the blessed Dove has been forced to fold His wings and be silent.

Our hearts tell us that these modern scribes who are long on interpretation are wrong in spirit. Our own longing souls tell us that the old saints and hymn writers and the devotional giants were right! ITB119-120

> *Come, Holy Spirit, heavenly Dove,*
> *With all Thy Quickening powers;*
> *Come shed abroad a Saviour's love;*
> *And that shall kindle ours.* HCL140

HOW WELL
DO I KNOW
MY HEART?

Create in me a clean heart, O God; and renew a right spirit within me.

—Psalm 51:10

None of us can really tell how weak and useless we are until God has exposed us—and no one wants to be exposed! But God knows so much better than we do that He must expose us for our own good.

Neither do any of us really know how unstable we are until we have been exposed by the Holy Ghost. Peter was a big, bold, strong fisherman, and it seemed easy for him to say to the Lord, "Let everyone else run away, but I will always stand by. You can count on me, Master!" I am sure it was hard for him to take the answer that Jesus gave him: "Before the rooster crows tonight you will say three times that you do not know me!" (See Matthew 26:33-34.) But Jesus knew the instability of the man who still tried to stand in his own strength and in his own self-trust.

We do not really know how unstable we are, and we often refuse to admit the truth when we find out, when we are exposed. That is why it is too dangerous to trust our good habits and our virtues—and that is why our distrust of ourselves must be the work of God's hand! ITB131-132

We must pass sentence upon our sinful heart and give God the right to cleanse it. CTBC, Vol. 5/313

"BE" FIRST, THEN "DO"

Every good tree bringeth forth good fruit; but a corrupt tree bringeth forth evil fruit.

—Matthew 7:17

*W*hile good deeds cannot make a man good, it is likewise true that everything a good man does is good because he is a good man. Holy deeds are holy not because they are one kind of deed instead of another, but because a holy man performs them. . . .

Every person should see to it that he is fully cleansed from all sin, entirely surrendered to the whole will of God and filled with the Holy Spirit. Then he will not be known as what he *does*, but as what he *is*. He will be a man of God first and anything else second: a man of God who paints or mines coal or farms or preaches . . . but always a man of God. That and not the kind of work he does will determine the quality of his deeds. WTA060

> *We need to remember that this world is not so much a place for doing things as for making character. Right in the midst of what some people call drudgery is the very best place to get the transformed, transfigured life.* JAS276
>
> *God weigheth more with how much love a man worketh, than how much he doeth. He doeth much that loveth much. He doeth much that doeth a thing well.* JAS276

GOD'S WAY IS BEST

In all thy ways acknowledge him, and he shall direct thy paths.

—Proverbs 3:6

The Christian who has in principle accepted God's truth as his standard of conduct and has submitted himself to Christ as his Lord, may yet be tempted to lay his own plans and even fight for them when they are challenged by the Word of God or the inner voice of the Spirit.

We humans are a calculating, planning race, and we like to say, "Tomorrow I will. . . ." But our Heavenly Father knows us too well to trust our way to our own planning, so He very often submits His own plans to us and requires that we accept them.

Right there a controversy is sometimes stirred up between the soul and God. But we had better not insist on our own way. It will always be bad for us in the long run. God's way is best.
WTA045

> *Instead of being supremely attached to God and the good of his kingdom, men are by nature "lovers of their own selves." Hence there is a controversy between man and his Maker. God requires men to regard His glory as the great object of their affections, and the ultimate end of their conduct.*
> DTC138

IRRITATING
OR
ATTRACTIVE?

Ye that love the LORD, hate evil: he preserveth the souls of his saints.

—Psalm 97:10

$\mathcal{S}$ometimes we Christians are opposed and persecuted for reasons other than our godliness. We like to think it is our spirituality that irritates people, when in reality, it may be our personality.

True, the spirit of this world is opposed to the Spirit of God; he that is born after the flesh will persecute him that is born of the Spirit. But making all allowances, it is still true that some Christians get into trouble through their faults instead of through their likeness to the character of Christ. We may as well admit this and do something about it. No good can come from trying to hide our unpleasant and annoying dispositional traits behind a verse of Scripture.

It is one of the strange facts of life that gross sins are often less offensive and always more attractive than spiritual ones. The world can tolerate a drunkard or a glutton or a smiling braggart but will turn in savage fury against the man of outwardly righteous life who is guilty of those refined sins, which he does not recognize as sins, but which may be more exceeding sinful than the sins of the flesh. WTA036

*In the sanctified heart, the hatred of sin is su-*preme. DTC094

DETACHED OR ATTACHED?

And Enoch walked with God: and he was not; for God took him.

—Genesis 5:24

*E*noch was a spiritual rebuke to his own generation. He fought off the wiles and the temptations of the devil. He purposed within himself: "I will walk with God by faith even if that means that I must be detached from my generation."

Are you really detached from your generation because you resist the devil and walk in the fullness of the Holy Spirit? Am I? That is a very personal question, and we dare not try to answer it for each other.

Our generation in this world system claims that there is no personal devil, no enemy of our souls. Yet, all the while, Satan is busy. He is using a successful, age-old tactic with many people. He is assuring them in a variety of ways that there is no urgency in the matters of faith. . . . "Put off a decision until you feel you are ready." That is the devil's urging to those who are lost. As a result, millions have waited. And in waiting, they have never come to God in repentance and faith. JAF026-027

> *As of old [Christ] hung on Calvary between two*
> *men that represented at once both heaven and hell,*
> *so still it is true that the cross of Jesus is the dividing*
> *line between lost and saved men.* CTBC, Vol. 3/322

ADD UP THE COLUMNS

But now being made free from sin, and become servants to God, ye have . . . everlasting life.

—Romans 6:22

$\mathcal{G}$od calls us into the joys and reality of eternal life. He calls us into purity of life and spirit, so that we may acceptably walk with Him. He calls us into a life of service and usefulness that brings glory to Himself as our God. He calls us into the sweetest fellowship possible on this earth—the fellowship of the family of God!

I hope I never hear any Christian bragging even a little bit about what he or she gave up and how much it cost him or her to answer the call of God. Anything that we were or any abilities that we possessed were as nothing compared to what God has called us into as His believing children.

Why is it so difficult in our churches for us to be honest about our lives and our condition as sinners alienated from God? We did not give up anything when God in His love and mercy called us unto Himself and into the blessings of grace and forgiveness and peace. JAF049

Counting is not the language of poetry or sentiment but of cold, unerring calculation. It adds up the columns thus: sorrow, temptation, difficulty, opposition, depression, desertion, danger, discouragement . . . but at the bottom of the column God's presence, God's will, God's joy, God's promise, God's recompense. ISS093

CELEBRATE DIVERSITY!

For as the body is one, and hath many members . . . so also is Christ. . . . For the body is not one member, but many.

—1 Corinthians 12:12, 14

$\mathcal{G}$od makes all of us different from one another, but by His Spirit He will bring divine illumination and power to our beings. . . . It is God's planned variety and not similarity that makes beauty and interest in our world.

We should thank God for giving us our own individual personalities and temperaments and abilities. We should never waste time and energy trying to fashion ourselves after someone else, no matter how much we admire that person. God does not expect us to become identical copies of our spiritual heroes. . . .

In only these respects should we all try to be alike: We should love God more than anything or anyone else, we should hate sin and iniquity even as Jesus hated them, and we should be willing always to obey God through the leading of His Word and His Spirit. Apart from that, it is perfectly natural for us to be ourselves, that is, different from each other. JAF068-069

> *He gives the Spirit to each of His servants. The differences among Christian workers are not due to favoritism or partiality on the part of God, but to the different way in which each follower of Christ improves His gift.* CTBC, Vol. 4/332

ONE ENEMY, ONE GOAL

Let us lay aside every weight, and . . . let us run with patience the race that is set before us.

—Hebrews 12:1

*A*ll of us Christians have a common enemy, that old devil, Satan. As we stand together, pray together, worship together, we repudiate him and his deceptions. He is our common foe, and he uses a variety of manipulations to hinder us in our spiritual lives.

When by faith we have entered this lifelong spiritual course, the Holy Spirit whispers, "Do you truly want to be among the victors in this discipline?" When we breathe our "Yes! Yes!" He whispers of ways that will aid us and carry us to certain victory.

The Spirit tells us to throw off everything that would hinder us in the race. He tells us to be aware of the little sins and errors that could divert us from the will of God as we run. But here is the important thing: He tells us to keep our eyes on Jesus, because He alone is our pacesetter and victorious example. JAF076-077

> *The secret of victory is to recognize the Conqueror within and the adversary as a conquered foe. . . . Satan has power only when he can make us dread him. He flees before the victorious faith and holy confidence.* HS546-547

ONE FOCUS, ONE GOAL

And if any man sin, we have an advocate with the Father, Jesus Christ the righteous.

—1 John 2:1

$\mathcal{I}$n a very real sense, faith is fixing our eyes on Jesus, keeping Jesus in full view regardless of what others may be doing all around us. This is excellent counsel, because as human beings we know we are not sufficient in ourselves. It is in our nature to look out—to look beyond ourselves for help. This world is big and deadly, and we are too weak and not wise enough to deal with it!

It is also a human trait to look beyond ourselves for assurance. We hope to find someone worthy of trust. We want someone who has made good, someone who has done what we would like to do.

The Hebrews writer points us to the perfect One, our eternal High Priest, seated now at the right hand of God. He is Jesus, the Pioneer and Perfecter of our faith. He has endured the cross and is now the eternal Victor and our Advocate in heaven.
JAF077

> *He who fought [the] battle once, comes still to fight it in our hearts. He who believed for Himself, now believes in us, and sustains in us the spirit of trust and victory.* CTBC, Vol. 3/194

June

MY ATTITUDE TO THE CROSS

But God forbid that I should glory, save in the cross of our Lord Jesus Christ.

—Galatians 6:14

$\mathcal{I}$ find a deep, compelling message in the words of an old hymn no longer sung. And I am concerned for the spiritual desire now seemingly lost with the hymn:

> Oh, for that flame of living fire
> Which shone so bright in saints of old,
> Which bade their souls to heaven aspire,
> Calm in distress, in danger bold.
>
> Where is that Spirit, Lord, which dwelt
> In Abram's breast and sealed him Thine,
> Which made Paul's heart with sorrow melt
> And glow with energy divine?
>
> That Spirit which from age to age
> Proclaimed Thy love and taught Thy ways,
> Brightened Isaiah's vivid page
> And breathed in David's hallowed lays.

. . . "Where is that Spirit, Lord?" Why must we cry in pathetic and plaintive manner, "Where is Thy Spirit, Lord?" I think it is because we differ from the saints of old in our relation to the cross—our attitude toward the cross. JAF081-082

> *[T]he cross on the hill must become the cross in our hearts.* JAF083

THE CROSS OF POWER

> *What things were gain to me,*
> *those I counted loss for Christ....*
> *that I may know ... the fellowship*
> *of his sufferings.*
>
> —Philippians 3:7, 10

*C*hristians have decided where to put the cross. They have made the cross objective instead of subjective. They have made the cross external instead of internal. They have made it institutional instead of experiential.

Now, the terrible thing is that they are so wrong because they are half right. They are right in making the cross objective. It was something that once stood on a hill with a man dying on it, the just for the unjust. They are right that it was an external cross—for on that cross God performed a judicial act that will last while the ages burn themselves out. . . .

But here is where they are wrong: They fail to see that there is a very real cross for you and me. There is a cross for every one of us—a cross that is subjective, internal, experiential. Our cross is an experience within. . . . When that cross on the hill has been transformed by the miraculous grace of the Holy Spirit into the cross in the heart, then we begin to know something of its true meaning and it will become to us the cross of power. JAF082-083

> *Our spiritual life is perfected by the constant rec-*
> *ognition of the cross and by our unceasing applica-*
> *tion of it to all our life and being.* CC031

WHAT WOULD JESUS DO?

Let the word of Christ dwell in you richly in all wisdom; teaching and admonishing one another.

—Colossians 3:16

$\mathcal{I}$ have known people who seemed to be terrified by God's loving desire that we should reflect His own holiness and goodness. As God's faithful children, we should be attracted to holiness, for holiness is God-likeness—likeness to God!

God encourages every Christian believer to follow after holiness. Holiness is to be our constant ambition—not as holy as God is holy, but holy because God is holy. We know who we are and God knows who He is. He does not ask us to be God, and He does not ask us to produce the holiness that only He Himself knows. Only God is holy absolutely; all other beings can be holy only in relative degrees.

The angels in heaven do not possess God's holiness. They are created beings and they are contented to reflect the glory of God. That is their holiness.

Holiness is not terrifying. Actually, it is amazing and wonderful that God should promise us the privilege of sharing in His nature. JAF089-090

> *To know Christ is the way to grow in holiness. Christianity is . . . the religion of the divine example. . . . Ask yourself . . . what would [Jesus] do if He were here? Nothing else will so surely lead us into the way of holy living.* JAS122

ONLY THE SPIRIT

No man can say that Jesus is the Lord, but by the Holy Ghost.

—1 Corinthians 12:3

I think that one of the most hopeless tasks in the world is that of trying to create some love for Christ our Savior among those who refuse and deny that there is a need for a definite spiritual experience of Jesus Christ in the human life.

I cannot understand the activities of many churches—their futile exercise of trying to whip up love and concern for Jesus Christ when there is no teaching of the new birth, no teaching of redemption through His blood, no dependence upon spiritual illumination by the Spirit of God!

No one can love the Lord Jesus Christ unless the Spirit of God is given opportunity to reveal Him in the life. No one can say that Jesus is Lord except the Holy Spirit enables him through spiritual life and experience. WPJ200

> *Those who have "put on the new man, which after God is created in righteousness and true holiness," love God because He is just such a God as He is. . . . The enemies of God may love Him for what they* imagine *Him to be; none but the real friends of God love Him for what* He *is.*
>
> DTC066-067

ME, MYSELF AND I

For as ye have yielded your members servants to uncleanness . . . even so now yield your members servants to righteousness unto holiness.

—Romans 6:19

*T*rue Christianity deals with the human problem of the self-life, with the basic matter of "me, myself and I." The Spirit of God deals with it by an intolerant and final destruction, saying, "This selfish *I* cannot live if God is to be glorified in this human life."

God Himself deals with this aspect of human nature—the sum of all our proud life—and pronounces a stern condemnation upon it, flatly and frankly disapproving of it, fully and completely rejecting it.

And what does God say about it? "I am God alone, and I will have nothing to do with man's selfish ego, in which I find the essence of rebellion and disobedience and unbelief. Man's nature in its pride of self and egotism is anti-God—and sinful, indeed!" WPJ161-162

He who is not a stranger to the spirit of self-denial, has learned to make his own interest bend to the interest of God's kingdom. . . . It is his great concern that God should be glorified, that His laws should be obeyed, His gospel loved, and the highest interest of His infinitely extended kingdom prevail and triumph. DTC142

HIGH PLANS FOR HUMANS

*W*hen the wonder of regeneration has taken place in our lives, then comes the lifetime of preparation with the guidance of the Holy Spirit.

God has told us that heaven and the glories of the heavenly kingdom are more than humans can ever dream or imagine. It will be neither an exhibition of the commonplace nor a democracy for the spiritually mediocre.

Why should we try to be detractors of God's gracious and rewarding plan of discipleship? God has high plans for all of His redeemed ones. It is inherent in His infinite being that His motives are love and goodness. His plans for us come out of His eternal and creative wisdom and power.

Beyond that is His knowledge and regard for the astonishing potential that lies resident in human nature, long asleep in sin but awakened by the Holy Spirit in regeneration. JAF093-094

Redemption puts God where He belongs—exalted to the throne—and man where he belongs—down in the dust—in order that God may . . . raise man to the throne. SAT138

A
DISCIPLE
IN TRAINING

Happy is the man that findeth wisdom, and the man that getteth understanding.

—Proverbs 3:13

A disciple is one who is in training. Being a disciple of Christ brings us to the day-by-day realities of such terms as discipline, rebuke, correction, hardship. Those are not pleasant words....

In times of testing and hardship, I have heard Christians cry in their discouragement, "How can I believe that God loves me?" The fact is, God loves us to such a degree that He will use every necessary means to mature us until we reach "unity of the faith" and attain "unto the measure of the stature of the fulness of Christ" (Ephesians 4:13).

A critic may cringe and charge that God is breaking our spirits, that we will be worth nothing as a result.... Oh, no! That is not true. What God plans is to bring us into accord with the wisdom and power and holiness that flow eternally from His throne. JAF094-095

> *How good it would be if we could learn that God is easy to live with.... He may sometimes chasten us, it is true, but even this He does with a smile.* ROR016

ONLY A REHEARSAL FOR HEAVEN

For I reckon that the sufferings of this present time are not worthy to be compared with the glory which shall be revealed.

—Romans 8:18

$\mathcal{G}$od's loving motive [in discipline] is to bring us into total harmony with Himself so that moral power and holy usefulness become ours in this world and in the world to come. . . .

My mind returns frequently to some of the old Christian saints who often prayed in their faith, "O God, we know this world is only a dressing room for the heaven to come!" They were very close to the truth in their vision of what God has planned for His children.

In summary: Down here the orchestra merely rehearses; over there we will give the concert. Here, we ready our garments of righteousness; over there we will wear them at the wedding of the Lamb. JAF095-096

> *God's richest blessings often require not only sacrifice, suffering and . . . conflict, but long delay and patient waiting. But the blessing grows with the delay. The interest gathers with the extended time, and God's ratio is always compound interest.* CTBC, Vol. 2/065

THE UNPARDONABLE SIN

For God sent not his Son into the world to condemn the world; but that the world through him might be saved.

—John 3:17

*T*here have been many backslidden Christians who have agonized over the possibility of having committed the unpardonable sin. I have discovered a very helpful rule in this matter. I believe it holds good throughout the whole Church of God around the world. *Anyone who is concerned about having committed the unpardonable sin may be sure he or she has not!*

Any person who has ever committed that dark and dread unpardonable sin feels no guilt and confesses no worry. Jesus dealt with the Pharisees . . . [b]ut His warning caused them no worry. They still believed themselves to be entirely righteous! They felt no need for repentance, no sorrow for sin, no guilt for unbelief. "Do not worry about us," was their attitude. "We do not have any problem!"

Returning to our rule for Christians with guilt and concern, the very fact that a person is worried and concerned indicates that the Spirit of God is still working in his or her life. JAF103

God not only forgives great sins as readily as little ones, but once He has forgiven them He starts anew right there and never brings up the old sins again. FBR112

THANKFUL FOR GRACE

My grace is sufficient for thee: for my strength is made perfect in weakness.

—2 Corinthians 12:9

$\mathcal{T}$he inspired Word of God insists that the reality and the blessings from the heart of the living Christ are not reserved for some future and heavenly age. . . .

We can meet God and His Spirit in blessed reality now! We can know and commune with our Lord Jesus Christ in our heart of hearts now! We may know the joy of sensing all around us God's innumerable company and the fellowship with the church of the Firstborn *now!*

As committed Christians, we know what we believe and we know what God has done for us. We want to make it plain to our own day and age that we are highly privileged to be part of a Christian church in God's plan and in God's will. We are thankful for the dimensions of His grace and love. JAF111-112

It is possible . . . for those who will indeed draw on their Lord's power . . . to live a life in which His promises are taken as they stand, and found to be true. It is possible to cast every care on Him, daily, and to be at peace amidst the pressure. It is possible to see the will of God in everything. . . . These are things divinely possible. JAS187

COMING TOGETHER— A BLESSED FELLOWSHIP

*As we have therefore opportu-
nity, let us do good unto all men,
especially unto them who are of
the household of faith.*

—Galatians 6:10

The church of Jesus Christ, His believing body on earth, recognizes that "our conversation is in heaven; from whence also we look for the Saviour, the Lord Jesus Christ" (Philippians 3:20). The believing Christian agrees that he or she is a migrant and a pilgrim.

To these believers, God has imparted His own nature. They have a distinct sense of belonging to one another while they live—almost as exiles—in an unfriendly world. These earthly citizens of heaven speak a common language—that of their constitution, which is the Bible, the Word of God. They love to sing the songs of Zion, for they are loyal to the same Lord and King. Thus the Christians come together where the life of the assembly is the life of Christ.

This is the Bible pattern. God the Father is there. Christ the Son is present. The Holy Spirit indwells each member. . . . The spirit within us can experience and taste the glories of God in a blessed fellowship now. Such is the joyful purpose of the Church! JAF118

> *Next to God Himself we need each other most. . . .
> [S]hould we for a moment lose sight of the Shep-
> herd we only have to go where His flock is to find
> Him again.* BAM114

COME!
COME
QUICKLY!

Whom having not seen, ye love; in whom, though now ye see him not, yet believing, ye rejoice with joy unspeakable and full of glory.

—1 Peter 1:8

The people of God ought to be the happiest people in all the wide world! People should be coming to us constantly and asking the source of our joy and delight—redeemed by the blood of the Lamb, our yesterdays behind us, our sin under the blood forever and a day, to be remembered against us no more forever. God is our Father, Christ is our Brother, the Holy Spirit our Advocate and Comforter. Our Brother has gone to the Father's house to prepare a place for us, leaving with us the promise that He will come again!

Don't send Moses, Lord, don't send Moses! He broke the tablets of stone. Don't send Elijah for me, Lord! I am afraid of Elijah—he called down fire from heaven.

Don't send Paul, Lord! He is so learned that I feel like a little boy when I read his epistles.

Oh, Lord Jesus, come Yourself! I am not afraid of You. You took the little children as lambs to Your fold. You forgave the woman taken in adultery. You healed the timid woman who reached out in the crowd to touch You. We are not afraid of You!

Even so, come, Lord Jesus!
Come quickly! WPJ154

ON THE HEAVENLY PLAIN

And hath raised us up together, and made us sit together in heavenly places in Christ Jesus.

—Ephesians 2:6

*E*arth may have been good enough for that creature who was created from the dust and clay, but it is not good enough for the living soul who is redeemed by royal blood!

Earth was fit and proper to be the eternal dwelling place for that creature who was made by God's hand, but it is not appropriate nor sufficient to be the eternal dwelling place of that redeemed being who is begotten of the Holy Spirit. Every born-again Christian has been lifted up—lifted up from the level of the fallen Adamic race to the heavenly plane of the unfallen and victorious Christ. He belongs up there! WPJ150

> *The children of God are partakers of the divine nature. From bearing the "image of the earthly," they now bear the "image of the heavenly." God has imparted to them a portion of His own loveliness. He has formed them new creatures.* DTC166

> *And I shall see Him face to face*
> *And tell the story—saved by grace:*
> *And I shall see Him face to face*
> *And tell the story—saved by grace.* HCL386

TRANSFORMED TO HIS IMAGE

Be ye transformed by the re-
newing of your mind, that ye may
prove what is that good, and ac-
ceptable, and perfect, will of God.

—Romans 12:2

Some people seem to think that Jesus came only to reclaim us or restore us so that we could regain the original image of Adam. . . . Christ did infinitely more in His death and resurrection than just undoing the damage of the fall. He came to raise us into the image of Jesus Christ. . . . The first man Adam was a living soul, the second man Adam was a life-giving Spirit. The first man Adam was made of the earth earthy, but the second man is the Lord from heaven!

Redemption in Christ, then, is not to pay back dollar-for-dollar or to straighten man out and restore him into Adamic grace. The purpose and work of redemption in Christ Jesus is to raise man as much above the level of Adam as Christ Himself is above the level of Adam. We are to gaze upon Christ, not Adam, and in so doing are being transformed by the Spirit of God into Christ's image.
WPJ149-150

> *We choose to be transformed to His image, but we cannot create that image by our own morality or struggles after righteousness. We must be created anew in His likeness by His own Spirit, and stamped with His resemblance by His heavenly seal impressed directly upon our hearts from His hand.* WS033

LOVE—
GOD IN
HUMAN FORM

*Oh how great is thy goodness,
which thou hast laid up for
them that fear thee.*

—Psalm 31:19

$\mathcal{T}$he Holy Spirit . . . helps us recognize the kind of love we received from Jesus Christ, who has freed us from our sins by His blood. Have you yet learned that love is not a thing of reason? Love tries to be reasonable, but it seldom succeeds. There is a sweet wisdom in love that is above reason—it rises above it and goes far beyond it. Who could ever imagine the God of all the universe condensing Himself into human form and, out of His love, dying for His alienated people? It seems an unreasonable thing to do, but it was reasonable in that it was the supreme wisdom of the mighty God!

The saintly Lady Julian, centuries ago, cherished this love that is ours in Christ. She wrote: "Out of His goodness, God made us. Out of His goodness, He keeps us. When man had sinned, He redeemed us again out of His goodness. Then do you not suppose that God will give His children the best of everything out of His goodness?" JIV045

> *God is not justice. God is not wisdom. God is not power. God has all these attributes but none of them is great enough to constitute His essence. But love is His very nature and in love all other attributes find their completeness.* CTBC, Vol. 6/361

FROM
INQUIRE
TO DESIRE

For the LORD knoweth the way
of the righteous: but the way of
the ungodly shall perish.

—Psalm 1:6

*I*t is not enough to inquire about the power of the crucified life and the Spirit-filled life. It is not enough to want it—it must be desired and claimed above everything else. There must be an abandonment to Jesus Christ to realize it. The individual must want the fullness of Christ with such desire that he will turn his back on whatever else matters in his life and walk straight to the arms of Jesus!

So much for the case of the rich young ruler. His veil was taken away and he turned from Jesus Christ. He was still the hypocrite, still a covetous man, a money-lover, a breaker of the law. Above all, he was still a sinner, and Christless.

He had to pay a great price to keep what he loved most. . . . We have no idea in terms of money and land and possessions what the rich young ruler paid in his refusal to follow Jesus. WPJ071

> *The secret of a Christlike life lies partly in the deep*
> *longing for it. We grow like the ideals that we ad-*
> *mire. We reach unconsciously at last the things we*
> *aspire to. Ask God to give you a high conception of*
> *the character of Christ and an intense desire to be*
> *like Him and you will never rest until you reach*
> *your ideal.* CTBC, Vol. 6/338-339

HONORING THE HOLY SPIRIT

He that hath an ear, let him hear what the Spirit saith unto the churches.

—Revelation 2:29

$\mathcal{T}$here is a question that should be answered in every Christian church: Are we honoring the Holy Spirit of God? That is, are we allowing Him to do what He wants to do in our midst today?

More than once in the Revelation John mentions the seven-fold Spirit of God and His presence before the heavenly throne. . . . Jesus did not begin His earthly ministry until at His water baptism the living Spirit of God had become all of those things to Him.

I have reason to suspect that many people are trying to give leadership in Christian churches today without ever having yielded to the wise and effective leading of the Holy Spirit. He truly is the Spirit of wisdom, understanding and counsel. He alone can bring the gracious presence of the living God into our lives and ministries. JIV047-048

> *[Jesus] has left to us the same power which He possessed. He has bequeathed to the Church the very Holy Spirit that lived and worked in Him. Let us accept this mighty gift.* HS314

MORE AND MORE, LESS AND LESS

And when he had said this, he breathed on them, and saith unto them, Receive ye the Holy Ghost.

—John 20:22

*I*n our churches today we are leaning too heavily upon human talents and educated abilities. We forget that the illumination of the Holy Spirit of God is a necessity, not only in our ministerial preparation, but in the administrative and leadership functions of our churches.

We need an enduement of the Spirit of God! We sorely need more of His wisdom, His counsel, His power, His knowledge. We need to reverence and fear the Almighty God. If we knew the full provision and the spiritual anointing that Jesus promised through the Holy Spirit, we would be far less dependent on so many other things.

Psychiatrists, psychologists, anthropologists, sociologists—and most of the other "ologists"—have their place in our society. I do not doubt that. But many of these professionals now have credentials in the church, and I fear that their counsel is put above the ministry of the Holy Spirit. I have said it before, and I say it now: We need the Holy Spirit more and more, and we need human helps less and less! JIV048

> [T]he Holy Spirit is the source of all spiritual power. He and He alone can . . . make us count for God and humanity, and the great purpose of our existence. HS321

ANYTHING YOU NEED

Put on the new man, which af-ter God is created in righteous-ness and true holiness.

—Ephesians 4:24

$\mathcal{G}$od holds no mental reservations about any of us when we become His children by faith. When He forgives us, He trusts us as though we had never sinned. When Satan comes around to taunt me about my past sins, I remind him that everything that had been charged against me came from him, and now everything I have—forgiveness and peace and freedom—I have freely received from my Lord Jesus Christ!

As long as you remain on this earth, God has not completed His work in you. The Spirit of God will help you discern when the chastening hand of God is upon you. But if it is the devil trying to tamper with your Christian life and testimony, dare to resist him in the victorious power of the living Christ. . . .

He has said to us, "Whatever your need, just come to the throne of grace. Anything you need, you may have!" Why not believe Him and exercise the dominion He has given you? JIV049-050

[W]e are compared with what we could be, not just what we should be. . . . [A]nything we ought to be we can be. Anything that God has declared that we should be we can be. RRR019-020

THE CHRIST QUESTION

And in the midst of the seven candlesticks one like unto the Son of man.

—Revelation 1:13

*T*hose celebrated European painters, whose works adorn the world's great art galleries, undoubtedly did their best to depict our Lord. They were limited, however, by their finite concepts of the Subject. To be frank, I do not want to hold in my mind an unworthy concept of my divine Savior. We Christians should earnestly desire the Holy Spirit to sketch a true and transforming portrait of Jesus Christ across our innermost beings! Our delight should be in the assurance that Christ lives within us, moment by moment. And that assurance must come from God's holy Word.

Do you personally desire with me that the Holy Spirit will dip His brush and begin to paint across the canvas of our souls a living portrayal of Jesus Christ, complete with blood and fire? JIV053-054

> *[U]ntil you receive Christ as God's Messenger and Channel of all blessing, you have not met the God of redemption. . . . The very first step in the Christian life is to come to Christ, to receive Christ, to become united to Christ, and to find Christ the Channel, Condition and Source of every blessing. . . . The question for every man is the Christ question.* CTBC, Vol. 5/420

GOD SEES ALL, KNOWS ALL

To him that overcometh will I give to eat of the tree of life, which is in the midst of the paradise of God.

—Revelation 2:7

*W*e have lived with unholiness so long that we are almost incapable of recognizing true holiness. The people of God in the churches of Jesus Christ ought to be a holy people. But ministers have largely given up preaching Bible-centered sermons on holiness. Maybe they would not know what to do with hearers who fell under the convicting power of God's Word. Preachers today would rather give their congregations tranquilizers. . . .

Our Lord is a holy Lord, and His eyes are as a flame of fire. His X-ray eyes can see right through everything! We can hide nothing from God. He sees all and knows all. But apparently we have a hard time with that fact—preachers and lay people alike. We seem to think our respectability should be accepted by our Lord as spirituality. JIV061-062

> *The basic principle in a spiritual life lies in its control. The Holy Spirit works to bring the Christian to refuse the further reign of self and to choose the sovereignty of Christ over his life by yielding to Him as Lord.*
>
> *You cannot get power from God until you receive holiness.* HS071

COME TO THE WATER

I thank God for Christian men and women who want to know the facts and the truths as they have come from God. Thank God, they are not just looking for someone to give them a relaxing religious massage! These are the facts—the blood of Jesus Christ cleanses. There is a purging element in Christianity. Then there is the Holy Spirit, the blessed Spirit of God who brings us the peace and tranquillity of the waters of Shiloah.

The living God invites us to the stream, the only perennial stream in the world, the only stream that never runs dry, the only stream that never overflows and destroys. WPJ047-048

> *There flows from Calvary a stream*
> *For every sinner's pain,*
> *And he that drinketh, Jesus said,*
> *Shall never thirst again.*
>
> *This stream from Calvary still flows*
> *To bless and cleanse and heal,*
> *And he that drinketh, Jesus said,*
> *New life and rest shall feel.* HCL516

IF I
MISS . . .

In my Father's house are many mansions: if it were not so, I would have told you. I go to prepare a place for you.

—John 14:2

If I miss the love and the mercy and the grace of God in this life, who is to be blamed? Certainly not the God who sits on the throne. He made full provision for my salvation. Certainly not the Lamb who stands before the throne. He died for my sins and rose again for my justification. Certainly not the radiant, flaming Holy Spirit who has accosted men and women all over the world, mediating to them the saving gospel of Christ.

Hear the words John heard on rocky Patmos as the Revelation of Jesus Christ concluded:

> And, behold, I come quickly; and my reward is with me, to give to every man according as his work shall be. . . . Blessed are they that do his commandments, that they may have right to the tree of life, and may enter in through the gates into the city. . . . And the Spirit and the bride say, Come. . . . And let him that is athirst come. And whosoever will, let him take the water of life freely. (22:12, 14, 17)

If I miss God's great salvation, has this life been worth the struggle? Personally, I think not! JIV076

> *[I]f we go to heaven it is because we have a nature that belongs there.* EFE103

THE ABILITY TO WAIT

Behold, I come quickly; and my reward is with me, to give every man according as his work shall be.

—Revelation 22:12

*W*hen Jesus was on earth 2,000 years ago, He told His hearers that the "day of the Lord" was coming. He said no one except the Father in heaven knew the day or the hour.

It is our understanding that God's patience and His time of grace will endure until the world's cup of iniquity overflows. According to the Scriptures, patience—the ability to wait—is one of the fruits of the Holy Spirit.

The human, natural part of us does not like to wait for anything. But the great God Almighty, who has all of eternity to accomplish His purposes, can afford to wait. In our creature impatience we are prone to cry out, "O God, how long? How long?"

And God replies, in effect, "Why are you in such a hurry? We have an eternity stretching before us." JIV094

> *It is not enough merely to know that Christ is coming, and to desire it. It is a great crisis in the life of a soul when it becomes truly centered there. The attraction of the soul is removed from earth to the heavens and learns to live under the power of the world to come.* HS360

GO
TO THE
BOOK!

My mouth shall praise thee
with joyful lips: when I re-
member thee upon my bed, and
meditate on thee.

—Psalm 63:5-6

*W*hat are we allowing the Word of God to say to us, and what is our reaction to that Word? Have we consumed and digested the Book? Have we absorbed the Word of God into our lives? . . .

When we, as Christians, love our Lord Jesus Christ with heart and soul and mind, the Word of God is on our side! If we could only grasp the fact that God's Word is more than a book! It is the revelation of divine truth from the person of God Himself. It has come as a divine communication in the sacred Scriptures. It has come to us in the guidance and conviction imparted by the divine Spirit of God within our beings. It has been modeled for us in Jesus Christ, the incarnate Word and the eternal Son. . . .

God is *not* silent, and His love for His creation is such that He has never been silent. JIV164-165

> *Every problem that touches us is answered in the*
> *Book—stay by the Word! . . . God is in this Book,*
> *the Holy Spirit is in this Book, and if you want to*
> *find Him, go into this Book.* COU136

AN
OLD
MESSAGE

*This Jesus hath God raised up,
whereof we all are witnesses.*

—Acts 2:32

*I*n our world are dozens of different kinds of Christianities. Certainly many of them do not seem to be busy and joyful in proclaiming the unique glories of Jesus Christ as the eternal Son of God. Some brands of Christianity will tell you very quickly that they are just trying to do a little bit of good on behalf of neglected people and neglected causes. Others will affirm that we can do more good by joining in the "contemporary dialogue" than by continuing to proclaim the "old, old story of the cross."

But we stand with the early Christian apostles. We believe that every Christian proclamation should be to the glory and the praise of the One whom God raised up after He had loosed the pains of death. . . . Peter considered it important to affirm that the risen Christ is now exalted at the right hand of God. He said that fact was the reason for the coming of the Holy Spirit. JMI004-005

> *Jesus of Nazareth, a man approved of God among you by miracles and wonders and signs, which God did by him in the midst of you, as ye yourselves also know: him . . . ye have taken, and by wicked hands have crucified and slain: whom God hath raised up, having loosed the pains of death: because it was not possible that he should be holden of it. (ACTS 2:22-24)*

ONLY ONE REVELATION

According to his mercy he saved us, by the washing of regeneration, and renewing of the Holy Ghost.

—Titus 3:5

I have always felt that when we read and study the Word of God we should have great expectations. We should ask the Holy Spirit to reveal the Person, the glory and the eternal ministry of our Lord Jesus Christ. Perhaps our problem is in our approach. Perhaps we have simply read our Bibles as we might read a piece of literature or a textbook.

In today's society, great numbers of people seem unable to deal with God's revelation in Christ. They run and hide, just as Adam and Eve did. Today, however, they do not hide behind trees but behind such things as philosophy and reason and even theology—believe it or not! This attitude is hard to understand.

In Jesus' death for our sins, God is offering far more than escape from a much-deserved hell. God is promising us an amazing future, an eternal future. . . . I often wonder if we are making it plain enough to our generation that there will be no other revelation from God except as He speaks it through our Lord Jesus Christ. JMI017-018

> *A real Christian is an odd number. . . . He feels supreme love for One whom he has never seen . . . dies so he can live . . . sees the invisible, hears the inaudible, and knows that which passeth knowledge.*
>
> ROR156

REVELATION— BY HIS SPIRIT, THROUGH HIS WORD

With my whole heart have I sought thee: O let me not wander from thy commandments.

—Psalm 119:10

*Y*ears ago my family and I enjoyed Christian fellowship with a Jewish medical doctor who had come to personal faith in Jesus, the Savior and Messiah. He gladly discussed with me his previous participation in Sabbath services in the synagogue. . . .

"I often think back on those years of reading from the Old Testament," he told me. "I had the haunting sense that it was good and true. I knew it explained the history of my people. But I had the feeling that something was missing." Then, with a beautiful, radiant smile he added, "When I found Jesus as my personal Savior and Messiah, I found Him to be the One to whom the Old Testament was in fact pointing. I found Him to be the answer to my completion as a Jew, as a person and as a believer."

Whether Jew or Gentile, we were made originally in God's image, and the revelation of God by His Spirit is a necessity. An understanding of the Word of God must come from the same Spirit who provided its inspiration. JMI019-020

> *The Holy Spirit never comes into a vacuum, but where the Word of God is, there is fuel, and the fire falls.* FBR028-029

THE HABITS OF A HOLY LIFE

Bodily exercise profiteth little: but godliness is profitable unto all things.

—1 Timothy 4:8

*L*et me return to the root of this whole matter—are we Christians willing to be regular in the habits of a holy life, thus learning from the Holy Spirit how to be dependable and faithful, unselfish and Christlike?

The crops in the field are regular, and the birds and the animals have a regularity of life. We see it in the rising and the setting of the sun, and in the regularity of the phases of the moon.

The Old Testament revelation itself was built around regularity. It is said of the old man of God that he went into the temple of God in the order of his course and everything in the temple was laid out in order.

God has ordained, as well, that order and regularity may be of immense value to the Christian life. . . . [L]earn to be regular in your prayer life, in your giving to God and His work and in your church attendance. WPJ025-026

> *God would have His people learn regular holy habits and follow them right along day by day. He doesn't ask us to become slaves to habits, but He does insist that our holy habits of life should become servants of His grace and glory.* WPJ027

"Do as I Do" —Jesus

I can do all things through Christ which strengtheneth me.

—Philippians 4:13

*T*here is a tendency for people to relegate everything in the realm of righteousness or iniquity to deity, whatever their concept of deity may be. For the true Christian, however, our risen Lord made a promise to us before His death and resurrection. That promise effectively removes our excuses and makes us responsible:

> Howbeit when he, the Spirit of truth, is come, he will guide you into all truth: for he shall not speak of himself; but whatsoever he shall hear, that shall he speak: and he will shew you things to come. He shall glorify me: for he shall receive of mine, and shall shew it unto you. All things that the Father hath are mine: therefore said I, that he shall take of mine, and shall shew it unto you. (John 16:13-15)

I will readily admit that we are not God. We cannot do in ourselves what God can do. But God created us as human beings, and if we have the anointing of the Holy Spirit and His presence in our lives, we should be able to do what Jesus, the Son of Man, was able to do in His earthly ministry. JMI059-060

Anyone can do the possible; add a bit of courage and zeal and some may do the phenomenal; only Christians are obliged to do the impossible. WOS012

July

THE FRAGRANT LIFE

Therefore God, thy God, hath anointed thee with the oil of gladness. . . . All thy garments smell of myrrh, and aloes, and cassia.

—Psalm 45:7-8

$\mathcal{I}$n the New Testament, when the Holy Spirit came, His presence fulfilled that whole list of fragrances found in the holy anointing oil. When New Testament believers were anointed, that anointing was evident. Read it in the book of Acts. "And they were all filled with the Holy Ghost" (Acts 2:4). "And they were all filled with the Holy Ghost, and they spake the word of God with boldness" (4:31). "But he [Stephen], being full of the Holy Ghost, looked up stedfastly into heaven" (7:55). "While Peter yet spake these words, the Holy Ghost fell on all them which heard the word" (10:44). The list goes on.

The Holy Spirit has not changed. His power and authority have not changed. He is still the third Person of the eternal Godhead. He is among us to teach us all we need to know about Jesus Christ, the eternal Son of God. I am suggesting—indeed, I am stating—that no one among us, man or woman, can be genuinely anointed with the Holy Spirit and hope to keep it a secret. His or her anointing will be evident. JMI062-063

> *All that God wants of any of us is room for Himself, the displacement of our self-consciousness and strength in sufficient measure to let Him have His way without resistance and interference.* SI111

FRAGRANCE CANNOT BE HIDDEN

Mary ... anointed the feet of Jesus ... and the house was filled with the odour of the ointment.

—John 12:3

A Christian brother once confided in me how he had tried to keep the fullness of the Spirit a secret within his own life. He had made a commitment of his life to God in faith. In answer to prayer, God had filled him with the Spirit. Within himself he said, "I cannot tell anyone about this!"

Three days passed. On the third day his wife touched him on the arm and asked, "Everett, what has happened to you? Something has happened to you!" And like a pent-up stream his testimony flowed out. He had received an anointing of the Holy Spirit. The fragrance could not be hidden. His wife knew it in the home. His life was changed. The spiritual graces and fruits of the consecrated life cannot be hidden. It is an anointing with the oil of gladness and joy. JMI063

> *A [person] anointed by the Holy Spirit, fed on the sweetness of Christ and bearing fruit for God and man, is not craving after self-aggrandizement. Empty glory can never fill the human heart; vanity and pride are no substitutes for the joy of the Lord, the fullness of the Spirit and the sweet rest we find at Jesus' feet.* CTBC, Vol. 2/194

LOVE RIGHTEOUSNESS, HATE INIQUITY

For he hath made him to be sin for us, who knew no sin; that we might be made the righteousness of God in him.

—2 Corinthians 5:21

I am happy to tell everyone that the power of the Spirit is glad power! Our Savior, Jesus Christ, lived His beautiful, holy life on earth and did His healing, saving deeds of power in the strength of this oil of gladness.

We must admit that there was more of the holy oil of God on the head of Jesus than on your head or mine—or on the head of anyone else who has ever lived. That is not to say that God will withhold His best from anyone. But the Spirit of God can only anoint in proportion to the willingness He finds in our lives.

In the case of Jesus, we are told that He had a special anointing because He loved righteousness and hated iniquity. That surely gives us the clue we need concerning the kind of persons we must be in order to receive the full anointing and blessing from Almighty God. JMI063-064

I claim nothing and my testimony is the same as Martin Luther's prayer: "Oh, Lord Jesus, Thou art my righteousness—I am Thy sin!" The only sin Jesus had was mine, Luther's and yours—and the only righteousness we can ever have is His. ITB135

LOVE GOOD, HATE EVIL

Hate the evil, and love the good, and establish judgment in the gate.

—Amos 5:15

$\mathcal{I}$f we are committed, consecrated Christians, truly disciples of the crucified and risen Christ, there are some things we must face.

We cannot love honesty without hating dishonesty. We cannot love purity without hating impurity. We cannot love truth without hating lying and deceitfulness.

If we belong to Jesus Christ, we must hate evil even as He hated evil in every form. The ability of Jesus Christ to hate that which was against God and to love that which was full of God was the force that made Him able to receive the anointing—the oil of gladness—in complete measure.

On our human side, it is our imperfection in loving the good and hating the evil that prevents us from receiving the Holy Spirit in complete measure. God withholds from us because we are unwilling to follow Jesus in His great poured-out love for what is right and His pure and holy hatred of what is evil. JMI064-065

> *We receive the Holy Spirit at the moment of surrender, but we do not realize the fullness of His power until we have been fully tested and have stood triumphant with Him in the conflict with evil.* CTBC, Vol. 2/311

LOVE GOD, HATE SIN

He that followeth after righteous-
ness and mercy findeth life, righ-
teousness, and honour.

—Proverbs 21:21

*P*eople remark how favored the church is in this country. It does not have to face persecution and rejection. If the truth were known, our freedom from persecution is because we have taken the easy, the popular way.

If we would love righteousness until it became an overpowering passion, if we would renounce everything that is evil, our day of popularity and pleasantness would quickly end. The world would soon turn on us.

We are too nice! We are too tolerant! We are too anxious to be popular! We are too quick to make excuses for sin in its many forms! If I could stir Christians around me to love God and hate sin, even to the point of being a bit of a nuisance, I would rejoice. . . . Vance Havner used to remark that too many are running for something when they ought to be standing for something. God's people should be willing to stand! JMI066-067

> *We Christians must stop apologizing for our moral*
> *position and start making our voices heard, exposing*
> *sin for the enemy of the human race which it surely*
> *is, and setting forth righteousness and true holiness*
> *as the only worthy pursuits for moral beings.* MDP048

PUT AWAY COMPROMISE

My righteousness I hold fast, and will not let it go: my heart shall not reproach me so long as I live.

—Job 27:6

*T*he way to spiritual power and favor with God is to be willing to put away the weak compromises and the tempting evils to which we are prone to cling. There is no Christian victory or blessing if we refuse to turn away from the things that God hates.

Even if your wife loves it, turn away from it. Even if your husband loves it, turn away from it. Even if it is accepted in the whole social class and system of which you are a part, turn away from it. Even if it is something that has come to be accepted by our whole generation, turn away from it if it is evil and wrong and an offense to our holy and righteous Savior. . . .

Every Christian holds the key to his or her own spiritual attainment. If he or she will not pay the price of being joyfully led by the Holy Spirit of God, if he or she refuses to hate sin and evil and wrong, our churches might as well be turned into lodges or clubs. JMI068

> *We need a revival! We need a revival of consecration to death, a revival of happy abandonment to the will of God that will laugh at sacrifice and count it a privilege to bear the cross through the heat and burden of the day. We are too much influenced by the world and too little controlled by the Spirit.*
> GTM159-160

GOD DOES NOT PLAY ON OUR EMOTIONS

Did not our heart burn within us, while he talked with us by the way . . . ?

—Luke 24:32

$\mathcal{I}$ do not know how familiar you are with the ways of God and the tender movings of His Spirit. But I will tell you this quite frankly: God does not play on our emotions to bring us to the point of spiritual decision.

God's Word, which is God's truth, and God's Spirit unite to arouse our highest emotions. Because He is God and worthy of our praise, we will find the ability to praise Him and to glorify Him. Some religious and evangelistic techniques are directed almost entirely to the emotions of those who are listening to the appeal. They are psychology, not Spirit-directed conviction. . . .

I have to disagree with religious appeal that supposes if someone in the audience can be moved to shed a tear, a saint has been made. . . . [T]here is no connection whatsoever between the human manipulation of our emotions, on the one hand, and, on the other, the confirmation of God's revealed truth in our beings through the ministry of His Holy Spirit. When in our Christian experience our emotions are raised, it must be the result of what God's truth is doing for us. JMI083-084

> *Whatever else it embraces, true Christian experience must always include a genuine encounter with God.* POM010

AN ATTRIBUTE CALLED OMNIPOTENCE

If thou canst believe, all things are possible to him that believeth.

—Mark 9:23

*G*od knows everything that can be known. He is perfect in wisdom. God never has to excuse Himself. . . . His ability to deliver on His promises is tied directly to His omnipotence. If God was not omnipotent, He would be unable to keep His promises. He could not give any of us assurance of salvation.

This attribute of God we call omnipotence does not really mean that God can do anything. It means that He is the only Being who can do anything He wills to do. . . .

Because holiness is God's being, He cannot lie. Because He is God, He cannot violate the holy nature of His being. God does not will to lie. He does not will to cheat. He does not will to deceive. He does not will to be false to His own dear people. . . .

Confidently knowing that the Lord God omnipotent reigns, and knowing that He is able to do all that He wills to do, I have no more doubts. I am safely held in the arms of the all-powerful God. JMI088-089

> *[There is] an innate conviction, strong as the everlasting foundations, that, if there is a God above us, all is well,* all must be well. JAS156

GOD
LOVES
HARD PLACES

Faithful is he that calleth you, who also will do it.

—1 Thessalonians 5:24

$\mathcal{W}$e are in the midst of the storm of life. The believing saints of God are on board the ship. Someone looks to the horizon and warns, "We are directly in the path of the typhoon! We are as good as dead. We will surely be dashed to pieces on the rocks!"

But calmly someone else advises, "Look down, look down! We have an anchor!" We look, but the depth is too great. We cannot see the anchor. But the anchor is there. It grips the immovable rock and holds fast. Thus the ship outrides the storm.

The Holy Spirit has assured us that we have an Anchor, steadfast and sure, that keeps the soul. . . . The Spirit is saying to us, "Keep on believing. Pursue holiness. Show diligence and hold full assurance of faith to the very end. Follow those who through faith and patience inherit what has been promised.

"He is faithful!" JMI089-090

> *Nearly all the great examples of faith and victorious grace which we find in the Scriptures came out of situations of extremity and distress. God loves hard places, and faith is usually born of danger and extremity.* WCC091

THE
HOLY SPIRIT
IS WAITING

Thy soul followeth hard after thee: thy right hand upholdeth me.

—Psalm 63:8

I am reminded that one old saint was asked, "Which is the more important: reading God's Word or praying?" To which he replied, "Which is more important to a bird: the right wing or the left?" The writer to the Hebrews was telling his readers—and telling us—that Christians must believe *all* there is to be believed. They are to do *all* that the Word commands them to do. Those two wings take the Christian up to God! . . .

God has purposefully given us a mental capacity with wide human boundaries. Beyond that, if we are justified, regenerated believers, He has given us an entirely new spiritual capacity. God wants us to believe, to think, to meditate, to consider His Word. He has promised that the Holy Spirit is waiting to teach us. He has assured us concerning all of our blessings in Jesus Christ. JMI104-105

> *O God, I have tasted Thy goodness, and it has both satisfied me and made me thirsty for more. . . . I want to want Thee; I long to be filled with longing; I thirst to be made more thirsty still. Show me Thy glory.* POG019

THE TRINITY WORKS TOGETHER

In the beginning was the Word, and the Word was with God, and the Word was God. The same was in the beginning with God.

—John 1:1-2

*C*ritics often have declared that the Bible contradicts itself in matters relating to the Trinity. For example, Genesis speaks of God's creating the heavens and the earth. The New Testament declares that the Word—God the Son—created all things. Still other references speak of the Holy Spirit's work in creation. These are not contradictions. Father, Son and Spirit worked together in the miracles of creation, just as they worked together in the planning and effecting of human redemption. The Father, Son and Holy Spirit are consubstantial . . . one in substance and cannot be separated.

When Jesus was to launch His earthly ministry, He went to John at the Jordan River to be baptized. The record speaks of the Trinity's involvement. As Jesus stood on the bank of the river following His baptism, the Holy Spirit descended as a dove upon Him and the voice of God the Father was heard from heaven saying, "This is my beloved Son, in whom I am well pleased" (Matthew 3:17). JMI106

> *Praise God from whom all blessings flow;*
> *Praise Him, all creatures here below;*
> *Praise Him above, ye heavenly host;*
> *Praise Father, Son, and Holy Ghost. AMEN.*
> HCL597

A PAIN FELT IN HEAVEN

When Jesus therefore had received the vinegar, he said, It is finished: and he bowed his head, and gave up the ghost.

—John 19:30

$\mathcal{T}$he Father in heaven so loved the world that He gave His only begotten Son. It was the love of the Father that sent the Son into our world to die for mankind. The Father and Son and Spirit were in perfect agreement that the eternal Son should die for the sins of the world. We are not wrong to believe—and proclaim—that while Mary's Son, Jesus, died alone, terribly alone, on that cross, the loving heart of God the Father was as deeply pained with suffering as was the heart of the holy, dying Son.

We must ask our Lord to help us comprehend what it meant to the Trinity for the Son to die alone on the cross. When the holy Father had to turn His back on the dying Son by the necessity of divine justice, I believe the pain for the Father was as great as the suffering of the Savior as He bore our sins in His body. When the soldier drove that Roman spear into the side of Jesus, I believe it was felt in heaven. JMI110

> *Well might the sun in darkness hide*
> *And shut His glories in,*
> *When Christ, the Mighty Maker, died*
> *For man, the creature's sin.* HCL085

TAKEN UP WITH CHRIST

To whom God would make known what is the riches of the glory of this mystery . . . which is Christ in you, the hope of glory.

—Colossians 1:27

*I*f we would please the indwelling Spirit we must be all taken up with Christ. The Spirit's present work is to honor Him, and everything He does has this for its ultimate purpose. And we must make our thoughts a clean sanctuary for His holy habitation.

He dwells in our thoughts, and soiled thoughts are as repugnant to Him as soiled linen to a king. Above all we must have a cheerful faith that will keep on believing however radical the fluctuation in our emotional states may be.

The Spirit indwelt life is not a special deluxe edition of Christianity to be enjoyed by a certain rare and privileged few who happen to be made of finer and more sensitive stuff than the rest. Rather, it is the normal state for every redeemed man and woman the world over. POM136-137

> *Is the glory of God the great end of your being? . . .*
> *Is your love to God supreme? Does it rise superior to the attachments of flesh and sense? What, whom do you love more than the everlasting God? . . . Supreme love to God is decisive evidence of the renewed heart.* DTC078-079

THE HOLY SPIRIT IS IN THE DETAILS

For ye are bought with a price: therefore glorify God in your body, and in your spirit, which are God's.

—1 Corinthians 6:20

$\mathcal{G}$od has given each of us an individual temperament and distinct characteristics. Therefore it is the office of the Holy Spirit to work out as He will the details in Christian experience. They will vary with the personality.

Certainly we can be sure of this: whenever a person truly meets God in faith and commitment to the gospel, he will have a consciousness and a sharp awareness of the details of that spiritual transaction. . . . The experience may have been brief, but the results will be evident in the life of the person touched as long as he or she lives. . . .

We can always trust the moving and the leading of the Holy Spirit in our lives and in our experiences. On the other hand, we cannot always trust our human leanings and our fleshly and carnal desires. MMG017-018

> *[A]re you sure you want to be possessed by a spirit other than your own? even though that spirit be the pure Spirit of God . . . even though He be wisdom personified, wisdom Himself? . . . That Spirit, if He ever possesses you, will be the Lord of your life!* HTB043

SOME WORRISOME CHARACTERISTICS

I have fed you with milk, and not with meat: for hitherto ye were not able to bear it.

—1 Corinthians 3:2

*R*eligion lies in the will and so does righteousness. God never intended that such a being as mankind should become the mere plaything of his or her feelings. The only good that God recognizes is the willed good. The only valid holiness is a willed holiness. That is why I am always a little suspicious of the overly bubbly Christian who talks too much about himself or herself and not enough about Jesus.

Then, I am always a little worried about the "hope-so" Christian who cannot tell me any of the details of his or her Christian experience.

And, finally, I am more than a little concerned about the professing Christian whose experience does not seem to have resulted in a true inner longing to be more like Jesus every day in thought, word and deed. MMG018

> *God wants us while we live to prove in our own experience all things that have been written in the Bible and to bind the Bible in a new and living edition of flesh and blood in our own lives.*
>
> TFG077

HAPPY WITH ONLY HIM!

The LORD is my strength and song . . . he is my God, and I will prepare him an habitation . . . and I will exalt him.

—Exodus 15:2

*B*eing lonely in this world will only drive you to a closer communion with the God who has promised never to leave you or forsake you. He is altogether good and He is faithful. He will never break His covenant or alter that which has gone from His mouth. He has promised to keep you as the apple of His eye. He has promised to watch over you as a mother watches over her child.

God's anxiety for you is real, and His pattern for you is plain. He says, "This is the sign of your pleasing My indwelling Spirit: you have been absorbed with Christ, you have made your thoughts a clean sanctuary for His holy habitation."

Build that invisible altar within. Let the Spirit of God produce the living, cleansing flame that marks your devotion to Christ, our Lord. MMG034-035

It is part of my belief that God wants to get us to a place where we would still be happy if we had only Him! We don't need God and something else. God does give us Himself and lets us have other things, too, but there is that inner loneliness until we reach the place where it is only God that we desire. COU082

HAPPY AND/OR HOLY

*O*ne may easily deceive himself by cultivating a religious joy without a correspondingly righteous life. No man should desire to be happy who is not at the same time holy. He should spend his efforts in seeking to know and do the will of God, leaving to Christ the matter of how happy he shall be.

For those who take this whole thing seriously I have a suggestion. Go to God and have an understanding. Tell Him that it is your desire to be holy at any cost and then ask Him never to give you more happiness than holiness. When your holiness becomes tarnished, let your joy become dim. And ask Him to make you holy whether you are happy or not.

Be assured that in the end you will be as happy as you are holy; but for the time being let your whole ambition be to serve God and be Christlike. PON03-039

> *The end of the Christian in the exercise of grace is the glory of God, and not merely his own present or future happiness.* DTC148

DIG
OUT THE
OLD WELLS

*Ye ask, and receive not, because
ye ask amiss, that ye may con-
sume it upon your lusts.*

—James 4:3

*F*riend, we must dig out the old wells! We must recognize our dryness of spirit, our coldness of heart. We must make the decision to renew our desire for God, for the outpouring of His Spirit and for the seasons of rejoicing as we become more like Jesus.

Many a congregation has been renewed and blessed when believers have been willing to reopen the Bible wells of reconciliation and confession. When Christians are harboring hard feelings against each other, they need to be reconciled. They need to confess and ask forgiveness.

I refer here to actual sins and faults. There are people in continual bondage to mere trifles and inconsequential matters. God has given us the Holy Spirit to be our prompter and our guide. And He has given us good sense as well to go along with our consciences. MMG042

> *We . . . [try] to substitute praying for obeying;
> and it simply will not work. . . . Prayer is never
> an acceptable substitute for obedience.* OGM055-056

REAL LIVING

Meditate upon these things; give thyself wholly to them; that thy profiting may appear to all.

—1 Timothy 4:15

*L*et me observe that some Christians think they can be disciples of Christ without ever a thought about the necessity of self-discipline and genuine commitment to Him. We must face the fact that many today are notoriously careless in their living. This attitude finds its way into the church. We have liberty, we have money, we live in comparative luxury. As a result, discipline practically has disappeared.

What would a violin solo sound like if the strings on the musician's instrument were all hanging loose, not stretched tight, not "disciplined"? Being an artist, the musician would not attempt to bring sound from that violin until each string had been tuned and tested and all was in perfect harmony.

In things that matter with God—important things—we need to be disciplined, pulled together, attuned to the Spirit until we are in harmony with all of God's planning for us. MMG043-044

> *The Spirit of Life dwells and fills men, permeates their being, sanctifies their nature, quickens their powers, vitalizes their mortal bodies and radiates their life. . . . Pentecost turned anemic believers into exuberant saints.* PRL041

IT'S A CHOICE

Choose you this day whom ye will serve. . . . God forbid that we should forsake the LORD, to serve other gods.

—Joshua 24:15-16

$\mathcal{I}$t is the spark of God within a person that troubles him or her. That spark is placed within by the Spirit of God. Conviction. Longing. Desire. That spark within does not save. But that spark must be there to lead the person on to salvation.

Why is it that some men and women seem never to have any awareness of that spark from God? They may be nice people, nice neighbors, nice friends. But they live every day without any spark of discontent, without any spark of need for God. . . .

God has made us with the right to make our own choices. We were not created to be robots. God made us in His own image, but with the right and the ability to choose. We are free moral agents.

When our first parents made the wrong choices, the human race became alienated from God. Since that time, every person has been faced with choices and decisions. MMG063-064

Happiness is nothing but that inward sweet delight, which will arise from the harmonious agreement between our wills and the will of God. JAS147

HOLY WOUNDS

Father, if thou be willing, remove this cup from me: nevertheless not my will, but thine, be done.

—Luke 22:42

*T*here are people within the ranks of Christianity who have been taught and who believe that Christ will shield His followers from wounds of every kind.

If the truth were known, the saints of God in every age were only effective after they had been wounded. They experienced the humbling wounds that brought contrition, compassion and a yearning for the knowledge of God. I could only wish that more among the followers of Christ knew what some of the early saints meant when they spoke of being wounded by the Holy Spirit.

Think for a moment about the apostle Paul. I suppose there is no theologian living or dead who quite knows what Paul meant when he said, "From henceforth let no man trouble me: for I bear in my body the marks of the Lord Jesus" (Galatians 6:17). Every commentary has a different idea. I think Paul referred to the wounds he suffered because of his faith and godly life. MMG059

If you are to sit with Christ upon His throne, you must go with Him through His Gethsemane.
CTBC, Vol. 2/065

HOLINESS IS GOD

Draw nigh to God, and he will draw nigh to you. Cleanse your hands . . . and purify your hearts.

—James 4:8

$\mathcal{G}$od Himself is the holiness and the purity we need. Some people think of holiness as something they have for a time, but suddenly God allows them to lose it. Holiness in the Christian life is nothing else but the Spirit of God dwelling, filling, satisfying the surrendered, committed, trusting believer.

When will we admit and confess that holiness comes with the presence of God? When will we believe that a true encounter with God brings purity of heart?

Christ is not just our Sanctifier. He is our sanctification. He Himself is our holiness. If Christ lives within our hearts, then just as the fire dwelt within the burning bush in living encounter and experience, so we will be cleansed and pure. How could it be otherwise if Christ who is holy and pure lives out His life in us? MMG074

> *We must consent to the work of cleansing. We must pass sentence upon our sinful heart and give God the right to cleanse it. . . . God will not take one step till we have handed ourselves over to Him unreservedly.* CTBC, Vol. 5/313

THE TEST OF TRUTH

Therefore whosoever heareth these sayings of mine, and doeth them, I will liken him unto a wise man, which built his house upon a rock.

—Matthew 7:24

*E*very activity now being carried on in the name of Christ must meet the last supreme test: Does it have biblical authority back of it? Is it according to the letter and the spirit of the Scripture? Is its spiritual content divinely given?

That it succeeds proves nothing. That it is popular proves less. Where are the proofs of its heavenly birth? Where are its scriptural credentials? What assurance does it give that it represents the operation of the Holy Spirit in the divine plan of the ages? These questions demand satisfactory answers.

No one should object to an honest examination of his work in the pure light of Scripture. No honest man will shrink from the light, nor will he defend beliefs and practices that cannot be justified by the test of truth. Rather he will eagerly seek to build according to the pattern shown him in the mount. PON088-089

> *While the moral quality of any act is imparted by the condition of the heart, there may be a world of religious activity . . . which would seem to have little or no moral content. Such religious conduct . . . stems from the current cult of commotion and possesses no sound inner life.* ROR076

A High and Holy Concept of God

O magnify the LORD with me, and let us exalt his name together.

—Psalm 34:3

*M*ankind has succeeded quite well in reducing God to a pitiful nothing! The God of the modern context is no God at all. He is simply a glorified chairman of the board, a kind of big businessman dealing in souls. The God portrayed in much of our church life today commands very little respect.

We must get back to the Bible and to the ministration of God's Spirit to regain a high and holy concept of God. Oh, this awesome, terrible God ! . . .

To know the Creator and the God of all the universe is to revere Him. It is to bow down before Him in wonder and awesome fear.

God wants to be an experience to us. We need to sense the possibility of being caught between the upper and lower millstones, knowing we can be ground to powder before Him. We need to know what it is to rise in humility out of our grief and nothingness, to know God in Jesus Christ forever and ever, to glorify Him and enjoy Him while the ages roll on. MMG080

God calls us to magnify Him, to see Him big.
SAT040

MAJESTY, WORSHIP HIS MAJESTY

Bless the LORD, O my soul. O LORD my God, thou art very great; thou art clothed with honour and majesty.

—Psalm 104:1

*T*here is neither preacher nor teacher anywhere in the world who can say, "Let me tell you all about God!" God told Moses and Israel, and He tells us, "Always there will be the cloud about Me. Always there will be a veil covering My person. While you are on My earth, you will sense this obscurity, for I Am who I Am!". . .

And I can say this from personal experience: After you have known God and walked with Him by faith for fifty years, growing daily in His grace and the knowledge of Him, you will still see a cloud on Mount Sinai. You will still sense the obscurity. Your mind and your spirit will still bow before Him. Your day of full comprehension is yet to come.

Innate within us is the need to kneel in reverence before something. When God appears to us, and, stunned and overcome, we are bumped to our knees, we have a right start in the life of the Spirit! MMG083

> "[I]n the contemplation of God's majesty, all eloquence is done." SAT039

GETTING PRIORITIES IN ORDER

O the depth of the riches both of the wisdom and knowledge of God!

—Romans 11:33

*O*ur Lord knows us very well. Yet He has given us the power of choice. I believe our Lord Jesus, by the Spirit of God, keeps whispering to us, "Watch out! It is very easy to put today's world first and spiritual treasures second—or last!"

We must make our choice in response. What will it be?

I confess that I feel a compulsion to cry out in prayer: "My Lord, I have so many earthly treasures! I must continually give thanks to Thee, my God, for Thy blessings. But I know that I am going to have to leave these things, to give them all up some day. Therefore, I do deliberately choose to earnestly seek spiritual treasures, putting them above all else. They are the only treasures that will not perish." . . .

He would have us continue to decide for Himself and His kingdom. MMG085

> *In the kingdom of God the surest way to lose something is to try to protect it, and the best way to keep it is to let it go.* BAM096

PLEASURES AND TREASURES

Set your affection on things above, not on things on the earth.

—Colossians 3:2

*L*et the Bible experts split it up however they will, let them divide and subdivide it, then tack on a couple of Greek verbs. But when they are through, I will still believe that the kingdom of God is the realm of the Holy Spirit into which men and women enter when they are born from above.

Yes, that invisible world that God has revealed is more real, more lasting, more eternal than this world we are in now. That is why God has given us the prophets and His revelation in His Word. He wants us to be able to look in on the coming world. . . .

Of all the calamities that have been visited upon this world and its inhabitants, the willing surrender of the human spirit to materialistic values is the worst!

We who were made for higher worlds are accepting the ways of this world as the ultimate. That is a tragedy of staggering proportions. MMG101-102

> *Moses turned his back on the pleasures and treasures of Egypt. Would we, could we turn our backs on the cash, the comforts, the conveniences we have in order to be the people of God?* MMG085

CORRECT DOCTRINE PLUS . . .

Who hath known the mind of the Lord, that he may instruct him? But we have the mind of Christ.

—1 Corinthians 2:16

*W*hen we see God with the eyes of our hearts, God is fulfilling His purpose to appear to us. To those who ask how this can be, I answer that He can appear to us because we were made in God's image.

In the Old Testament, the writer of the Proverbs taught that true spiritual knowledge is the result of a visitation of heavenly wisdom. It is a kind of baptism of the Spirit of Truth that comes to God-fearing men. This wisdom always is associated with righteousness and humility. It is never found apart from godliness and true holiness of life.

We need to learn and to declare again the mystery of wisdom from above. Truth consists not merely in correct doctrine but in correct doctrine to which is added the inward enlightenment of the Holy Spirit. MMG124

> *[T]ruth, to be understood, must be lived; . . . Bible doctrine is wholly ineffective until it has been digested and assimilated by the total life.* TIC109

ONE
WAY TO
TRUTH

*The entrance of thy words giv-
eth light; it giveth understanding unto the simple.*

—Psalm 119:130

$\mathcal{I}$t is apparent that we cannot know God by the logic of reason. Through reason we can only know about God. Through
the light of nature, our moral reason may be enlightened, but
the deeper mysteries of God remain hidden to us until we have
received illumination from above.

John the Baptist gave his questioners a brief sentence that I
have called the hope and despair of mankind. He said, "A man
can receive nothing, except it be given him from heaven" (John
3:27).

He was not referring to men's gifts. He was speaking of spiritual truth. Divine truth is of the nature of the Holy Spirit, and
for that reason it can be received only by spiritual revelation.
MMG124

*We will go far to simplify our religious concepts
and unify our lives if we remember [this]: . . .
truth is a spiritual entity and can be grasped in its
inner essence only as the Spirit of truth enlightens
our hearts and teaches us.* SIZ114

IN THE IMAGE OF GOD

Herein is love, not that we loved God, but that he loved us, and sent his Son to be the propitiation for our sins.

—1 John 4:10

$\mathcal{E}$very person who is born into the world begins to see God in some ways as soon as he or she is old enough to comprehend. If that person does not repent and experience the renewal of regeneration through the working of the Holy Spirit, he or she is lost and will be lost forever. I believe that with all my heart.

But I also believe that human beings, made in the image of God, continue to keep upon themselves something of that image of deity. It is that residual image that permits God to incarnate Himself in us without incongruity or inconsistency.

So it was that the eternal Son, Himself God, could become flesh in Jesus Christ without inconsistency. MMG125-126

"You matter to the living and loving God of all creation. Above everyone else in the whole universe, He cares for you and calls to you and has gracious plans for you! . . . ." What a message for the sinner! CES094

That He should leave His place on high
And come for sinful man to die,
You count it strange?
So once did I Before I knew my Saviour. HCL507

SETTING UP A QUOTA SYSTEM

For we preach not ourselves, but Christ Jesus the Lord; and ourselves your servants for Jesus' sake.

—2 Corinthians 4:5

I have thanked God many times for the sweet, winsome ways of the Holy Spirit in dealing with the heart of this untaught lad when I was only seventeen. We had a neighbor by the name of Holman. . . . [O]ne day I was walking up the street with this friendly neighbor. Suddenly, he put his hand on my shoulder.

"You know," he said, "I have been wondering about you. I have been wondering if you are a Christian, if you are converted. I just wanted the chance to talk it over with you."

"No, Mr. Holman," I answered, "I am not converted, but I thank you for saying this to me. I am going to give it some serious thought." . . .

Some Christians set up a quota system for their witnessing. I would hate to think that I was Mr. Holman's quota for the day! Witnessing is a matter in which we need the guidance and concern of God through His Holy Spirit. MMG127-128

> *When seeking to bring the lost to Christ we must pray continually that they may receive the gift of seeing. And we must pit our prayer against that dark spirit who blinds the hearts of men.* BAM063

August

A FORGOTTEN YESTERDAY, AN UNBORN TOMORROW

The LORD searcheth all hearts, and understandeth all the imaginations of the thoughts: if thou seek him, he will be found of thee.

—1 Chronicles 28:9

*I*f you . . . trace [the] word everlasting in the Hebrew language, you will find that it can mean "time out of mind," or it can mean "always," or it can mean "to the vanishing point." It can also mean "to the beginningless past."

From everlasting to everlasting, God is God! From the beginningless past to the endless future, God is God! That is what the Holy Ghost says about the person and the eternal nature of God.

Now, if you have one of those mousetrap minds—open and shut—you will . . . dismiss it and leave it, or tuck it away in your memory among the unused items in the attic of your soul.

But . . . if . . . the Holy Ghost is allowed to bring His radiance to it, there can be great meaning; for we are between the everlasting vanishing point of a forgotten yesterday and the equally everlasting vanishing point of an unborn tomorrow. CES051-052

If you accept the gospel of Jesus Christ, you will have all the power of God back of you to defend you; all the will of God on your side; all the justice and righteousness of God pledged to your defense, as well as all the infinite love and mercy of God to welcome and bless you. CTBC, Vol. 2/100

THE ABSENCE OF LOVE

I will love thee, O LORD, my strength.

—Psalm 18:1

*T*he thirteenth chapter of First Corinthians may tell us what Christ is like, but let us not forget that it also tells us what we must be like to avoid spiritual tragedy. Let us not turn our back on this critically important teaching.

Without love, the kind described by Paul, my whole Christian life is a barren fig tree. It's a neat trick to apply Paul's words to Christ only; but it isn't honest, and it is dangerous.

It is the Holy Spirit who sheds abroad the love of God in our hearts (Romans 5:5) and love is declared to be a fruit of the Spirit (Galatians 5:22). But if our daily lives reveal that the fruit is not there we dare not assume that it is—"because the Bible says so."

The absence of love as described in First Corinthians 13 is proof of the absence of the Spirit, or at least that He is inoperative within us. That's the only honest conclusion. We can't afford to be less than candid about the whole thing. PON129

> *[The] gospel breathes the spirit of love. Love is the fulfilling of its precepts, the pledge of its joy, and the evidence of its power.* DTC165

APPRAISE,
THEN
ACT

Prove all things; hold fast that which is good.

—1 Thessalonians 5:21

𝓜any tender-minded Christians fear to sin against love by daring to inquire into anything that comes wearing the cloak of Christianity and breathing the name of Jesus. They dare not examine the credentials of the latest prophet to hit their town lest they be guilty of rejecting something which may be of God. . . . This is supposed to indicate a high degree of spirituality. But in sober fact it indicates no such thing. It may indeed be evidence of the absence of the Holy Spirit.

Gullibility is not synonymous with spirituality. Faith is not a mental habit leading its possessor to open his mouth and swallow everything that has about it the color of the supernatural. Faith keeps its heart open to whatever is of God, and rejects everything that is not of God, however wonderful it may be.

"Try the spirits" is a command of the Holy Spirit to the Church (1 John 4:1). We may sin as certainly by approving the spurious as by rejecting the genuine. . . . To appraise things with a heart of love and then to act on the results is an obligation resting upon every Christian in the world. SOS025

Can you renounce everything which is inconsistent with the glory of God and the highest good of your fellowmen? DTC149-150

ENERGY FROM INDWELLING POWER

He that raised up Christ from the dead shall also quicken your mortal bodies by his Spirit that dwelleth in you.

—Romans 8:11

*O*ur Lord was able to work with a minimum of weariness because He was a man completely possessed by the Holy Spirit. As a man He did grow tired and had to sleep and rest to refresh Himself, but the strain and the exhaustion that He would otherwise have suffered were spared Him by the constant quickening of the Holy Spirit.

Peter explained that Christ "went about doing good, and healing all that were oppressed of the devil," *after* God had "anointed [Him] with the Holy Ghost and with power" (Acts 10:38).

It is possible to work far beyond the normal strength of the human constitution and yet experience little or no fatigue because the energy for the work has been provided, not by the burning up of human tissue, but by the indwelling Spirit of power. This has been realized by a few unusual souls, and the pity is that they *are* unusual. SIZ184

> *To live in the Spirit is to receive the . . . life of the Holy Spirit in our physical being and to find in Him the source of constant stimulus and strength for . . . our mind and all the functions of our body.*
> ISS007

SEIZE THE DAY

That the life also of Jesus might be made manifest in our mortal flesh.

—2 Corinthians 4:11

$\mathcal{T}$oday is our day. No one at any time has ever had any spiritual graces that we at this time cannot enjoy if we will meet the terms on which they are given. If these times are morally darker, they but provide a background against which we can shine the brighter.

Our God is the God of today as well as of yesterday, and we may be sure that wherever our tomorrows may carry us, our faithful God will be with us as He was with Abraham and David and Paul.

Those great men did not need us then, and we cannot have them with us now. Amen. So be it. And God be praised. We cannot have them, but we can have that which is infinitely better—we can have their God and Father, and we can have their Savior, and we can have the same blessed Holy Spirit that made them great. NCA024

> *The surest method of arriving at a knowledge of God's eternal purposes about us is to be found in the right use of the present moment. . . . It is our business to piece it together, and to* live *it into one orderly vocation.* JAS128

GLORIOUS FUTURE, BLESSED TOMORROW

I press toward the mark for the prize of the high calling of God in Christ Jesus.

—Philippians 3:14

The normal Bible direction is not backward, it is always forward. Jacob returned to the altar, but in doing so he did not go back, he went forward. The Prodigal Son did not say, "I will go back"; he said, "I will arise and go to my father."

From where he was, going to his father's house was a forward step in his moral activities. It represented no retreat, but a distinct advance over his previous conduct.

The will of God is always the proper goal for every one of us. Where God is must be the place of desire. Any motion toward God is a forward motion. Even repentance is not a retreat toward the past but a decided march into a more glorious future. Restitution is not a return to yesterday but a step into a blessed tomorrow. . . .

If we find that we have gone back, then we should immediately reverse the direction and again go forward. NCA024-025

God's purpose in all His dealings with us is to make us grow into something higher. The greatest calamity that can come to a soul is to be satisfied with its present condition. CTBC, Vol. 5/015

DRAW IT IN, GIVE IT OUT

And hope maketh not ashamed;
because the love of God is shed
abroad in our hearts by the Holy
Ghost which is given unto us.

—Romans 5:5

The human heart can love the human Jesus as it can love the human Lincoln, but the spiritual love of Jesus is something altogether different from and infinitely superior to the purest love the human heart can know.

Indeed it is not possible to love Jesus rightly except by the Holy Spirit. Only the Third Person of the Trinity can love the Second Person in a manner pleasing to the Father. The spiritual love of Jesus is nothing else but the Spirit in us loving Christ the Eternal Son.

Christ, after the flesh, receives a great deal of fawning attention . . . , but love that is not the outflow of the indwelling Holy Spirit is not true spiritual love and cannot be acceptable to God. We do Christ no honor when we do no more than to give Him the best of our human love. . . . He is not rightly loved until . . . the Spirit within us does the loving. NCA031-032

We are not love, and we never expect to love by our
own impulses. . . . But Jesus is the heart of love. Je-
sus is love itself, and Jesus is ours. His love is ours.
We draw it in and give it out. CTAB060

MARKS OF LOVE

And now abideth faith, hope, charity, these three; but the greatest of these is charity.

—1 Corinthians 13:13

$\mathcal{W}$hile the all-important distinction between the human and the spiritual love of Jesus is one that must be *discerned*, and one which can scarcely be *explained*, we yet venture to point out some marks which may distinguish the two.

Reverence, for one thing, will always be present in the heart of the one who loves Christ in the Spirit. The Spirit gives a holy solemnity to every thought of Jesus, so that it is psychologically impossible to think of the true Christ with humor or levity. Neither can there be any unbecoming familiarity. The Person of Christ precludes all such.

Then, self-abasement is always found in the heart that loves Jesus with true spiritual love. When Paul saw Jesus, he fell on his face. John fell down as dead, and every soul that ever saw and felt the terror and wonder of His glorious Presence, has known some such experience of self-abasement.

It is most important that we know whether our relation to Jesus is divine or human. It will pay us to find out now. NCA032-033

Love is the loveliest thing in this world and the thing that speaks most for God in your life. Everybody can understand it. WL007

FOR THE SOLITARY HEART

Now to him that is of power to stablish you ... to God only wise, be glory through Jesus Christ for ever. Amen.

—Romans 16:25, 27

*T*he man that *will* have God's best becomes at once the object of the personal attention of the Holy Spirit. Such a man will not be required to wait for the rest of the church to come alive. He will not be penalized for the failures of his fellow Christians, nor be asked to forego the blessing till his sleepy brethren catch up.

God deals with the individual heart as exclusively as if only one existed.

If this should seem to be an unduly individualistic approach to revival, let it be remembered that religion is personal before it can be social. . . .

The plain Christian of today must experience personal revival before he can hope to bring renewed spiritual life to his church.

It is a matter for the solitary heart. SIZ015

It is certainly not speculative that God is able to manifest Himself most in the lives of those who passionately love Him (see John 14:21). . . . And He will do that. ROL091

THINGS SEEN AND UNSEEN

The things which are seen are temporal; but the things which are not seen are eternal.

—2 Corinthians 4:18

*I*ndeed it may be truthfully said that everything of lasting value in the Christian life is unseen and eternal. Things seen are of little real significance in the light of God's presence. He pays small attention to the beauty of a woman or the strength of a man. With Him the heart is all that matters. The rest of the life comes into notice only because it represents the dwelling place of the inner eternal being.

The solution to life's problems is spiritual because the essence of life is spiritual. It is astonishing how many difficulties clear up without any effort when the inner life gets straightened out.

If half the time we spend trying to fix up outward things were spent in getting our hearts right, we would be delighted with the result. NCA082-083

> *Christ will not dwell in our hearts, if we fill our hearts with things which He hates. . . . To do wilfully and knowingly what God hates, destroys faith, and hope, and love.* JAS133

KNOW YOUR GIFT

Now ye are the body of Christ, and members in particular.

—1 Corinthians 12:27

*T*he task of the church is too great for any one person to compass and too varied for the skill of any one person to accomplish.

God has met this difficulty by dividing the task and giving to every man gifts that enable him to do his part. By distributing the work, He lightens the burden for all and makes possible the smooth carrying out of His purposes among men. That is undoubtedly the reason behind the gifts of the Spirit given to the various members of the Christian community. Here, as elsewhere, the manifold wisdom of God is revealed. . . .

Blessed is the man who knows his gift and who seeks to exercise it toward the other members of the body of Christ "as good stewards of the manifold grace of God" (1 Peter 4:10). NCA080

> *[T]he Holy Spirit desires to take us and control us and use us as instruments and organs through whom He can express Himself in the body of Christ. . . . The Spirit of God, His presence and His gifts are not simply desirable in our Christian congregations; they are absolutely imperative.* TRA030, 027

FLOWERS AND FRUIT DO NOT GROW IN THIN AIR!

But the fruit of the Spirit is love, joy, peace, longsuffering, gentleness, goodness, faith, meekness, temperance.

—Galatians 5:22-23

I would like to be able to ask every Christian in the world this question: Are you really interested in God's producing in you the beautiful fruits and fragrances of the Holy Spirit?

For every affirmative answer, I would quickly recommend: Then look to your own willingness to be regular in the habits of a holy life—for flowers and fruit do not grow in thin air! They grow and come up out of a root and "the root of the righteous yieldeth fruit" (Proverbs 12:12).

For every beautiful garden that you see, whose fragrance comes out to welcome you, has its roots down into the hard earth. The beautiful flowers and blooms will grow and appear and flourish only when there are deep roots and strong stalks. If you take the roots away, the blossom and flower will endure perhaps one day. The sun will scorch them and they will be gone. WPJ015-016

What is the special likeness of Christ that He would reproduce in me? What are the features of His life that He calls me to imitate? What pattern would He set before me in my work, my circumstances, my difficulties? What are the inspirations of grace that He would urge me to cultivate and cherish? JAS188

DEALING WITH THE ROOT

Lest any root of bitterness springing up trouble you, and thereby many be defiled.

—Hebrews 12:15

Strange as it may seem, harmony within our own hearts depends mostly upon our getting into harmony with God. Morning comes not by our pushing out the darkness but by waiting for the coming of the sun.

Church difficulties are spiritual also and admit of a spiritual answer. Whatever may be wrong in the life of any church may be cleared up by recognizing the quality of the trouble and dealing with it at the root.

Prayer, humility and a generous application of the Spirit of Christ will cure just about any disease in the body of believers. Yet this is usually the last thing we think about when difficulties arise. We often attempt to cure spiritual ills with carnal medicines, and the results are more than disappointing. NCA083

What God wants today in His Church and in His work is not so much that the world shall see the power of the Church as the power of her Lord and the presence of Him who goes forth with His weakest servants and becomes their mighty Victor. CFD091

REAPING
FOLLOWS
SOWING

Good understanding giveth fa-
vour: but the way of transgres-
sors is hard.

—Proverbs 13:15

$\mathcal{W}$e may sow to the flesh if we will. There will be no interference from above. Thus to sow is our privilege—if we want to reap the harvest of corruption which must inevitably follow, a harvest no man in his right mind could deliberately choose.

No, the snare lies in choosing the pleasures of sowing with the secret hope that in some way we can escape the sorrows of the reaping; but never since the beginning of the world has it been possible to separate the one from the other.

The way to deal with a law of God is to work along with it. By faith and obedience we can put every divine law to work for us. And the law of sowing and reaping may be brought to our service and made to toil for our everlasting good.

So kind is God and so thoughtful of His creatures. NCA086-087

Disobedience always leads to danger. The way of wrong is the way of peril; the way of transgressors is hard. God has said so, and you can never make it otherwise. CTBC, Vol. 4/598

THE HARVEST
OF A LIFE
WELL LIVED

He that soweth to the Spirit shall of the Spirit reap life everlasting.

—Galatians 6:8

*W*e have but to submit *to* [the Holy Spirit] to gain *from* [Him] an everlasting reward. Deeds done in the Spirit, in obedience to Christ and with the purpose of bringing honor to the Triune God, are seeds of endless blessedness.

The first gift of life is not by works, but by faith in the work of a sufficient Redeemer; but after the miracle of the new birth has been accomplished, the Christian to a large extent carries his future in his hands. If he denies himself and takes up his cross in meek obedience, his deeds will become seeds of life and everlasting glory.

He may forget his deeds of love or think them small and useless, but God is not unmindful. He never forgets.

The sweet harvest of a life well lived will be there to meet the sower after the toil is ended and the heat of the day is past.
NCA087

> *If you would constantly enjoy [God's] approving smile, let Him see a spirit of single-hearted devotion to Jesus and uncompromising and unqualified obedience to His will.* WL041

THE SECRET SANCTUARY

Whereby are given unto us exceeding great and precious promises: that by these ye might be partakers of the divine nature.

—2 Peter 1:4

$\mathscr{I}$t is the teaching of Meister Eckhart that there is something far inside the mysterious depths of a human life which is unknown except as God and the individual know it. This he called the "ground" of the soul.

This "ground" is, according to Eckhart, the stuff which once received the image of God at creation. The lesser powers of the soul are the instruments through which this mysterious primal stuff makes itself felt in the world. These powers are imagination, reason, the faculty of speech and the creative powers. . . .

In this far-in secret sanctuary, God reveals Himself to the individual as a "birth," bringing forth a new creation by the regenerating act of the Holy Spirit. Thus we receive from Christ the very nature of God (2 Peter 1:4) and are spiritually prepared for the full revelation of Christ in us, the hope of glory. NCA102

In that blessed moment of appropriating faith [Christ] gives Himself to us as our complete life, covering all our future need, and day by day we just enter into it step by step. SI019

THE FINE TOUCH OF THE SPIRIT

And God is able to make all grace abound toward you; that ye . . . may abound to every good work.

—2 Corinthians 9:8

$\mathcal{T}$he Holy Spirit never differs from Himself, and wherever He touches a human mind His sure marks are always present so plainly that there can be no mistaking them.

Anyone familiar with the work of the French artist Millet will notice a similarity in everything he painted, as if the very breathing personality of the man had somehow gotten into the paint and onto the canvas.

So the Holy Spirit teaches the same thing to everyone; however different the subjects may be from each other, the fine touch of the Spirit's hand may be detected on each one. NCA103

> *O fire of God, begin in me;*
> *Burn out the dross of self and sin,*
> *Burn off my fetters, set me free,*
> *And make my heart a heaven within.*
>
> *Baptize with fire this soul of mine;*
> *Endue me with Thy Spirit's might*
> *And make me by Thy power divine*
> *A burning and a shining light.* HCL246

INSIST ON SAINTHOOD

Holding the mystery of the faith in a pure conscience.

—1 Timothy 3:9

*T*he fact is that we are not today producing saints. We are making converts to an effete type of Christianity that bears little resemblance to that of the New Testament. The average so-called Bible Christian in our times is but a wretched parody of true sainthood. Yet we put millions of dollars behind movements to perpetuate this degenerate form of religion and attack the man who dares to challenge the wisdom of it.

Clearly we must begin to produce better Christians. We must insist on New Testament sainthood for our converts, nothing less; and we must lead them into a state of heart purity, fiery love, separation from the world and poured-out devotion to the Person of Christ. Only in this way can the low level of spirituality be raised again to where it should be in the light of the Scriptures and of eternal values. OGM009

> *It is well to remember that a new heart is one thing, and a pure heart is another. They are not synonymous. Any man can have a new heart which loves God and yet not possess a pure heart from which self, man-fear, love of praise and other like things are banished.* SAN005-006

FROM WITHIN OR ABOVE

If any man speak, let him speak as the oracles of God; if any man minister, let him do it as of the ability which God giveth.

—1 Peter 4:11

*T*he Church at this moment needs men, the right kind of men—bold men. The talk is that we need revival, that we need a baptism of the Spirit—and God knows we must have both; but God will not revive mice. He will not fill rabbits with the Holy Spirit.

We languish for men who feel themselves expendable in the warfare of the soul, who cannot be frightened by threats of death because they have already died to the allurements of this world. Such men will be free from the compulsions that control weaker men. They will not be forced to do things by the squeeze of circumstances; their only compulsion will come from within—or from above. OGM011

> *God does ask us and expect us to be holy men and women of God, because we are the children of God, who is holy. . . . [T]he provision of God by His pure and gentle and loving Spirit is still the positive answer for those who hunger and thirst for a life and spirit well-pleasing to God.* ICH068

NOT I, BUT CHRIST

> . . . *that in all things he might have the preeminence. For it pleased the Father that in him should all fulness dwell.*
>
> —Colossians 1:18-19

$\mathcal{S}$omeone wrote the godly Macarius of Optino that his spiritual counsel had been helpful.

"This cannot be," Macarius wrote in reply. "Only the mistakes are mine. All good advice is the advice of the Spirit of God; His advice that I happen to have heard rightly and to have passed on without distorting it."

There is an excellent lesson here which we must not allow to go unregarded. It is the sweet humility of the man of God. . . . In this day when shimmering personalities carry on the Lord's work after the methods of the entertainment world, it is refreshing to associate for a moment even in the pages of a book with a sincere and humble man who keeps his own personality out of sight and places the emphasis upon the inner working of God. OGM015-016

> *Oh, to be saved from myself, dear Lord!*
> *Oh, to be lost in Thee!*
> *Oh, that it might be no more I, but*
> *Christ that lives in me!* HCL264

A HIGH NOTE OF HOLY JOY

Walk in the statutes of life, without committing iniquity; he shall surely live, he shall not die.

—Ezekiel 33:15

*O*ur religion must interfere with our private lives [because] we live in the world, the Bible name for human society. The regenerated man has been inwardly separated from society as Israel was separated from Egypt at the crossing of the Red Sea.

The Christian is a man of heaven temporarily living on earth. Though in spirit divided from the race of fallen men, he must yet in the flesh live among them. In many things he is like them, but in others he differs so radically from them that they cannot but see and resent it. . . .

But we must not get the impression that the Christian life is one continuous conflict, one unbroken irritating struggle against the world, the flesh and the devil. A thousand times no. The heart that learns to die with Christ soon knows the blessed experience of rising with Him, and all the world's persecutions cannot still the high note of holy joy that springs up in the soul that has become the dwelling place of the Holy Spirit. OGM042

> *There is never a day so dreary,*
> *There is never a night so long,*
> *But the soul that is trusting Jesus*
> *Will somewhere find a song.* HCL528

TEMPERANCE— A BEAUTIFUL WORD

And [add] to knowledge temperance; and to temperance patience; and to patience godliness.

—2 Peter 1:6

*T*he beautiful word temperance occurs strategically in the theology of the New Testament. Temperance is the helmsman in easy control of the powerful ship as it ploughs through the sea with all parts working in harmony.

Temperance is that in the Christian man's life which brings every faculty into harmony with every other, and the total personality into accord with God's plan for the whole man. In a life so directed there can be no place for excess. . . .

[T]emperance is not automatic. It is listed among the fruit of the Spirit, but it requires prayer, Bible reading, cross-bearing, hard discipline, obedience and self-denial before it can become a fixed part of the Christian's character. WOS084

> *Those who are in the flesh . . . live unto themselves; those who are in the Spirit . . . live unto Christ. There are but two moral characters that are essentially different, and this is the radical difference between them.* DTC147

HOLINESS FOR TAINTED SOULS

The fear of the LORD is the beginning of wisdom: and the knowledge of the holy is understanding.

—Proverbs 9:10

We come into the presence of God with tainted souls. We come with our own concept of morality, having learned it from books, from the newspaper and from school. We come to God dirty . . . and do nothing about it!

If we came to God dirty, but trembling and shocked and awestruck in His presence, if we knelt at His feet and cried with Isaiah, "I am undone; because I am a man of unclean lips" (Isaiah 6:5), then I could understand. But we skip into His awful presence. We're dirty, but we have a book called *Seven Steps to Salvation* that gives us seven verses to get us out of our problems. And each year we have more Christians, more people going to church, more church buildings, more money—and less spirituality and less holiness. We're forgetting "holiness, without which no man shall see the Lord" (Hebrews 12:14). I tell you this: I want God to be what God is: the impeccably holy, unapproachable Holy Thing, the All-Holy One. I want Him to be and remain *THE HOLY*. AOG171-172

Lay aside the garments that are stained with sin
And be washed in the blood of the Lamb;
There's a fountain flowing for the soul unclean;
Oh, be washed in the blood of the Lamb. HCL513

AS HAPPY
AS YOU
ARE HOLY

Happy is he that hath the God of Jacob for his help, whose hope is in the LORD his God.

—Psalm 146:5

*T*he childish clamor after happiness can become a real snare. One may easily deceive himself by cultivating a religious joy without a correspondingly righteous life.

No man should desire to be happy who is not at the same time holy. He should spend his efforts in seeking to know and do the will of God, leaving to Christ the matter of how happy he shall be.

For those who take this whole thing seriously, I have a suggestion: Go to God and have an understanding. Tell Him that it is your desire to be holy at any cost, and then ask Him never to give you more happiness than holiness. When your holiness becomes tarnished, let your joy become dim. And ask Him to make you holy whether you are happy or not.

Be assured that in the end you will be as happy as you are holy. OGM049-050

> *The work of the Holy Spirit is, among other things, to rescue the redeemed man's emotions, to restring his harp and open again the wells of sacred joy which have been stopped by sin.* POM112

FAITH IN FAITH

I thank my God through Jesus Christ for you all, that your faith is spoken of throughout the whole world.

—Romans 1:8

$\mathcal{T}$rue faith requires that we believe everything God has said about Himself, but also that we believe everything He has said about *us*. Until we believe that we are as bad as God says we are, we can never believe that He will do for us what He says He will do.

Right here is where popular religion breaks down. It never quite accepts the severity of God or the depravity of man. It stresses the goodness of God and man's misfortune. Sin is a pardonable frailty and God is not too much concerned about it. He merely wants us to trust in His goodness.

To believe thus is to ground faith upon falsehood and build our eternal hope upon sand. No man has any right to pick and choose among revealed truths. God has spoken. . . .

Faith in faith is faith astray. To hope for heaven by means of such faith is to drive in the dark across a deep chasm on a bridge that doesn't quite reach the other side. OGM061-062

The first act of faith is to believe what God says about sin. SI006

FAITH IN WHICH JESUS?

Righteous art thou, O LORD, and upright are thy judgments. Thy testimonies that thou hast commanded are righteous and very faithful.

—Psalm 119:137-138

To manipulate the Scriptures so as to make them excuse us, compliment us and console us is to do despite to the written Word and to reject the Living Word. To believe savingly in Jesus Christ is to believe all He has said about Himself and all that the prophets and apostles have said about Him. Let us beware that the Jesus we "accept" is not one we have created out of the dust of our imagination and formed after our own likeness.

True faith commits us to obedience. "[W]e have received grace and apostleship," says Paul, "for obedience to the faith among all nations, for his name" (Romans 1:5). That dreamy, sentimental faith which ignores the judgments of God against us and listens to the affirmations of the soul is as deadly as cyanide.

That faith which passively accepts all the pleasant texts of the Scriptures while it overlooks or rejects the stern warnings and commandments of those same Scriptures is not the faith of which Christ and His apostles spoke. OGM062

> *[F]aith is simply that which takes hold of the promise and the fullness of Christ.* SI123

TRUE CHRISTIAN EQUALS PRACTICING CHRISTIAN

We have a building of God, an house not made with hands, eternal in the heavens.

—2 Corinthians 5:1

The supreme purpose of the Christian religion is to make men like God in order that they may act like God. In Christ the verbs *to be* and *to do* follow each other in that order.

True religion leads to moral action. The only true Christian is the practicing Christian.

Such a one is in very reality an incarnation of Christ as Christ is the incarnation of God; not in the same degree and fullness of perfection, for there is nothing in the moral universe equal to that awful mystery of godliness which joined God and man in eternal union in the person of the Man Christ Jesus; but as the fullness of the Godhead was and is in Christ, so Christ is in the nature of the one who believes in Him in the manner prescribed in the Scriptures. OGM063

> *It appears that too many Christians want to enjoy the thrill of feeling right but are not willing to endure the inconvenience of being right.* ROR052-053

GOD ALWAYS ACTS LIKE HIMSELF

Exalt the LORD our God, and worship at his holy hill; for the LORD our God is holy.

—Psalm 99:9

*G*od always acts like Himself wherever He may be and whatever He may be doing. When God became flesh and dwelt among us He did not cease to act as He had been acting from eternity. "He veiled His deity but He did not void it." The ancient name dimmed down to spare the helpless eyes of mortal men, but as much as was seen was true fire.

Christ restrained His powers but He did not violate His holiness. In whatsoever He did He was holy, harmless, separate from sinners and higher than the highest heaven.

Just as in eternity God acted like Himself and when incarnated in human flesh still continued in all His conduct to be true to His holiness, so does He when He enters the nature of a believing man. This is the method by which He makes the redeemed man holy. OGM063-064

We can only become holy through the holiness of God. CTBC, Vol. 1/200

MAGNIFY,
MORTIFY,
SIMPLIFY

If ye through the Spirit do mortify the deeds of the body, ye shall live.

—Romans 8:13

*C*hrist calls men to carry a cross; we call them to have fun in His Name. He calls them to forsake the world; we assure them that if they but accept Jesus the world is their oyster. He calls them to suffer; we call them to enjoy all the bourgeois comforts modern civilization affords. He calls them to self-abnegation and death. We call them to spread themselves like green bay trees or perchance even to become stars in a pitiful fifth-rate religious zodiac. He calls them to holiness; we call them to a cheap and tawdry happiness that would have been rejected with scorn by the least of the Stoic philosophers.

In a world like this, with conditions being what they are, what should a serious-minded Christian do? The answer is easy to give but hard to follow. First, accept the truth concerning yourself. . . . Seek the kingdom of God and His righteousness. Seek through Jesus Christ a right relationship to your fellow man. Set about reverently to amend your doings. Magnify God, mortify the flesh, simplify your life. wos079-080

> *We must obey God. What a joy it brings to the soul to be thus consciously submissive and doing the whole will of God. . . . Satan feels helpless before a man with faith in heart and perfect obedience to God in life.* SAN074

FRUIT, NOT TREES

Either make the tree good, and his fruit good; or else make the tree corrupt, and his fruit corrupt: for the tree is known by his fruit.

—Matthew 12:33

$\mathcal{R}$ightly understood, faith is not a substitute for moral conduct but a means toward it. The tree does not serve in lieu of fruit but as an agent by which fruit is secured. Fruit, not trees, is the end God has in mind in yonder orchard; so Christlike conduct is the end of Christian faith.

To oppose faith to works is to make the fruit the enemy to the tree; yet that is exactly what we have managed to do. And the consequences have been disastrous.

A miscalculation in laying the foundation of a building will throw the whole superstructure out of plumb, and the error that gave us faith as a substitute for action instead of faith in action has raised up in our day unsymmetrical and ugly temples of which we may well be ashamed and for which we shall surely give a strict account in the day when Christ judges the secrets of our hearts. OGM065

> *If there is true faith within, there will be obedience to God without. They walk together and they go down together. When faith fails, disobedience sets in.* SAN072

OF FAITH AND FEAR

This is the victory that overcometh the world, even our faith.

—1 John 5:4

$\mathcal{N}$o matter what the circumstances, we Christians should keep our heads. God has not given us the spirit of fear, but of power, of love and of a sound mind. It is a dismal thing to see a son of heaven cringe in terror before the sons of earth. We are taught by the Holy Spirit in Scriptures of truth that fear is a kind of prison for the mind and that by it we may spend a lifetime in bondage.

To recoil from the approach of mental or physical pain is natural, but to allow our minds to become terrorized is quite another thing. The first is a reflex action; the latter is the result of sin and is a work of the devil to bring us into bondage. Terror is or should be foreign to the redeemed mind.

True faith delivers from fear by consciously interposing God between it and the object that would make it afraid. The soul that lives in God is surrounded by the divine Presence so that no enemy can approach it without first disposing of God, a palpable impossibility. WOS052-053

This is the victory that overcometh low spirits, a sinking heart, whispers of the devil and all the discouragements of this lower world—even our faith. SAN072

September

THE WAR NEVER ENDS

Thou art my beloved Son, in whom I am well pleased.

—Mark 1:11

It is the Spirit of Christ in us that will draw Satan's fire. The people of the world will not much care what we believe and they will stare vacantly at our religious forms, but there is one thing they will never forgive us—the presence of God's Spirit in our hearts.

They may not know the cause of that strange feeling of antagonism which rises within them, but it will be nonetheless real and dangerous. Satan will never cease to make war on the Man-child, and the soul in which dwells the Spirit of Christ will continue to be the target for his attacks. WOSO04

> *Immediately after a person has received the witness of the Spirit, . . . the adversary charges down upon the soul. . . . It is well for all such assaulted individuals to remember that just as soon as the Son of God received the . . . baptism of the Holy Ghost on the banks of the Jordan, that He was immediately afterwards driven into the wilderness and there tempted forty days by the devil. He conquered by faith and in the use of the Word of God. We can do the same.* SAN066

STEADY INWARD FIRE

I will pour out in those days of my Spirit; and they shall prophesy.

—Acts 2:18

$\mathcal{G}$od dwells in a state of perpetual enthusiasm. He is delighted with all that is good and lovingly concerned about all that is wrong.

He pursues His labors always in a fullness of holy zeal. No wonder the Spirit came at Pentecost as the sound of a rushing mighty wind and sat in tongues of fire on every forehead. In so doing He was acting as one of the Persons of the blessed Godhead.

Whatever else happened at Pentecost, one thing that cannot be missed by the most casual observer was the sudden upsurging of moral enthusiasm.

Those first disciples burned with a steady, inward fire. They were enthusiastic to the point of complete abandon. OGM005-006

> *With [the disciples'] baptism in the Spirit, their whole demeanor changed. The sadness left their hearts. The minor key left their worship. Their self-imposed righteousness was turned into life in the Spirit.* JJJ310

CHEAP SUBSTITUTE FOR THE REAL THING

They measuring themselves by themselves, and comparing themselves among themselves, are not wise.

—2 Corinthians 10:12

$\mathcal{W}$e may as well face it: the whole level of spirituality among us is low. We have measured ourselves by ourselves until the incentive to seek higher plateaus in the things of the Spirit is all but gone.

Large and influential sections of the world of fundamental Christianity have gone overboard for practices wholly unscriptural, altogether unjustifiable in the light of historic Christian truth and deeply damaging to the inner life of the individual Christian.

They have imitated the world, sought popular favor, manufactured delights to substitute for the joy of the Lord and produced a cheap and synthetic power to substitute for the power of the Holy Spirit. The glowworm has taken the place of the bush that burned, and scintillating personalities now answer to the fire that fell at Pentecost. OGM008-009

The Holy Spirit, whom Jesus also called the Spirit of Truth, has not come into the world to fool around; He will be found wherever the Lord's people meet, and in confirming the Word and the Person of Jesus Christ, He will demand moral action! TTPII, Book 8/029

IN SILENCE OR IN STORM

The desire of our soul is to thy name, and to the remembrance of thee.

—Isaiah 26:8

$\mathcal{I}$f God knows that your intention is to worship Him with every part of your being, He has promised to cooperate with you. On His side is the love and grace, the promises and the atonement, the constant help and the presence of the Holy Spirit.

On your side there is determination, seeking, yielding, believing. Your heart becomes a chamber, a sanctuary, a shrine in which there may be continuous, unbroken fellowship and communion with God. Your worship rises to God moment by moment.

Two of Spurgeon's greatest sermons were "God in The Silence" and "God in The Storm." The heart that knows God can find God anywhere. I surely join with Spurgeon in the truth that a person filled with the Spirit of God, a person who has met God in a living encounter can know the joy of worshiping Him, whether in the silences of life or in the storms of life. There really is no argument. We know what God wants us to be. He wants us to be worshipers! WHT127-128

It is not the man who spends his time in the crowd and merely reflects the opinion, spirit and attainments of men who most benefits the world, but the man who listens to and speak of things that have their birth beyond and far above the street. SAN104

SINNING WITH SILENCE?

He was in the world . . . and the world knew him not. He came unto his own, and his own received him not.

—John 1:10-11

*A*t this hour in world history the state of religion is such that the Church is in grave danger of losing [the spiritual treasures of God's wisdom]. Her gold is being turned to copper and her diamonds to glass. The religion of Cain is now in the ascendency—and marching under the banner of the cross.

Even among those who make a great noise about believing the Bible, that Bible has virtually no practical influence left. Fiction, films, fun, frolic, religious entertainment, Hollywood ideals, big business techniques and cheap, worldly philosophies now overrun the sanctuary. The grieved Holy Spirit broods over the chaos but no light breaks forth. "Revivals" come without rousing the hostility of organized sin and pass without raising the moral level of the community or purifying the lives of professing Christians. Why?

Could it be that too many of God's true children . . . are sinning against God by guilty silence? When those whose eyes are opened by the touch of Christ become vocal and active God may begin to fight again on the side of truth. GTM179-180

THE NAME AND THE NATURE

*Exalt ye the LORD our God,
and worship at his footstool; for
he is holy.*

—Psalm 99:5

Study the Bible carefully with the help of the Holy Spirit and you will find that the name and the nature of Jesus are one. It is not enough to know how to spell Jesus' name. If we have come to be like Him in nature, if we have come to the place of being able to ask in accordance with His will, He will give us the good things we desire and need. We do not worship in name only. We worship God as the result of a birth from above in which God has been pleased to give us more than a name. He has given us a nature transformed. . . .

Why should we delude ourselves about pleasing God in worship? If I live like a worldly and carnal tramp all day and then find myself in a time of crisis at midnight, how do I pray to a God who is holy? How do I address the One who has asked me to worship Him in spirit and in truth? Do I get on my knees and call on the name of Jesus because I believe there is some magic in that name? WHT126

> *I have come to believe that no worship is wholly pleasing to God until there is nothing in us displeasing to God.* RDAJan8

SUNDAY AND MONDAY

*I will extol thee, my God, O king;
and I will bless thy name for ever
and ever. Every day will I bless
thee; and I will praise thy name
for ever and ever.*

—Psalm 145:1-2

$\mathcal{M}$y brother or sister, if we are believing children of God in whom the Holy Spirit nurtures continual joy, delight and wonder, we will not need a storm on the mountain to show us how glorious our Lord really is.

It is a delusion to think that because we suddenly feel expansive and poetic in the presence of the storm or stars or space that we are spiritual. I need only remind you that drunkards or tyrants or criminals can have those "sublime" feelings, too. Let us not imagine that they constitute worship.

I can offer no worship wholly pleasing to God if I know that I am harboring elements in my life that are displeasing to Him. I cannot truly and joyfully worship God on Sunday and not worship Him on Monday. I cannot worship God with a glad song on Sunday and then knowingly displease Him in my business dealings on Monday and Tuesday. WHT124-125

> *[I]f you will not worship God seven days a week, you do not worship Him on one day a week.* TTPI, Book 1/051

A LIFE IN HARMONY

And whatsoever ye do in word or deed, do all in the name of the Lord Jesus, giving thanks to God and the Father by him.

—Colossians 3:17

$\mathcal{T}$he Bible is among other things a book of revealed truth. That is, certain facts are revealed that could not be discovered by the most brilliant mind. These facts are of such a nature as to be past finding out. They were hidden behind a veil, and until certain men who spoke as they were moved by the Holy Spirit took away that veil no mortal man could know them.

This lifting of the veil of unknowing from undiscoverable things we call divine revelation.

The Bible, however, is more than a volume of hitherto unknown facts about God, man and the universe. It is a book of exhortation based upon those facts. By far the greater portion of the book is devoted to an urgent effort to persuade people to alter their ways and bring their lives into harmony with the will of God as set forth in its pages. OGM025-026

> *Out of His goodness, God made us. Out of His goodness, He keeps us. When the man had sinned, He redeemed us again out of His goodness.* JIV045

ON
LOSING
THE "OH!"

*Keep not thou silence, O God:
hold not thy peace, and be not
still, O God.*

—Psalm 83:1

*T*heology seeks to reduce what may be known of God to intellectual terms, and as long as the intellect can comprehend it can find words to express itself.

When God Himself appears before the mind, awesome, vast and incomprehensible, then the mind sinks into silence and the heart cries out "O Lord God!" There is the difference between theological knowledge and spiritual experience, the difference between knowing God by hearsay and knowing Him by acquaintance. . . .

We Christians should watch lest we lose the "Oh!" from our hearts. There is real danger these days that we shall fall victim to the prophets of poise and the purveyors of tranquility, and our Christianity be reduced to a mere evangelical humanism that is never disturbed about anything nor overcome by and "trances of thought and mountings of the mind." . . .

When the calm listing of requests and the courteous giving of proper thanks take the place of the burdened prayer that finds utterance difficult we should beware the next step, for our direction is surely down whether we know it or not. BAM086-087

> *The chief thing is not to listen to yourself, but silently to list to God.* JAS171

BE THOU EXALTED

> *And he is before all things, and by him all things consist. . . . That in all things he might have the pre-eminence.*
>
> —Colossians 1:17-18

*F*ather, I want to know Thee, but my cowardly heart fears to give up its toys. I cannot part with them without inward bleeding, and I do not try to hide from Thee the terror of the parting. I come trembling, but I do come. Please root from my heart all those things which I have cherished so long and which have become a very part of my living self, so that Thou mayest enter and dwell there without a rival. Then shalt Thou make the place of Thy feet glorious. Then shall my heart have no need of the sun to shine in it, for Thyself wilt be the light of it, and there shall be no night there.

Lord, how excellent are Thy ways, and how devious and dark are the ways of man. Show us how to die, that we may rise again to newness of life. Rend the veil of our self-life from the top down as Thou didst rend the veil of the Temple. We would draw near in full assurance of faith. We would dwell with Thee in daily experience here on this earth so that we may be accustomed to the glory when we enter Thy heaven to dwell with Thee there. POG030, 044

> *Rise, O lord, into Thy proper place of honor, above my ambitions, above my likes and dislikes. . . . Let me sink that Thou mayest rise above.* POG099-100

FUNCTION JOYFULLY

*In thy presence is fulness of joy;
at thy right hand there are
pleasures for evermore.*

—Psalm 16:11

$\mathcal{M}$y Christian brother or sister, thank God always for the blessed gifts of sensitivity and conscience and human choice He has given you. Are you being faithful as a Christian believer where He has placed you?

If God has called you out of darkness into His light, you should be worshiping Him. If He has shown you that you are to show forth the excellencies, the virtues, the beauties of the Lord who has called you, then you should be humbly and gladly worshiping Him with the radiance and the blessing of the Holy Spirit in your life.

It is sad that we humans do not always function joyfully for God in the place He has marked out for us. We may even allow trifling things and minor incidents to disturb our fellowship with God and our spiritual witness for Him who is our Savior.

WHT100-101

> *Outward trials and troubles do not cease because the soul is baptized with the Holy Ghost. The disciples abounded in affliction after their sanctification, although they also abounded in joy.* SAN047

NOT HOW HAPPY, BUT HOW HOLY

What then? shall we sin, because we are not under the law, but under grace? God forbid.

—Romans 6:15

A selfish desire for happiness is as sinful as any other selfish desire. Its root is in the flesh which can never have any standing before God. . . . People are coming more and more to excuse every sort of wrongdoing on the grounds that they are "just trying to secure a little happiness . . . ."

The effect of this modern hedonism is felt also among the people of God. The gospel is too often presented as a means toward happiness, to peace of mind or security. There are even those who use the Bible to "relax" them, as if it were a drug.

How far wrong all this is will be discovered easily by the simple act of reading the New Testament through once with meditation. There the emphasis is not upon happiness but upon holiness. God is more concerned with the state of people's hearts than with the state of their feelings. Undoubtedly the will of God brings final happiness to those who obey, but the most important matter is not how happy we are but how holy. OGM047, 049

> *The whole matter of personal holiness is highly important to God! . . . Morally, we dare not ignore this commandment, "Be ye holy."* ICH061-062

THE NEVER-FAILING PRESENCE

And suddenly there came a sound from heaven as of a rushing mighty wind, and it filled all the house where they were sitting.

—Acts 2:2

$\mathcal{P}$entecost did not come and go; Pentecost came and stayed. Chronologically the day may be found on the historic calendar; dynamically it remains with us still in all its fullness of power....

Our insensibility to the presence of the Spirit is one of the greatest losses our unbelief and preoccupation have cost us. We have made Him a tenet in our creed, we have enclosed Him in a religious word, but we have known Him very little in personal experience.

Satan has hindered us all he could by raising conflicting opinions about the Spirit, by making Him a topic of hot and uncharitable debate between Christians. In the meanwhile, our hearts crave Him, and we hardly know what the craving means.

It would help us if we could remember that the Spirit is Himself God, the very true Nature of the Godhead subsisting in a form that can impart Himself to our consciousness.... It is His light upon the face of Christ which enables us to know Him. TET095-096

> *Augustine says it is amazing that anyone should live apart from [God,] apart from whom he cannot live at all.* BME058

CODDLED OR CRUCIFIED?

Knowing this, that our old man is crucified with him, that the body of sin might be destroyed, that henceforth we should not serve sin.

—Romans 6:6

The spiritual giants of old would not take their religion the easy way nor offer unto God that which cost them nothing. They sought not comfort but holiness, and the pages of history are still wet with their blood and their tears.

We now live in softer times. Woe unto us, for we have become adept in the art of comforting ourselves without power. . . . Those who will justify themselves in that kind of dodging are not likely to be much affected by anything I can say or write. . . .

But to those who will hear I would say with all the urgency at my command: Though the cross of Christ has been beautified by the poet and the artist, the avid seeker after God is likely to find it the same savage implement of destruction it was in the days of old. The way of the cross is still the pain-wracked path to spiritual power and fruitfulness.

So do not seek to hide from it. Do not accept an easy way. Do not allow yourself to be patted to sleep in a comfortable church, void of power and barren of fruit. TET083-084

> *Let [the cross] slay you utterly. Seek God. Seek to be holy and fear none of those things which thou shalt suffer.* TET084

NOT GOOD OR BAD, BUT ALIVE

Now if any man have not the Spirit of Christ, he is none of his.

—Romans 8:9

There are religious persons who have the name of Christ but whose spirit is the spirit of Adam. They belong to the old order which perishes, not to the new order of life in Christ Jesus. The point is not that they are good or bad but that they are dead. Their direction is wrong; they are on their way to the grave, not on their way out of it.

It is not that I plant, but what I plant that matters. A man could plant glass beads for a lifetime and have nothing to show for his trouble. . . .

Christ makes the difference between death and life, always and everywhere. He is the Prince of Life, and whatever He touches lives. The fabled Midas had a magic power which made everything he touched turn to gold. It is not fable, but wondrously true and real, that the power to give life belongs to Christ. Nothing He touches can ever die, and whatever is dead has only to be touched by Him and it lives again forever. TET059-060

> *We who bear the name of Christ should give ourselves no rest till we are sure that we possess the Spirit of Christ. . . . Without that Spirit no man can speak a living word or do an immortal deed.*
> TET060

A THANKFUL HEART AND TONGUE

> *Therefore I will give thanks unto thee, O LORD, among the heathen, and I will sing praises unto thy name.*
>
> —2 Samuel 22:50

*A*ll good and beneficial things the world affords are gifts of Almighty God and come to us out of His lovingkindness. Add to these all the wealth of grace which comes to us through blood atonement: revelation, redemption, mercy, the gift of eternal life and in the indwelling Spirit. For all this, for everything we are in debt to God forever. We can never repay our heavenly Father for the least of His goodness.

In view of all these things, a thankless man must be a bad man if for no other reason than that he is thankless. Ingratitude is a major sin.

The man of enlightened mind will always feel deeply humbled when he considers God's goodness and his own insignificance. He is likely to be very modest about demanding anything further; he will be too conscious that he already enjoys far more than the circumstances warrant. TET003-004

> *There are . . . holy tongues, yielded to the Holy Spirit and under the control of the fire of Pentecost. The good tongue is often a silent tongue. We all talk too much. Hand your tongue over to God; ask Him to take it and help you to remember it is not your own.* PC070

WARM HEARTS AND COOL HEADS

We have such an high priest, who is set on the right hand of the throne of the Majesty in the heavens.

—Hebrews 8:1

*T*he warmest hearts and the coolest heads anywhere at any time should always belong to the Christians. There are sound reasons for this. The Christian is seated "above." His fortunes do not depend upon earthly circumstances, but upon Christ who has conquered everything. . . .

For the warmth of his heart the Christian has the love of God which is "shed abroad" by the Holy Ghost, while from his vantage point in the "heavenly places" he is able to look down calmly upon the excited happenings of men. In his flesh he may be a part of the human scene, but in his spirit he is far above it all and is never at any time too much moved by what he sees. . . .

Since he is a part of God's eternal purpose, he knows he must win at last, and he can afford to be calm even when the battle seems to be temporarily going against him. The world has no such "blissful center" upon which to rest and is therefore constantly shifting about, greatly elated today, terribly cast down tomorrow and wildly excited the next day. TET041-042

We know that in the natural world the mightiest forces are those we do not see. . . . So in the spiritual world faith is the power to attach ourselves to God. PC018

A NEW PERSON IN AN OLD WORLD

And he shall stand and feed in the strength of the LORD, in the majesty of the name of the LORD his God.

—Micah 5:4

*T*he Christian who has dedicated his life to God and has shouldered his cross need not be surprised at the conflict in which he at once finds himself engaged. Such conflict is logical; it results from the nature of God and of man and of Christianity.

He will, for instance, discover that the ways of God and the ways of men are not equal. He will find that the skills he learned in Adam's world are of very little use to him in the spiritual realm. His tried and proven methods for getting things done will fail him when he attempts to apply them to the work of the Spirit. The new Adam will not surrender to the old Adam nor gear His new creation to the methods of the world. God will not share His glory with another. The seeking Christian must learn the hard way that it is "Not by might, nor by power, but by my spirit, saith the LORD of hosts" (Zechariah 4:6). OGM067

> *Oh, how long we struggle!*
> *Oh, how hard we try!*
> *Helplessly we labor,*
> *Helplessly we sigh*
> *Till Thy Spirit gives us*
> *Power from on high.* HCL249

THE BLISSFUL CENTER

He openeth also their ear to discipline, and commandeth that they return from iniquity.... Behold, God exalteth by his power.

—Job 36: 10, 22

*T*he work of God is not finished when the first act of inward adjustment has been done. The Spirit would go on from there to bring the total life into harmony with that "blissful center." This is wrought in the believer by the Word and by prayer and discipline and suffering.

It could be done by a short course in things spiritual if we were more pliable, less self-willed and stubborn; but it usually takes some time before we learn the hard lessons of faith and obedience sufficiently well to permit the work to be done within us with anything near to perfection.

In bringing many sons unto glory God works with whatever He has in whatever way He can and by whatever means He can, respecting always His own gift to us, the freedom of our wills. But of all means He uses, the Bible is the best. OGM072-073

> *The threefold purpose of the Bible is to inform, to inspire faith and to secure obedience. . . . The Holy Scriptures will do us good only as we present an open mind to be taught, a tender heart to believe and a surrendered will to obey.* NCA093

BEWARE THE FILE-CARD MENTALITY

Pure religion and undefiled . . . is this, To visit the fatherless and widows . . . and to keep himself unspotted from the world.

—James 1:27

The essence of true religion is spontaneity, the sovereign movings of the Holy Spirit upon and in the free spirit of redeemed men. This has through the years of human history been the hallmark of spiritual excellency, the evidence of reality in a world of unreality.

When religion loses its sovereign character and becomes mere form, this spontaneity is lost also, and in its place come precedent, propriety, system—and the file-card mentality.

Back of the file-card mentality is the belief that spirituality can be organized. Then is introduced into religion those ideas which never belong there—numbers, statistics, the law of averages, and other such natural human things.

And creeping death always follows. OGM079

> *[T]here are churches so completely out of the hands of God that if the Holy Spirit withdrew from them, they wouldn't find it out for many months.* COU052

HERE'S HOW IT WORKS

Pray without ceasing. In every thing give thanks: for this is the will of God in Christ Jesus concerning you.

—1 Thessalonians 5:17-18

*H*ere's how the file card works when it gets into the Christian life and begins to create mental habits: It divides the Bible into sections fitted to the days of the year, and compels the Christian to read according to rule. No matter what the Holy Spirit may be trying to say to a man, still he goes on reading where the card tells him, dutifully checking it off each day....

Inevitably the calendar crowds out the Spirit and the face of the clock hides the face of God. Prayer ceases to be the free breath of a ransomed soul and becomes a duty to be fulfilled. And even if under such circumstances he succeeds in making his prayer amount to something, still he is suffering tragic losses and binding upon his soul a yoke from which Christ died to set him free. OGM080-081

> *It is the privilege of every Christian to live so fully in God that he never gets out of the experienced Presence for one moment. . . . The whole life becomes a prayer . . . thoughts become mental prayers, deeds become prayers in action and even sleep may be but unconscious prayer.* NCA090

CONFRONT WITH KINDNESS

Be instant in season, out of season; reprove, rebuke, exhort with all longsuffering and doctrine.

—2 Timothy 4:2

$\mathcal{I}$t is quite natural, and even spiritual, to feel sorrow and heaviness when we see the professed followers of Christ walking in the ways of the world. And our first impulse may easily be to go straight to them and upbraid them indignantly.

But such methods are seldom successful. The heat in our spirit may not be from the Holy Spirit, and if it is not then it can very well do more harm than good. . . .

In this as in everything else Christ is our perfect example. A prayerful, face-down meditation on the life of Christ will show us how to oppose with kindness and reprove with charity. And the power of the Holy Spirit within us will enable us to follow His blessed example. OGM110-111

> *The baptism of the Holy Spirit will always bring a spirit of love . . . and . . . sweetness and charity toward all men.* HS377

BLESSINGS THROUGH OBEDIENCE

So will I save you, and ye shall be a blessing: fear not, but let your hands be strong.

—Zechariah 8:13

Christ is to His people so many wonderful things and brings to them such a wealth of benefits as the mind cannot comprehend nor the heart find words to express.

These treasures are both present and to come. The Spirit of Truth, speaking through Paul, assures us that God has in Christ blessed us with all spiritual blessings. These are ours as sons of the new creation and are made available to us now by the obedience of faith.

Peter, moved by the same Spirit, tells us of an inheritance guaranteed us by the resurrection of Christ, an inheritance incorruptible, undefiled and unfading, reserved in heaven for us.

There is no contradiction here, for one apostle speaks of present benefits and the other of benefits yet to be conferred upon us at the coming of Christ. And both exhaust human speech to celebrate the many blessings which we have already received. OGM153-154

> *[A]s soon as thou givest thyself to God from thy whole heart, and seekest neither this nor that, . . . thou shalt find thyself united and at peace.* JAS115

THE GLORIOUS PURSUIT

For there are three that bear record in heaven, the Father, the Word, and the Holy Ghost: and these three are one.

—1 John 5:7

*Y*ou and I are in little (our sins excepted) what God is in large. Being made in His image we have within us the capacity to know Him. In our sins we lack only the power. The moment the Spirit has quickened us to life in regeneration our whole being senses its kinship to God and leaps up in joyous recognition. That is the heavenly birth without which we cannot see the Kingdom of God. It is, however, not an end but an inception, for now begins the glorious pursuit, the heart's happy exploration of the infinite riches of the Godhead. That is where we begin, I say, but where we stop no man has yet discovered, for there is in the awful and mysterious depths of the Triune God neither limit nor end.

> *Shoreless Ocean, who can sound Thee?*
> *Thine own eternity is round Thee,*
> *Majesty divine!* POG014

> *Jehovah—Father, Spirit, Son—*
> *Mysterious Godhead, Three-in-One,*
> *Before Thy throne we sinners bend;*
> *Grace, pardon, life to us extend. AMEN.* HCL004

THE PARADOX OF LOVE

...my soul thirsteth for thee, my flesh longeth for thee ... to see thy power and thy glory, so as I have seen thee in the sanctuary.

—Psalm 63:1-2

*T*o have found God and still to pursue Him is the soul's paradox of love, scorned indeed by the too-easily-satisfied religionist, but justified in happy experience by the children of the burning heart. St. Bernard stated this holy paradox in a musical quatrain that will be instantly understood by every worshiping soul:

> *We taste Thee, O Thou Living Bread,*
> *And long to feast upon Thee still:*
> *We drink of Thee, the Fountainhead*
> *And thirst our souls from Thee to fill.* POG014-015

Each of [the fruits of the Spirit] is but a phase of love. Joy is love exulting; peace is love reposing; patience is love enduring; goodness is the good manners of love; kindness is love in action; faithfulness is love confiding; gentleness is love yielding; and self-control is true self-love. WL005

THE MANIFEST PRESENCE

The eyes of the LORD are in every place, beholding the evil and the good.

—Proverbs 15:3

$\mathcal{T}$he omnipresence of the Lord is one thing, and is a solemn fact necessary to His perfection.

The manifest Presence is another thing altogether, and from that Presence we have fled, like Adam, to hide among the trees of the garden, or like Peter, to shrink away crying, "Depart from me; for I am a sinful man, O Lord" (Luke 5:8).

So the life of man upon the earth is a life away from the Presence, wrenched loose from that "blissful center" which is our right and proper dwelling place, our first estate which we kept not, the loss of which is the cause of our unceasing restlessness.

POG032-033

The Holy Spirit is God, and the most important thing is that the Holy Spirit is present now. There is unseen deity present. I cannot bring Him to you; I can only tell you that He is here. QTB111

SAVED TO WORSHIP

Thine, O LORD, is the greatness, and the power, and the glory, and the victory, and the majesty.

—1 Chronicles 29:11

I believe a local church exists to do corporately what each Christian believer should be doing individually—and that is to worship God. . . .

We are saved to worship God. All that Christ has done for us in the past and all that He is doing now leads to this one end. If we are denying this truth and if we are saying that worship is not really important, we can blame our attitudes for the great wave of arrested development in our Christian fellowships.

Why should the church of Jesus Christ be a spiritual school where hardly anyone ever graduates from the first grade? WHT093-094

> *Do you love Jesus for the divine glories of His person, for the excellence of His life, for the benefits of His death, for the prevalence of His intercession, for His resurrection, His dominion over the world, and His office as the supreme and final Judge? Are the feelings of your heart drawn out towards Christ as your chief joy? Can you sit down under His shadow with great delight, and find His fruit sweet to your taste?* DTC115

WHEN GOD BREAKS THROUGH

I am with thee to deliver thee, saith the LORD. Then the LORD put forth his hand, and touched my mouth.

—Jeremiah 1:8-9

$\mathcal{P}$ascal wrote on a piece of paper a brief account of his experience, folded the paper and kept it in a pocket close to his heart, apparently as a reminder of what he had felt. Those who attended him at his death found the worn, creased paper. In Pascal's own hand it read:

> From about half-past ten at night to about half-after midnight—fire! O God of Abraham, God of Isaac, God of Jacob—not the God of the philosophers and the wise. The God of Jesus Christ who can be known only in the ways of the gospel. Security—feeling—peace—joy—tears of joy. Amen.

Were these the expressions of a fanatic, an extremist? No. Pascal's mind was one of the greatest. But the living God had broken through and beyond all that was human and intellectual and philosophical. The astonished Pascal could only describe in one word the visitation in his spirit: "Fire!" . . . .

What we need among us is a genuine visitation of the Spirit.
WHT090-091

Nothing can prevent the spiritual rejuvenation of the soul that insists upon having it. SIZ015

THE BEING AND THE SEEING

They shall know that I am the LORD their God... that I may dwell among them: I am the LORD their God.

—Exodus 29:46

*A*dam sinned and, in his panic, frantically tried to do the impossible; he tried to hide from the presence of God. David also must have had wild thoughts of trying to escape from the Presence, for he wrote, "Whither shall I go from thy spirit? or whither shall I flee from thy presence?" (Psalm 139:7).

Then he proceeded through one of his most beautiful psalms to celebrate the glory of the divine immanence. "If I ascend up into heaven, thou art there: if I make my bed in hell, behold, thou art there. If I take the wings of the morning, and dwell in the uttermost parts of the sea; even there shall thy hand lead me, and thy right hand shall hold me" (139:8-10).

And he knew that God's *being* and God's *seeing* are the same, that the seeing Presence had been with him even before he was born, watching the mystery of unfolding life. POG057

> *At the heart of the Christian message is God Himself waiting for His redeemed children to push in to conscious awareness of His presence.*
>
> POG034-035

GOD WILL MANIFEST HIMSELF

And the LORD God called unto Adam, and said unto him, Where art thou?

—Genesis 3:9

*I*f God is present at every point in space, if we cannot go where He is not, cannot even conceive of a place where He is not, why then has not that Presence become the one universally celebrated fact of the world? . . .

The Presence and the manifestation of the Presence are not the same. There can be the one without the other. God is here when we are wholly unaware of it. He is manifest only when and as we are aware of His presence.

On our part, there must be surrender to the Spirit of God, for His work is to show us the Father and the Son. If we cooperate with Him in loving obedience, God will manifest Himself to us, and that manifestation will be the difference between a nominal Christian life and a life radiant with the light of His face. POG057-058

Oh, may He come to us now and light up the sanctuary of our hearts until they shall shine like the chambers above! . . . May He open to our vision . . . His own immediate, everlasting presence! Amen! CTAB061

October

THE VOLUNTARY SELLOUT

My sheep hear my voice, and I know them, and they follow me: and I give unto them eternal life.

—John 10:27-28

Let no one imagine that he will lose anything of human dignity by this voluntary sell-out of his all to his God. He does not by this degrade himself as a man; rather he finds his right place of high honor as one made in the image of his Creator. His deep disgrace lay in his moral derangement, his unnatural usurpation of the place of God. His honor will be proved by restoring again that stolen throne. In exalting God over all he finds his own highest honor upheld.

Anyone who might feel reluctant to surrender his will to the will of another should remember Jesus' words, "Whosoever committeth sin is the servant of sin" (John 8:34). We must of necessity be servant to someone, either to God or to sin. . . . The man who surrenders to Christ exchanges a cruel slave driver for a kind and gentle Master whose yoke is easy and whose burden is light. POG095-096

> *The spirit of the carnal mind is an independent spirit. . . . But a sense of perfect dependence is a grateful guest of the broken and contrite heart.* DTC120

CITIZENS OF TWO WORLDS

We should live soberly, righteously, and godly, in this present world.

—Titus 2:12

O ur trouble springs from the fact that we who follow Christ inhabit at once two worlds—the spiritual and the natural. As children of Adam we live our lives on earth subject to the limitations of the flesh and the weaknesses and ills to which human nature is heir. Merely to live among men requires of us years of hard toil and much care and attention to the things of this world.

In sharp contrast to this is our life in the Spirit. There we enjoy another and higher kind of life—we are children of God; we possess heavenly status and enjoy intimate fellowship with Christ.

This tends to divide our total life into two departments. We come unconsciously to recognize two sets of actions [the sacred and the secular]. . . . [But] the sacred-secular antithesis has no foundation in the New Testament. . . . Paul's exhortation to "do all to the glory of God" (1 Corinthians 10:31) is more than pious idealism. . . . It opens before us the possibility of making every act of our lives contribute to the glory of God. POG109-110

> *[Christ] will not use us to establish His kingdom in the world until He occupies the throne of our entire being and becomes the King of our affections, our motives, our will and all our heart.* NJ088

ADORE—
A PRECIOUS
WORD

Sing, O heavens; and be joyful, O earth; and break forth into singing, O mountains: for the LORD hath comforted his people.

—Isaiah 49:13

𝓕ascination with God must necessarily have an element of adoration. You may ask me for a definition of adoration in this context. I will say that when we adore God, all of the beautiful ingredients of worship are brought to white, incandescent heat with the fire of the Holy Spirit. To adore God means we love Him with all the powers within us. We love Him with fear and wonder and yearning and awe.

The admonition to "love the Lord thy God with all thy heart, ... and with all thy mind" (Matthew 22:37) can mean only one thing. It means to adore Him.

I use the word "adore" sparingly, for it is a precious word. I love babies and I love people, but I cannot say I adore them. Adoration I keep for the only One who deserves it. In no other presence and before no other being can I kneel in reverent fear and wonder and yearning and feel the sense of possessiveness that cries "Mine, mine!" WHT088-089

> *God's child wants nothing more than the opportunity to pour out his or her love at the Savior's feet.* WHT089

NEEDED: A RADICAL SHIFT

Now unto him that is able to do exceeding abundantly above all that we ask or think ... unto him be glory.

—Ephesians 3:20-21

*J*he truth received in power shifts the bases of life from Adam to Christ and a new set of motives goes to work within the soul. A new and different Spirit enters the personality and makes the believing man new in every department of his being.

His interests shift from things external to things internal, from things on earth to things in heaven. He loses faith in the soundness of external values, he sees clearly the deceptiveness of outward appearances and his love for and confidence in the unseen and eternal world become stronger as his experience widens.

With the ideas here expressed most Christians will agree, but the gulf between theory and practice is so great as to be terrifying. For the gospel is too often preached and accepted without power, and the radical shift which the truth demands is never made. POM020-021

> *Anyone can do the possible; add a bit of courage and zeal and some may do the phenomenal; only Christians are obliged to do the impossible.* WOS012

FROM
SELF
TO GOD

*If any man will come after me,
let him deny himself, and take
up his cross, and follow me.*

—Matthew 16:24

$\mathcal{I}$t is a distressing thing that a truth so beautiful [as justification by faith] should have been so perverted. But perversion is the price we pay for failure to emphasize the moral content of truth; it is the curse that follows rational orthodoxy when it has quenched or rejected the Spirit of Truth.

In asserting that faith in the gospel effects a change of life-motive from self to God I am but stating the sober facts.

Every man with moral intelligence must be aware of the curse that afflicts him inwardly; he must be conscious of the thing we call *ego*, by the Bible called *flesh* or *self*, but by whatever name called, a cruel master and a deadly foe. POM026

> *Affections that do not terminate on God, terminate on self. Men who do not "seek the things that are Jesus Christ's," seek their own. Inordinate self-love is the ruling passion of their hearts and the governing principle of their lives. . . . The glory of God the Christian must seek.* DTC141, 143

THE DIVINE DISPLACEMENT

Sanctify the Lord God in your hearts: and be ready always to give an answer to every man that asketh.

—1 Peter 3:15

*W*ith [the] desire to please men so deeply implanted within us how can we uproot it and shift our life-drive from pleasing men to pleasing God?

Well, no one can do it alone, nor can he do it with the help of others, nor by education nor by training nor by any other method known under the sun. What is required is a reversal of nature (that it is a fallen nature does not make it any the less powerful) and this reversal must be a supernatural act.

That act the Spirit performs through the power of the gospel when it is received in living faith. Then He displaces the old with the new. Then He invades the life as sunlight invades a landscape and drives out the old motives as light drives away darkness from the sky. POM029-030

We ought never to confound the things we do with what God does. We get ready for Him. We place ourselves in position, and the fire descends. We sanctify ourselves that He might sanctify us. It is God's work. SAN017

A Switch in Pleasure Source

And they overcame him by the blood of the Lamb, and . . . they loved not their lives unto the death.

—Revelation 12:11

$\mathcal{T}$he way [faith] works in experience is something like this: The believing man is overwhelmed suddenly by a powerful feeling that *only God matters;* soon this works itself out into his mental life and conditions all his judgments and all his values.

Now he finds himself free from slavery to man's opinions. Soon he learns to love above all else the assurance that he is well-pleasing to the Father in heaven.

It is this complete switch in their pleasure source that has made believing men invincible. So could saints and martyrs stand alone, deserted by every earthly friend, and die for Christ under the universal displeasure of mankind. . . .

[T]he gospel has power to deliver men from the tyranny of social approval and make them free to do the will of God. POM030

Nothing is too dear to give to Christ, nothing too great to be cheerfully sacrificed to the promotion of His glory. Such is the disposition of good men, that they place their happiness in the glory of God and the prosperity of His kingdom. DTC143

ACCEPTING AND DECIDING

He that overcometh . . . shall be clothed in white raiment . . . I will confess his name before my Father, and before his angels.

—Revelation 3:5

$\mathcal{I}$t is time for us to seek again the leadership of the Holy Ghost. Man's lordship has cost us too much. Man's intrusive will has introduced such a multiplicity of unscriptural ways and unscriptural activities as positively to threaten the life of the Church. These divert annually millions of dollars from the true work of God and waste Christian man-hours in such vast numbers as to be heartbreaking.

There is another and worse evil which springs from this basic failure to grasp the radical difference between the natures of two worlds. It is the habit of languidly "accepting" salvation as if it were a small matter and one wholly in our hands. Men are exhorted to think things over and "decide" for Christ. . . . By a complete misunderstanding of the noble and true doctrine of the freedom of the human will, salvation is made to depend perilously upon the will of man instead of upon the will of God.
POM037-038

> *There is no genuine repentance where there is no forsaking of sin. Still to go on in sin, to practice iniquity with greediness, with constancy, and with perseverance, is incompatible with the nature of that sorrow which is unto salvation.* DTC093-094

How Badly Do You Want God?

He that cometh to me shall never hunger; and he that believeth on me shall never thirst.

—John 6:35

"Blessed are they which do hunger and thirst after righteousness: for they shall be filled" (Matthew 5:6). Hunger and thirst are physical sensations which, in their acute stages, may become real pain.

It has been the experience of countless seekers after God that when their desires become a pain they were suddenly and wonderfully filled. The problem is not to persuade God to fill us, but to want God sufficiently to permit Him to do so.

The average Christian is so cold and so contented with his wretched condition that there is no vacuum of desire into which the blessed Spirit can rush in satisfying fullness. BAM008

Child of the kingdom, be filled with the Spirit.
Nothing but fullness thy longing can meet;
'Tis the enduement for life and for service—
Thine is the promise, so certain, so sweet.

"I will pour water on him who is thirsty,
I will pour floods upon the dry ground;
Open your heart for the gift I am bringing,
While ye are seeking me, I will be found." HCL243

ALONE . . .
TOGETHER

*And they, continuing daily with
one accord in the temple . . . did
eat their meat with gladness
and singleness of heart.*

—Acts 2:46

*T*here are other experiences deep and wholly inward that cannot be shared with any other: Jacob at Bethel and Peniel, Moses at the burning bush, Christ in the garden, John in the Isle of Patmos are Bible examples, and Christian biography will reveal many more.

A community of believers must be composed of persons who have each one met God in individual experience. No matter how large the family, each child must be born individually. . . . So it is in the local church. Each member must be born of the Spirit individually.

It will not escape the discerning reader that while each child is born separate from the rest it is born into a family, and after that must live in the fellowship of the rest of the household. . . .

The church is called the household of God, and it is the ideal place to rear young Christians. BAM112-113

> *Next to God Himself we need each other most.
> We are His sheep and it is our nature to live with
> the flock.* BAM114

WORSHIPER FIRST

Enter into his gates with thanksgiving, and into his courts with praise: be thankful unto him, and bless his name.

—Psalm 100:4

Our Lord commands us to pray the Lord of the harvest that He will send forth laborers into His harvest field. What we are overlooking is that no one can be a worker who is not first a worshiper. Labor that does not spring out of worship is futile. . . .

It may be set down as an axiom that if we do not worship we cannot work acceptably. The Holy Spirit can work through a worshiping heart and through no other kind. We may go through the motions and delude ourselves by our religious activity, but we are setting ourselves up for a shocking disillusionment some day.

Without doubt the emphasis in Christian teaching today should be on worship. There is little danger that we shall become merely worshipers and neglect the practical implications of the gospel. . . . Fellowship with God leads straight to obedience and good works. That is the divine order, and it can never be reversed.

BAM125-126

Christian work must ever be subordinate to Christian worship, and our service must be under the control and inspiration of our deeper life and fellowship with the Lord Jesus Christ. CTBC, Vol. 1/232-233

AN INTIMATE AND PRIVATE PLACE

My voice shalt thou hear in the morning, O LORD; in the morning will I direct my prayer unto thee, and will look up.

—Psalm 5:3

One of the most liberating declarations in the New Testament is this: "[T]he true worshippers shall worship the Father in spirit and in truth: for the Father seeketh such to worship him. God is a Spirit: and they that worship him must worship him in spirit and in truth" (John 4:23-24). Here the nature of worship is shown to be wholly spiritual. . . .

From man's standpoint the most tragic loss suffered in the Fall was the vacating of this inner sanctum by the Spirit of God. At the far-in hidden center of man's being is a bush fitted to be the dwelling place of the Triune God.

There God planned to rest and glow with moral and spiritual fire. Man by his sin forfeited this indescribably wonderful privilege and must now dwell there alone. For so intimately private is the place that no creature can intrude; no one can enter but Christ, and He will enter only by the invitation of faith. MDP010

[G]et alone with God and His Word every day. I recommend that you turn off the radio and the television and let your soul delight in the fellowship and the mercies of God. TTPII, Book 6/074

THE HOLY SPIRIT IS NOT OPTIONAL

For thou, LORD, wilt bless the righteous; with favour wilt thou compass him as with a shield.

—Psalm 5:12

*T*he stark, tragic fact is that the efforts of many people to worship are unacceptable to God. Without an infusion of the Holy Spirit there can be no true worship. This is serious. It is hard for me to rest peacefully at night knowing that millions of cultured, religious people are merely carrying on church traditions and religious customs and they are not actually reaching God at all.

We must humbly worship God in spirit and in truth. Each one of us stands before the truth to be judged. Is it not now plain that the presence and the power of the Holy Spirit of God, far from being an optional luxury in our Christian lives, is a necessity? WHT046

> *The fellowship of God is delightful beyond all telling. He communes with His redeemed ones in an easy, uninhibited fellowship that is restful and healing to the soul. He is not sensitive nor selfish nor temperamental. What He is today we shall find Him tomorrow and the next day and the next year. . . . He loves us for ourselves and values our love more than galaxies of new created worlds.* ROR015

WALKING MYSTERY . . . WALKING MIRACLE

Who among us shall dwell with the devouring fire? who among us shall dwell with everlasting burnings?

—Isaiah 33:14

*O*ur Lord does not expect us to behave like zombies when we become Christians. But He does expect that we will have our soul open to the mystery that is God. I think it is proper for us to say that a genuine Christian should be a walking mystery because he surely is a walking miracle.

Through the leading and the power of the Holy Spirit, the Christian is involved in a daily life and habit that cannot be explained. A Christian should have upon him an element that is beyond psychology—beyond all natural laws and into spiritual laws. . . .

I think in our witness and ministries, we Christians should be men and women out of the fire. Because our God is holy, He is actively hostile to sin. God can only burn on and on against sin forever. WHT075

> *It matters not how great the sin. . . . To us the message is given, and we may echo it back to the Throne of Grace. It is the deep and inspired petition breathed long ago from the lips of David: "For thy name's sake, O LORD, pardon mine iniquity; for it is great" (Psalm 25:11).* LCL100

SAVED TO WORSHIP

For we are the circumcision, which worship God in the spirit . . . and have no confidence in the flesh.

—Philippians 3:3

*E*ven in our Christian circles we are prone to depend upon techniques and methods in the work that Christ has given us to do. Without a complete dependence upon the Holy Spirit we can only fail. If we have been misled to believe that we can do Christ's work ourselves, it will never be done.

The man whom God will use must be undone. He must be a man who has seen the King in His beauty. Let us never take anything for granted about ourselves, my brother or sister. . . .

I tell you again that God has saved us to be worshipers. May God show us a vision of ourselves that will disvalue us to the point of total devaluation. From there He can raise us up to worship Him and to praise Him and to witness. WHT077-078

> *There is no part of our existence which [God] cannot touch. There is no place in our varied experience where He cannot meet us. His humanity is as broad as ours. . . . This is the secret of all-sufficiency—the friendship of Jesus, the indwelling life of Christ, our union heart to heart with One who, as no other friend could possibly do, lives out His very life in ours.* PSP098-099

No Worship without the Holy Spirit

God is the King of all the earth: sing ye praises with understanding.... God sitteth upon the throne of his holiness.

—Psalm 47:7-8

$\mathcal{W}$e find much of spiritual astonishment and wonder in the book of Acts. You will always find these elements present when the Holy Spirit directs believing men and women.

On the other hand, you will not find astonished wonder among men and women when the Holy Spirit is not present.

Engineers can do many great things in their fields, but no mere human force or direction can work the mysteries of God among men.

If there is no wonder, no experience of mystery, our efforts to worship will be futile. There will be no worship without the Spirit. WHT065

> *Worship has to be in the Spirit and by the Spirit. The notion that just anybody can worship is all wrong. The notion that we can worship without the Spirit is all wrong. The notion that we can crowd the Spirit into a corner and ignore Him, quench Him, resist Him and yet worship God acceptably is a great heresy which we need to correct.* TWE041

CULTIVATION MEANS FRUITFULNESS

Charity suffereth long, and is kind; charity envieth not; charity vaunteth not itself, is not puffed up.

—1 Corinthians 13:4

This is the problem. We try to arrive at the fruits of Christianity by a shortcut. . . . Everybody wants to be known as being spiritual, close to God and walking in the Truth. . . . This is the answer. Every flower and every fruit has a stalk and every stalk has a root, and long before there is any bloom there must be a careful tending of the root and the stalk. This is where the misunderstanding lies—we think that we get the flower and the fragrance and the fruit by some kind of magic, instead of by cultivation. . . .

"Be ye therefore followers of God . . . and walk in love, as Christ also hath loved us . . . " (Ephesians 5:1-2). This is the likeness of Christ in the human heart and life—and our neighbors are waiting to see Him in our lives! WPJ020

What a multitude of words the Holy Spirit has given us for the various forms of love and patience. The list includes: love, charity, brotherly kindness, tenderness, meekness, longsuffering, patience, forbearance, unity, gentleness. They are like many shades of a color—all in the same class, yet no two exactly alike. LCL147

A
SUPERNATURAL
RADIANCE

These things have I spoken unto you, that my joy might remain in you, and that your joy might be full.

—John 15:11

*O*ne distinguishing mark of those first Christians was a supernatural radiance that shined out from within them. The sun had come up in their hearts and its warmth and light made unnecessary any secondary sources of assurance.

They had the inner witness. They knew with an immediate awareness that required no jockeying of evidence to give them a feeling of certainty. Great power and great grace marked their lives, enabling them to rejoice to suffer shame for the name of Jesus.

It is obvious that the average evangelical Christian today is without this radiance. The efforts of some of our teachers to cheer up our drooping spirits are futile because those same teachers reject the very phenomenon that would naturally produce joy, namely, the inner witness . . . : "He that believeth on the Son of God hath the witness in himself" (1 John 5:10). BAM013

> *[D]ivine joy is the privilege of all consecrated believers. . . . The world must see the light of heaven in our faces if it would believe in the reality of our religion.* ISS089

ALTOGETHER HIS

Thou shalt love the Lord thy God with all thy heart, and with all thy soul, and with all thy strength, and with all thy mind.

—Luke 10:27

*L*ord, I would trust Thee completely; I would be altogether Thine; I would exalt Thee above all.

I desire that I may feel no sense of possessing anything outside of Thee. I want constantly to be aware of Thy overshadowing presence and to heart Thy speaking voice.

I long to live in restful sincerity of heart.

I want to live so fully in the Spirit that all my thoughts may be as sweet incense ascending to Thee and every act of my life may be an act of worship. Therefore I pray in the words of Thy great servant of old, "I beseech Thee so for to cleanse the intent of mind heart with the unspeakable gift of Thy grace, that I may perfectly love Thee and worthily praise thee."

And all this I confidently believe Thou wilt grant me through the merits of Jesus Christ Thy Son. Amen. POG118

A distinguishing characteristic of true love to God is that it is supreme. *"No man can serve two masters." There cannot be two objects of supreme regard. . . . The love of God is paramount to every other principle. . . every desire subservient to that of promoting His glory.* DTC071-072

THE HOLY SPIRIT ACTS LIKE JESUS

God, who is rich in mercy . . . even when we were dead in sins, hath quickened us together with Christ.

—Ephesians 2:4-5

*T*he Holy Spirit is the Spirit of life and light and love. In His uncreated nature He is a boundless sea of fire, flowing, moving ever, performing as He moves the eternal purposes of God.

Toward nature He performs one sort of work, toward the world another and toward the Church still another. And every act of His accords with the will of the Triune God. Never does He act on impulse nor move after a quick or arbitrary decision.

Since He is the Spirit of the Father He feels toward His people exactly as the Father feels, so there need be on our part no sense of strangeness in His presence. He will always act like Jesus, toward sinners in compassion, toward saints in warm affection, toward human suffering in tenderest pity and love. POM071

What Christ did for us on the cross, the Spirit must do in us as a personal experience. CDP095

He has offered us Himself as the life and power to be obedient and to be holy, and nothing less than his own perfect example should ever satisfy our holy ambition! LCL060

THE RESULT OF REVIVAL

I am the Almighty God; walk before me, and be thou perfect. . . . And Abram fell on his face: and God talked with him.

—Genesis 17:1, 3

*W*hat [happens] in a Christian church when a fresh and vital working of the Spirit of God brings revival?

In my study and observations, a revival generally results in a sudden bestowment of a spirit of worship. This is not the result of engineering or of manipulation. It is something God bestows on people hungering and thirsting for Him. With spiritual renewing will come a blessed spirit of loving worship.

These believers worship gladly because they have a high view of God. In some circles, God has been abridged, reduced, modified, edited, changed and amended until He is no longer the God whom Isaiah saw, high and lifted up. Because He has been reduced in the minds of so many people, we no longer have that boundless confidence in His character that we used to have. WHTW086

> *The one mark . . . which forever distinguishes man from all other forms of life on earth is that he is a worshiper; he has a bent toward and a capacity for worship.* TIC153

TIME TO REPENT

Let the wicked forsake his way, and the unrighteous man his thoughts: and let him return unto the LORD.

—Isaiah 55:7

$\mathcal{I}$t is time for us to repent, for our transgressions against the blessed Third Person have been many and much aggravated. We have bitterly mistreated Him in the house of His friends. We have crucified Him in His own temple as they crucified the Eternal Son on the hill above Jerusalem. And the nails we used were not of iron, but of finer and more precious stuff of which human life is made.

Out of our hearts we took the refined metals of will and feeling and thought, and from them we fashioned the nails of suspicion and rebellion and neglect.

By unworthy thoughts about Him and unfriendly attitudes toward Him we grieved and quenched Him days without end.

The truest and most acceptable repentance is to reverse the acts and attitudes of which we repent. POM071-072

> *Worship rises or falls . . . depending upon the attitude we take toward God, whether we see God big or whether we see Him little. . . . [I]f there is one terrible disease in the Church of Christ, it is that . . . [w]e're too familiar with God.* WMJ021

WELCOME, HOLY SPIRIT!

In all their affliction he was afflicted . . . and in his pity he redeemed them. . . . But they . . . vexed his holy Spirit.

—Isaiah 63:9-10

*W*e can best repent our neglect by neglecting [the Holy Spirit] no more.

Let us begin to think of Him as One to be worshiped and obeyed.

Let us throw open every door and invite Him in.

Let us surrender to Him every room in the temple of our hearts and insist that He enter and occupy as Lord and Master within His own dwelling.

And let us remember that He is drawn to the sweet name of Jesus as bees are drawn to the fragrance of clover.

Where Christ is honored the Spirit is sure to feel welcome; where Christ is glorified He will move about freely, pleased and at home. POM072

When the Scripture says, "And grieve not the holy Spirit of God" (Ephesians 4:30), it is telling us that He loves us so much that when we insult Him, He is grieved; when we ignore Him, He is grieved; when we resist Him, He is grieved; and when we doubt Him, He is grieved. COU052

AS THEY ARE, SO HE IS

*Behold my servant, whom I
have chosen; my beloved, in
whom my soul is well pleased: I
will put my spirit upon him.*

—Matthew 12:18

To the reverent question, "What is God like?" a proper answer will always be, "He is like Christ." For Christ is God, and the Man who walked among men in Palestine was God acting like Himself in the familiar situation where His incarnation placed Him.

To the question, "What is the Spirit like?" the answer must always be, "He is like Christ." For the Spirit is the essence of the Father and the Son. As they are, so is He. As we feel toward Christ and toward our Father who art in heaven, so should we feel toward the Spirit of the Father and the Son. POM070-071

> *Holy Father, Holy Son, Holy Spirit—*
> *Three we name Thee;*
> *Though in essence only one,*
> *Undivided God we claim Thee,*
> *And adoring bend the knee*
> *While we sing our praise to Thee.* AMEN. HCL006

> *Somebody pointed out that hymnody took a down-ward trend when we left the great objective hymns that talked about God and began to sing the gospel songs that talk about us.* TWE096

THE EXPERIENCE OF KNOWING

The natural man receiveth not the things of the Spirit of God ... because they are spiritually discerned.

—1 Corinthians 2:14

*W*hen the Spirit illuminates the heart, then a part of the man sees which never saw before; a part of him knows which never knew before, and that with a kind of knowing which the most acute thinker cannot imitate. He knows now in a deep and authoritative way, and what he knows needs no reasoned proof. His experience of knowing is above reason, immediate, perfectly convincing and inwardly satisfying.

"A man can receive nothing." That is the burden of the Bible. Whatever men may think of human reason, God takes a low view of it. . . .

The inability of human reason as an organ of divine knowledge arises not from its own weakness but from its unfittedness for the task by its own nature. It was not given as an organ by which to know God. POM076

It takes the Holy Spirit to unlock the Book. He who reads simply with the eye of the Intellect will miss the glory of the Book, and never realize the soulfood with which it is stored. It is well to ask the light and blessing of the Holy Ghost upon us each time that we read. SAN117

NO TRUTH
APART FROM
THE SPIRIT

Thou couldest have no power at all against me, except it were given thee from above.

—John 19:11

*E*verywhere . . . we find persons who are Bible-taught but not Spirit-taught. They conceive truth to be something which they can grasp with the mind.

If a man holds to the fundamentals of the Christian faith he is thought to possess divine truth. But it does not follow. There is no truth apart from the Spirit.

The most brilliant intellect may be imbecilic when confronted with the mysteries of God. For a man to understand revealed truth requires an act of God equal to the original act which inspired the text.

"Except it were given thee from above" (John 19:11). Here is the other side of the truth; here is hope for all, for these words do certainly mean that there is such a thing as a gift of knowing, a gift that comes from heaven. POM077

> *It is blessed to be sanctified, and even more blessed to be intelligently sanctified. Happy is the man who enjoys the blessing of perfect love in connection with an informed mind, experienced head and sound judgment.* SAN167

WISDOM—CORRECT DOCTRINE PLUS

Lead me in thy truth, and teach me: for thou art the God of my salvation; on thee do I wait all the day.

—Psalm 25:5

*T*he old Jewish believers of pre-Christian times who gave us the (to modern Protestants little-known) books, the Wisdom of Solomon and Ecclesiasticus, believed that it is impossible for an impure heart to know divine truth.

> For into a malicious soul wisdom will not enter; nor dwell in the body that is subject unto sin. For the holy spirit of discipline will flee deceit, and remove from thoughts that are without understanding, and will not abide when unrighteousness cometh in.

These books, along with our familiar book of Proverbs, teach that true spiritual knowledge is the result of a visitation of heavenly wisdom, a kind of baptism of the Spirit of Truth which comes to God-fearing men.

This wisdom is always associated with righteousness and humility and is never found apart from godliness and true holiness of life. POM083-084

> *We need to learn that truth consists not in correct doctrine, but in correct doctrine* plus the inward enlightenment of the Holy Spirit. POM084

THE SPIRIT AS POWER

> *But ye shall receive power, after that the Holy Ghost is come upon you.*
>
> —Acts 1:8

Some good Christians have misread this text and have assumed that Christ told His disciples that they were to receive the Holy Spirit *and* power, the power to come after the coming of the Spirit. . . . [B]ut the truth is that Christ taught not the coming of the Holy Spirit *as* power; the power and the Spirit are the same. . . .

Our Lord before His ascension said to His disciples, "Tarry ye in the city of Jerusalem, until ye be endued with power from on high" (Luke 24:49). That word *until* is a time-word; it indicates a point in relation to which everything is either before or after.

So the experience of those disciples could be stated like this: Up to that point they *had not* received the power; at that point they *did* receive the power; after that point they *had* received the power. . . . That power, still active in the Church, has enabled her to exist for nearly twenty centuries. POM085, 087

> *Christianity takes for granted the absence of any self-help and offers a power which is nothing less than the power of God.* POM088

A SUPERNATURAL POTENCY

Now the God of hope fill you with all joy and peace in believing, that ye may abound in hope, through the power of the Holy Ghost.

—Romans 15:13

"Ye shall receive power." By those words our Lord raised the expectation of His disciples and taught them to look forward to the coming of a supernatural potency into their natures. . . . It was to be nothing less than God Himself entering into them with the purpose of ultimately reproducing His own likeness within them.

Here is the dividing line that separates Christianity from all occultism and from every kind of oriental cult. . . . They each advise, "Get in tune with the infinite," or "Wake the giant within you," or "Tune in to your hidden potential" or "Learn to think creatively."

All this may have some fleeting value as a psychological shot in the arm, but its results are not permanent because at its best it builds its hopes upon the fallen nature of man and knows no invasion from above. POM088

> *Oh, how long we struggle! Oh, how hard we try!*
> *Helplessly we labor, Helplessly we sigh*
> *Till Thy Spirit gives us*
> *Power from on high.* HCL249

NOT A
SELF-HELP
RELIGION

He that soweth to his flesh shall
of the flesh reap corruption; but
he that soweth to the Spirit shall
of the Spirit reap life everlasting.
—Galatians 6:8

Christianity takes for granted the absence of any self-help and offers a power which is nothing less than the power of God. This power is to come upon powerless men as a gentle but resistless invasion from another world, bringing a moral potency infinitely beyond anything that might be stirred up from within. This power is sufficient . . . for it is the Holy Spirit of God come where the weakness lay to supply power and grace to meet the moral need.

Set over against such a mighty provision as this ethical Christianity (if I may be allowed the term) is . . . [a]n infantile copying of Christ's "ideals," a pitiable effort to carry out the teachings of the Sermon on the Mount! All this is but religious child's play and is not the faith of Christ and the New Testament. POM088-089

> *You cannot know whether your self-denial is*
> *genuine or whether it is spurious, without know-*
> *ing whether it is founded upon a supreme attach-*
> *ment to the glory of God. To deny yourself from a*
> *supreme regard to a higher interest than your*
> *own, is to possess the spirit of the gospel.* DTC149

GOD'S KIND OF POWER

> *I am the vine, ye are the branches . . . without me ye can do nothing.*
>
> —John 15:5

"*Y*e shall receive power." This was and is a unique afflatus, an enduement of supernatural energy affecting every department of the believer's life and remaining with him forever. It is not physical power nor even mental power though it may touch everything both mental and physical in its benign outworking.

It is, too, another kind of power than that seen in nature, in the lunar attraction that creates the tides or the angry flash that splits the great oak during a storm.

This power from God operates on another level and affects another department of His wide creation. It is spiritual power. It is the kind of power that God is.

It is the ability to achieve spiritual and moral ends. Its long-range result is to produce Godlike character in men and women who were once wholly evil by nature and by choice.

POM089-090

> *[The] renovation of character and conduct is only in and through Christ Himself. . . . The cleansed temple must be possessed and occupied by the Lord of the temple.* UNKNOWN

November

PRESSURE ON THE HEART

Thus shall ye do in the fear of the LORD, faithfully, and with a perfect heart. . . . Deal courageously, and the LORD shall be with the good.

—2 Chronicles 19:9, 11

$\mathcal{N}$ow how does this power operate? At its purest it is an unmediated force directly applied by the Spirit of God to the spirit of man.

The wrestler achieves his ends by the pressure of his physical body upon the body of his opponent; the teacher by the pressure of ideas upon the mind of the student; the moralist by the pressure of duty upon the conscience of the disciple. So the Holy Spirit performs His blessed work by direct contact with the human spirit. . . .

The Spirit of God may use a song, a sermon, a good deed, a text or the mystery and majesty of nature, but always the final work will be done by the pressure of the inliving Spirit upon the human heart. POM090-091

The Spirit's first work is to cleanse us, to separate us, to sanctify us, to dedicate us wholly to God. Then as the property of God, He takes possession of us for God and uses us for His service and glory alone. HS071

A
VOLATILE
ESSENCE

*The wind bloweth where it listeth,
and thou hearest the sound
thereof, but canst not tell whence
it cometh, and whither it goeth.*

—John 3:8

*O*ne meaning of the word "power" is "ability to do." There precisely is the wonder of the Spirit's work in the Church and in the hearts of Christians, His sure ability to make spiritual things real to the soul.

This power can go straight to its object with piercing directness; it can diffuse itself through the mind like an infinitely fine volatile essence securing ends above and beyond the limits of the intellect.

Reality is its subject matter, reality in heaven and upon earth. It does not create objects which are not there but reveals objects already present and hidden from the soul.

In actual human experience this is likely to be first felt in a heightened sense of the presence of Christ. He is felt to be a real Person and to be intimately, ravishingly near. Then all other spiritual objects begin to stand out clearly before the mind. POM092

> *The Holy Spirit creates in us a new life and a
> new set of spiritual senses altogether, through
> which we discern, understand, and enter into the
> life of God and the spiritual realm.* HS344

ESTABLISHING THE DIRECTION

But grow in grace, and in the knowledge of our Lord and Saviour Jesus Christ. To him be glory both now and for ever. Amen.

—2 Peter 3:18

*O*nce the Holy Spirit's work in our heart begins, grace, forgiveness, cleansing take on a form of almost bodily clearness.

Prayer loses its unmeaning quality and becomes a sweet conversation with Someone actually there. Love for God and for the children of God takes possession of the soul. We feel ourselves near to heaven and it is now the earth and the world that begin to seem unreal. . . .

Then the whole life changes to suit the new reality and the change is permanent. Slight fluctuations there may be like the rise and dip of the line on a graph, but the established direction is upward and the ground taken is held.

This is not all, but it will give a fair idea of what is meant when the New Testament speaks of *power*, and perhaps by contrast we may learn how little of the power we enjoy. POM092-093

In every thing that belongs to the excellence of real religion, the true believer is in a state of progression. He seeks and strives, he wrestles and fights. He is ever aiming at the prize. . . . His obedience, though not perfect, is habitual. DTC192, 204

POWER— THE GREAT NEED

But the manifestation of the Spirit is given to every man to profit withal.

—1 Corinthians 12:7

J think there can be no doubt that the need above all other needs in the Church of God at this moment is the power of the Holy Spirit. More education, better organization, finer equipment, more advanced methods—all are unavailing.

It is like bringing a better respirator after the patient is dead. Good as these are they can never give life. "It is the spirit that quickeneth" (John 6:63). Good as they are they can never bring power. "Power belongeth unto God" (Psalm 62:11).

Protestantism is on the wrong road when it tries to win merely by means of a "united front." It is not organizational unity we need most; the great need is power. POM093

> *The power of God is at our disposal, waiting for us to call it into action by meeting the conditions which are plainly laid down. God is ready to send down floods of blessing upon us as we begin to obey His plain instructions.* PTP029

> *There is no divine incoming until there is the human emptying. How is it possible to fill us until we are first emptied? . . . Emptied first, filled afterward is the order.* SAN035

SILENCE AND SELF-EXAMINATION

*Stand in awe, and sin not: com-
mune with your own heart upon
your bed, and be still. Selah.*

—Psalm 4:4

I should like to suggest that we Bible-believing Christians announce a moratorium on religious activity and set our house in order preparatory to the coming of an afflatus from above.

So carnal is the body of Christians which composes the conservative wing of the Church, so shockingly irreverent are our public services in some quarters, so degraded are our religious tastes in still others that the need for power could scarcely have been greater at any time in history. I believe we should profit immensely were we to declare a period of silence and self-examination during which each one of us searched his own heart and sought to meet every condition for a real baptism of power from on high. POM094

> *More spiritual progress can be made in one short moment of speechless silence in the awesome presence of God than in years of mere study. . . . The exposure may be brief, but the results are permanent.* ROR146

> *Jesus calls us o'er the tumult*
> *Of our life's wild, restless sea;*
> *Day by day His sweet voice soundeth,*
> *Saying, "Christian, follow Me."* HCL221

ONLY THE SPIRIT

Receive thy sight, and be filled with the Holy Ghost. And immediately . . . he received sight forthwith.

—Acts 9:17-18

$\mathcal{W}$e may be sure of one thing, that for our deep trouble there is no cure apart from a visitation, yes, an *invasion* of power from above.

Only the Spirit Himself can show us what is wrong with us and only the Spirit can prescribe the cure.

Only the Spirit can save us from the numbing unreality of Spiritless Christianity.

Only the Spirit can show us the Father and the Son.

Only the inworking of the Spirit's power can discover to us the solemn majesty and the heart ravishing mystery of the Triune God. POM094

> *This is what the Holy Spirit brings to us, the vision of the Lord, power to see divine things as God sees them. Not only does He give knowledge of the truth, but He gives the realization of it. Not only does He reveal to us the promises, but He enables us to appropriate them. . . . The Spirit also thinks in us by giving us divine instincts, intuitions and enablements.* HS571-572

PEOPLE OF THE FIRE

He that cometh after me is mightier than I . . . he shall baptize you with the Holy Ghost, and with fire.

—Matthew 3:11

With the coming of the Holy Spirit at Pentecost the same imagery (fire) was continued. "And there appeared unto them cloven tongues like as of fire, and it sat upon each of them" (Acts 2:3). That which came upon the disciples in that upper room was nothing less than God Himself.

To their mortal eyes He appeared as fire, and may we not safely conclude that those Scripture-taught believers knew at once what it meant? The God who had appeared to them as fire throughout all their long history was now dwelling in them as fire. He had moved from without to the interior of their lives. The Shekinah that had once blazed over the mercy seat now blazed on their foreheads as an external emblem of the fire that had invaded their natures.

This was Deity giving Himself to ransomed men. The flame was the seal of a new union. They were now men and women of the Fire. POM099-100

> *A new heart comes with regeneration, the pure heart by the baptism of the Holy Ghost and of fire. We are born into one and baptized into the other.* SAN006

BACK INTO THE HEART OF GOD

. . . for the temple of God is holy, which temple ye are. . . . And ye are Christ's; and Christ is God's.

—1 Corinthians 3:17, 23

$\mathcal{D}$eity indwelling men! That, I say, is Christianity, and no man has experienced rightly the power of Christian belief until he has known this for himself as a living reality. Everything else is preliminary to this.

Incarnation, atonement, justification, regeneration—what are these but acts of God preparatory to the work of invading and the act of indwelling the redeemed human soul? Man, who moved out of the heart of God by sin, now moves back into the heart of God by redemption. God, who moved out of the heart of man because of sin, now enters again His ancient dwelling to drive out His enemies and once more make the place of His feet glorious. POM100-101

> *Regeneration is like building a house and having the work done well. Sanctification is having the owner come and dwell in the house and fill it with gladness and life and beauty.* TFG025

> *Shut in with Thee, O Lord, forever,*
> *My wayward feet no more to roam;*
> *What power from Thee my soul can sever?*
> *The center of God's will my home.* HCL215

HOLINESS IS A MORAL FLAME

[God] hath saved us, and called us with an holy calling . . . according to his own purpose and grace.

—2 Timothy 1:9

One of the most telling blows which the enemy ever struck at the life of the Church was to create in her a fear of the Holy Spirit. No one who mingles with Christians in these times will deny that such a fear exists. Few there are who without restraint will open their whole heart to the blessed Comforter. He has been and is so widely misunderstood that the very mention of His name in some circles is enough to frighten many people into resistance. . . . Perhaps we may help to destroy its power over us if we examine that fire which is the symbol of the Spirit's Person and presence.

The Holy Spirit is first of all a *moral flame*. It is not an accident of language that He is called the *Holy* Spirit, for whatever else the word *holy* may mean it does undoubtedly carry with it the idea of moral purity. And the Spirit, being God, must be absolutely and infinitely pure. With Him there are not (as with men) grades and degrees of holiness. He is holiness itself, the sum and essence of all that is unspeakably pure. POM101-102

> *Holiness is Christ, our Sanctification, enthroned as Life of our life. It is Christ, the Holy One, in us, living, speaking, walking.* PRL211-212

BE YE HOLY

*Cleanse your hands, ye sinners;
and purify your hearts, ye double minded. Be afflicted, and
mourn, and weep.*

—James 4:8-9

*W*hoever would be filled and indwelt by the Spirit should first judge his life for any hidden iniquities; he should courageously expel from his heart everything which is out of accord with the character of God as revealed by the Holy Scriptures.

At the base of all true Christian experience must lie a sound and sane morality. No joys are valid, no delights legitimate where sin is allowed to live in life or conduct. No transgression of pure righteousness dare excuse itself on the ground of superior religious experience.

To seek high emotional states while living in sin is to throw our whole life open to self-deception and the judgment of God. "Be ye holy" is not a mere motto to be framed and hung on the wall. It is a serious commandment from the Lord of the whole earth. POM102

The true Christian ideal is not to be happy but to be holy. The holy heart alone can be the habitation of the Holy Ghost. POM103

THE HOLY SPIRIT IS A SPIRITUAL FLAME

For the good that I would I do not: but the evil which I would not, that I do.

—Romans 7:19

*T*he Holy Spirit is also a *spiritual flame*. He alone can raise our worship to true spiritual levels. For we might as well know once for all that morality and ethics, however lofty, are still not Christianity.

The faith of Christ undertakes to raise the soul to actual communion with God, to introduce into our religious experiences a supra-rational element as far above mere goodness as the heavens are above the earth. . . .

The joy of the first Christians was not the joy of logic working on facts. They did not reason, "Christ is risen from the dead; therefore we ought to be glad." Their gladness was as great a miracle as the resurrection itself; indeed these were and are organically related. The moral happiness of the Creator had taken residence in the breasts of redeemed creatures and they could not but be glad. POM103-104

The continuous and unembarrassed interchange of love and thought between God and the soul of the redeemed man is the throbbing heart of New Testament religion. POG013

THE SPIRIT IS INTELLECTUAL

They received the word with all readiness of mind, and searched the scriptures daily, whether those things were so.

—Acts 17:11

*T*he flame of the Spirit is also *intellectual*. Reason, say the theologians, is one of the divine attributes. There need be no incompatibility between the deepest experiences of the Spirit and the highest attainments of the human intellect.

It is only required that the Christian intellect be fully surrendered to God and there need be no limit to its activities beyond those imposed upon it by its own strength and size.

How cold and deadly is the unblessed intellect. A superior brain without the saving essence of godliness may turn against the human race and drench the world with blood, or worse, it may loose ideas into the earth which will continue to curse mankind for centuries after it has turned to dust again.

But a Spirit-filled mind is a joy to God and a delight to all men of good will. POM104

> *God's method is first to fill the man with the facts of salvation and then send the baptism of fire upon him. . . . God's order is facts and fire.* SAN120

IN PRAISE OF VIRTUE

$\mathcal{W}$e naturally shy away from superlatives and from comparisons which praise one virtue at the expense of another, yet I wonder whether there is on earth anything as exquisitely lovely as a brilliant mind aglow with the love of God.

Such a mind sheds a mild and healing ray which can actually be *felt* by those who come near it. Virtue goes forth from it and blesses those who merely touch the hem of its garment. One has, for instance, but to read *The Celestial Country* by Bernard of Cluny to understand what I mean. There a sensitive and shining intellect warm with the fire of the inliving Spirit writes with a vast and tender sympathy of those longings for immortality. . . .

This same feeling of near-inspiration is experienced also in the letters of Samuel Rutherford, in the *Te Deum*, in many of the hymns of Watts and Wesley and occasionally in a work of some lesser-known saint whose limited gifts may have been for one joyous moment made incandescent by the fire of the indwelling Spirit. POM104-106

> *Those who love the divine character necessarily
> desire to promote the divine glory.* DTC069

DOCTRINE WITHOUT LOVE

My little children, let us not love in word, neither in tongue; but in deed and in truth.

—1 John 3:18

*T*he blight of the Pharisee's heart in olden times was doctrine without love. With the teachings of the Pharisees Christ had little quarrel, but with the pharisaic spirit He carried on unceasing warfare to the end.

It was religion that put Christ on the cross, religion without the indwelling Spirit. . . . An unblessed soul filled with the letter of truth may actually be worse off than a pagan kneeling before a fetish.

We are safe only when the love of God is shed abroad in our hearts by the Holy Ghost, only when our intellects are indwelt by the loving Fire that came at Pentecost. For the Holy Spirit is not a luxury, not something added now and again to produce a deluxe type of Christian once in a generation.

No, He is for every child of God a vital necessity, and that He fill and indwell His people is more than a languid hope. It is rather an inescapable imperative. POM106

They that walk in the King's holy way must have pure hearts, gentle tongues, loving ways, happy faces and restful lives. SAN048

THE SPIRIT IS A VOLITIONAL FLAME

Now the Lord is that Spirit: and where the Spirit of the Lord is, there is liberty.

—2 Corinthians 3:17

$\mathcal{T}$he Spirit is also a *volitional flame*. Here as elsewhere the imagery is inadequate to express all the truth, and unless care is taken we may easily gain a wrong impression from its use. For fire as we see and know it every day is a *thing*, not a person, and for that reason it has no will of its own.

But the Holy Spirit is a Person, having those attributes of personality of which volition is one. He does not, upon entering the human soul, void any of His attributes, nor does He surrender them in part or in full to the soul into which He enters. Remember, the Holy Spirit is Lord. . . .

Now it hardly need be said that the Sovereign Lord will never abandon the prerogatives of His Godhood. Wherever He is He must continue to act like Himself. When He enters the human heart He will be there what He has always been, Lord in His own right. POM106-107

> *The yielding up of the soul to the disposal of Christ, is an act of the mind which cannot be separated from living faith.* DTC108

DISEASE OF THE HEART

Love not the world, neither the things that are in the world. If any man love the world, the love of the Father is not in him.

—1 John 2:15

$\mathcal{T}$he deep disease of the human heart is a will broken loose from its center, like a planet which has left its central sun and started to revolve around some strange body from outer space which may have moved in close enough to draw it away. When Satan said, "I will," he broke loose from his normal center, and the disease with which he has infected the human race is the disease of disobedience and revolt. Any inadequate scheme of redemption must take into account this revolt and must undertake to restore again the human will to its proper place in the will of God. POM107-108

> *The spirit of the world is incompatible with the spirit of the gospel. It is the spirit of pride, and not humility—of self-indulgence rather than self-denial. Riches, honors and pleasure form the great object of pursuit with the men of the world. . . . This spirit the Christian has mortified.* DTC173-174

> *Not I but Christ be honored, loved, exalted;*
> *Not I but Christ be seen, be known, be heard;*
> *Not I but Christ in every look and action;*
> *Not I but Christ in every thought and word.*
> HCL264

A
GRACIOUS
INVASION

If thou canst believe, all things are possible to him that believeth. . . . Lord, I believe; help thou mine unbelief.

—Mark 9:23-24

$\mathcal{T}$he Holy Spirit, when He effects His gracious invasion of the believing heart, must win that heart to glad and voluntary obedience to the whole will of God. The cure must be wrought from within; no outward conformity will do.

Until the will is sanctified the man is still a rebel just as an outlaw is still an outlaw at heart even though he may be yielding grudging obedience to the sheriff who is taking him to prison. The Holy Spirit achieves this inward cure by merging the will of the redeemed man with His own. This is not accomplished at one stroke.

There must be, it is true, some kind of overall surrender of the will to Christ before any work of grace can be done, but the full mergence of every part of life with the life of God in the Spirit is likely to be a longer process than we in our creature impatience would wish. POM108

> *[N]o sin [is] so sweet that [the sanctified person] is not willing and resolved to forsake. He takes up the cross at the hazard of everything.*
> DTC142-143

WILLING THE WILL OF GOD

If any man will do his will, he shall know of the doctrine, whether it be of God.

—John 7:17

$\mathcal{T}$he most advanced soul may be shocked and chagrined to discover some private area within his life where he had been, unknown to himself, acting as lord and proprietor of that which he thought he had given to God. It is the work of the in-living Spirit to point out these moral discrepancies and correct them. He does not . . . "break" the human will, but He does invade it and bring it gently to a joyous union with the will of God.

To will the will of God is to do more than give unprotesting consent to it; it is rather to choose God's will with positive determination. As the work of God advances, the Christian finds himself free to choose whatever he will, and he gladly chooses the will of God as his highest conceivable good. Such a man has found life's highest goal. He has been placed beyond the little disappointments that plague the rest of men. Whatever happens to him is the will of God for him and that is just what he most ardently desires. POM108-109

> *Can you renounce everything which is inconsistent with the glory of God and the highest good of your fellowmen? Are these the natural breathings of your heart, "Thy kingdom come; thy will be done?"* DTC149-150

THE SPIRIT IS EMOTION

If we love one another, God dwelleth in us, and his love is perfected in us.

—1 John 4:12

*A*nother quality of the indwelling Fire is *emotion*. . . . What God is in His unique essence cannot be discovered by the mind nor uttered by the lips, but those qualities in God which may be termed rational, and so received by the intellect, have been freely set forth in the sacred Scriptures.

They do not tell us what God is, but they do tell us what God is like, and the sum of them constitute a mental picture of the Divine Being seen, as it were, afar off and through a glass darkly.

Now the Bible teaches that there is something in God which is like emotion. He experiences something which is like our love, something that is like our grief, that is like our joy. And we need not fear to go along with this conception of what God is like. . . . *God has said certain things about Himself, and these furnish all the grounds we require.* POM109-110

> *Once the seeking heart finds God in personal experience there will be no further problem about loving Him. To know Him is to love Him and to know Him better is to love Him more.* ROR143

EMOTION ON A HIGH PLAIN

The LORD thy God in the midst of thee is mighty; he will save, he will rejoice over thee with joy; he will rest in his love.

—Zephaniah 3:17

*T*his is but one verse among thousands which serve to form our rational picture of what God is like, and they tell us plainly that God feels something like our love, like our joy, and what He feels makes Him act very much as we would in a similar situation; He rejoices over His loved ones with joy and singing.

Here is emotion on as high a plane as it can ever be seen, emotion flowing out of the heart of God Himself. Feeling, then, is not the degenerate son of unbelief that is often painted by some of our Bible teachers. Our ability to feel is one of the marks of our divine origin. We need not be ashamed of either tears or laughter. The Christian stoic who has crushed his feelings is only two-thirds of a man; an important third part has been repudiated. POM110-111

> *The language of those who love God is that of rejoicing: "I will greatly rejoice in the Lord; my soul shall be joyful in my God."* DTC080

> *Spirit-filled souls are ablaze for God. They love with a love that glows. They believe with a faith that kinds. They serve with a devotion that consumes. . . . They rejoice with a joy that radiates.*
> PRL042

REJOICING WITH THE BRIDE

He brought me to the banquet-ing house, and his banner over me was love.

—Song of Solomon 2:4

*H*oly feeling had an important place in the life of our Lord. "For the joy that was set before him" (Hebrews 12:2) He endured the cross and despised its shame. He pictured Himself crying, "Rejoice with me; for I have found my sheep which was lost" (Luke 15:6).

On the night of His agony He "sang a hymn" before going out to the Mount of Olives. After His resurrection He sang among His brethren in the great congregation. (See Psalm 22:22.)

And if the Song of Solomon refers to Christ (as most Christians believe it does) then how are we to miss the sound of His rejoicing as He brings His Bride home after the night has ended and the shadows have fled away? POM111

> *Walk in the light! and you shall know*
> *That fellowship of love,*
> *His Spirit only can bestow*
> *Who reigns in light above.* HCL281

OPENING THE SACRED WELLS

Fear not, little flock; for it is your Father's good pleasure to give you the kingdom.

—Luke 12:32

*O*ne of the very greatest calamities which sin has brought upon us is the debasement of our normal emotions. We laugh at things which are not funny; we find pleasure in acts which are beneath our human dignity; and we rejoice in objects which should have no place in our affections.

The objection to "sinful pleasures," which has always been characteristic of the true saint, is at bottom simply a protest against the degradation of our human emotions. . . .

The world's artificial pleasures are all but evidence that the human race has to a large extent lost its power to enjoy the true pleasures of life and is forced to substitute for them false and degrading thrills.

The work of the Holy Spirit is, among other things, to rescue the redeemed man's emotions, to restring his harp and open again the wells of sacred joy which have been stopped by sin. POM112

> *Happiness is nothing but that inward sweet delight, which will arise from the harmonious agreement between our wills and the will of God.* JAS147

BORN OF THE SPIRIT

Examine yourselves, whether ye be in the faith; prove your own selves.

—2 Corinthians 13:5

A Christian is what he is not by ecclesiastical manipulation but by the new birth. He is a Christian because of a Spirit which dwells in him.

Only that which is born of the Spirit is spirit. The flesh can never be converted into spirit, no matter how many church dignitaries work on it.

Confirmation, baptism, holy communion, confession of faith—none of these nor all of them together can turn flesh into spirit nor make a son of Adam a son of God.

"Because ye are sons," wrote Paul to the Galatians, "God hath sent forth the Spirit of his Son into your hearts, crying, Abba, Father" (Galatians 4:6).... And to the Romans: "But ye are not in the flesh, but in the Spirit, if so be that the Spirit of God dwell in you. Now if any man have not the Spirit of Christ, he is none of his" (Romans 8:9). POM116-117

> *A sinner cannot grow into repentance. God's power puts him there, and being there, then he grows in grace.* SAN014

ON
REMOVING
THE DOUBTS

He that believeth on me, as the scripture hath said, out of his belly shall flow rivers of living water.

—John 7:38

$\mathcal{T}$hat every Christian can be and should be filled with the Holy Spirit would hardly seem to be a matter for debate among Christians. Yet some will argue that the Holy Spirit is not for plain Christians. . . .

I want here boldly to assert that it is my happy belief that every Christian can have a copious outpouring of the Holy Spirit in a measure far beyond that received at conversion, and I might also say, far beyond that enjoyed by the rank and file of orthodox believers today.

It is important that we get this straight, for until doubts are removed faith is impossible. God will not surprise a doubting heart with an effusion of the Holy Spirit, nor will He fill anyone who has doctrinal questions about the possibility of being filled. POM129-130

> *Doubt . . . opens the door to Satan and he rushes in to sow tears in the wheat. . . . But faith keeps the door of the heart; faith retains the grace and presence of God . . . and so the just not only shall, but do, live by faith.* SAN068

TOUGH QUESTIONS

*For ye were sometimes dark-
ness, but now are ye light in the
Lord: walk as children of light.*

—Ephesians 5:8

$\mathcal{B}$efore a [person] can be filled with the Spirit *he must be sure he wants to be*. . . . Let us imagine that we are talking to an inquirer, some eager young Christian, let us say, who has sought us out to learn about the Spirit-filled life.

As gently as possible, considering the pointed nature of the questions, we would probe his soul somewhat as follows: "Are you sure you want to be filled with a Spirit who, though He is like Jesus in His gentleness and love, will nevertheless demand to be Lord of your life? Are you willing to let your personality be taken over by another, even if that other be the Spirit of God Himself?"

If the Spirit takes charge of your life He will expect unquestioning obedience in everything. He will not tolerate in you the self-sins even though they are permitted and excused by most Christians. By the self-sins I mean self-love, self-pity, self-seeking, self-confidence, self-righteousness, self-aggrandizement, self-defense. POM131-132

> *Self-denial consists in the voluntary renunciation of every thing which is inconsistent with the glory of God and highest good of our fellow men.* DTC139

THE PRIMACY OF DESIRE

Desire the sincere milk of the word, that ye may grow thereby: if so be ye have tasted that the Lord is gracious.

—1 Peter 2:2-3

*B*efore we can be filled with the Spirit *the desire to be filled must be all-consuming.* It must be for the time the biggest thing in life, so acute, so intrusive as to crowd out everything else.

The degree of fullness in any life accords perfectly with the intensity of true desire. We have as much of God as we actually want. One great hindrance to the Spirit-filled life is the theology of complacency so widely accepted among gospel Christians today.

According to this view acute desire is an evidence of unbelief and proof of lack of knowledge of the Scriptures. A sufficient refutation of this position is afforded by the Word of God itself and by the fact that it always fails to produce real saintliness among those who hold it. POM133

> *I have met Christians who have been wanting to be filled, in a vague sort of way, for many years. The reason they have not been filled with the Spirit is because they have other things they want more.* QTB114

NOT REPEATED, BUT PERPETUATED

And they were all filled with the Holy Ghost, and began to speak with other tongues, as the Spirit gave them utterance.

—Acts 2:4

I do not believe in a repetition of Pentecost, but I do believe in a perpetuation of Pentecost—and there is a vast difference between the two. . . . Pentecost did not come and go, but . . . Pentecost came and stayed. . . .

What is the eternal and abiding element in Pentecost? Was something given, was there a deposit made? What came to pass that was internal, heavenly, permanent and lasting?

In order to discover what this element was, we must find out what was promised. According to John 14:16, Jesus said, "I will pray the Father, and he shall give you another Comforter." . . .

The wind, the fire and the appearance have never been repeated, as far as I know. But the Comforter came. He came and filled them. He came to abide in them. He came to make Jesus real. He came to give them inward moral ability to do right, and inward ability to do God's work. That stayed, and it is still here.

TTPI, Book 2/052, 057-058

> *The humblest Christian is called to live a miracle, a life that is a moral and spiritual life with such intensity and such purity that no human being can do it—only Jesus Christ can do it.* TTPI, Book 2/060

DESPAIR— A GOOD FRIEND

Our fathers trusted in thee: they trusted, and thou didst deliver them. They cried unto thee, and were delivered.

—Psalm 22:4-5

*T*he Christian who is seeking better things and who has to his consternation found himself in a state of complete self-despair need not be discouraged.

Despair with self, where it is accompanied by faith, is a good friend, for it destroys one of the heart's most potent enemies and prepares the soul for the ministration of the Comforter. . . .

He will never leave us nor forsake us, nor will He be wroth with us nor rebuke us.

He will not break His covenant nor alter that which has gone out of His mouth.

He will keep us as the apple of His eye and watch over us as a mother watches over her child.

His love will not fail even while He is taking us through this experience of self-crucifixion. POM134-135

> *This, indeed, is the true secret of sanctification and self-crucifixion: the expulsive power of the Holy Spirit's presence is the only true antidote to the power of self and Satan.* CTAB025

STEPS TO THE FILLING

If ye then be risen with Christ, seek those things which are above. . . . For ye are dead, and your life is hid with Christ in God.

—Colossians 3:1, 3

Now let us keep our theology straight about all this. There is not in this painful stripping one remote thought of human merit. The "dark night of the soul" knows not one dim ray of the treacherous light of self-righteousness. We do not by suffering earn the anointing for which we yearn, nor does this devastation of soul make us dear to God nor give us additional favor in His eyes.

The value of the stripping experience lies in its power to detach us from life's passing interests and to throw us back upon eternity. It serves to empty our earthly vessels and prepare us for the inpouring of the Holy Spirit.

The filling with the Spirit, then, requires that we give up our all, that we undergo an inward death, that we rid our hearts of that centuries-old accumulation of Adamic trash and open all rooms to the heavenly Guest. POM135

> *[T]he Holy Spirit is God's purifying messenger to us, bringing the water and the fire that will make us white as snow. Let us trust Him, let us obey Him, let us receive Him.* CTAB042

TOWARD THE GREATER

... Walk in the Spirit, and ye shall not fulfil the lust of the flesh. ... If we live in the Spirit, let us also walk in the Spirit.

—Galatians 5:16, 25

$\mathcal{T}$he Holy Spirit is a living Person and should be treated as a person. We must never think of Him as a blind energy nor as an impersonal force. He hears and sees and feels as any person does. He speaks and hears us speak.

We can please Him or grieve Him or silence Him as we can any other person. He will respond to our timid effort to know Him and will ever meet us over half the way.

However wonderful the crisis experience of being filled with the Spirit, we should remember that it is only a means toward something greater: that greater thing is the lifelong walk in the Spirit, indwelt, directed, taught and empowered by His mighty Person. And to continue thus to walk in the Spirit requires that we meet certain conditions.

These are laid down for us in the sacred Scriptures and are there for all to see. POM135-136

> *The highest point of Christian experience is to press forward. It is a distinguishing trait in the character of every good man, that he* grows in grace. DTC185

December

NOT WHO, BUT WHAT

And if Christ be in you, the body is dead because of sin; but the Spirit is life because of righteousness.

—Romans 8:10

*W*hat is the Holy Spirit? Not *who*, but *what*? The answer is that the Holy Spirit is a Being dwelling in another mode of existence. He has not weight, nor measure, nor size, nor any color, no extension in space, but He nevertheless exists as surely as you exist.

The Holy Spirit is not enthusiasm. I have found enthusiasm that hummed with excitement, and the Holy Spirit was nowhere to be found there at all; and I have found the Holy Ghost when there has not been much of what we call enthusiasm present.

Neither is the Holy Spirit another name for genius. We talk about the spirit of Beethoven and say, "This or that artist played with great spirit. He interpreted the spirit of the master." The Holy Spirit is none of these things. Now what is He?

He is a Person. Put that down in capital letters . . . He is Himself a Person, with all the qualities and powers of personality. HTB011-012

[T]he Spirit is Himself God, the very true Nature of the Godhead subsisting in a form that can impart Himself to our consciousness. TET096

THE HOLY SPIRIT IS A PERSON

When he, the Spirit of truth, is come, he will guide you into all truth: for he shall not speak of himself.

—John 16:13

*T*he Holy Spirit is often thought of as a beneficent wind that blows across the Church. If you think of the Holy Spirit as being literally a wind, a breath, then you think of Him as nonpersonal and nonindividual. But the Holy Spirit has will and intelligence and feeling and knowledge and sympathy and ability to love and see and think and hear and speak and desire the same as any person has. . . .

Many of us have grown up on the theology that accepts the Holy Spirit as a Person, and even as a divine Person, but for some reason it never did us any good. We are as empty as ever, we are as joyless as ever, we are as far from peace as ever, we are as weak as ever.

What I want to do is to tell you the old things, but while I am doing it, to encourage your heart to make them yours now, and to walk into the living, throbbing, vibrating heart of them, so that from here on your life will be altogether different. HTB012-013

If we should know the full comfort of the Holy Spirit we must cooperate with Him. WCC082

SIMPLY, PLAINLY, INTIMATELY

As the Father hath loved me, so have I loved you: continue ye in my love.

—John 15:9

$\mathcal{G}$od takes great pleasure in having a helpless soul come to Him simply and plainly and intimately. He takes pleasure in having us come to Him. This kind of Christianity doesn't draw big crowds. It draws only those who have their hearts set on God, who want God more than they want anything else in the world. These people want the spiritual experience that comes from knowing for Himself. They could have everything stripped away from them and still have God.

These people are not vastly numerous in any given locality. This kind of Christianity doesn't draw big crowds, but it is likely to draw the hungriest ones, and thirstiest ones and some of the best ones.

And so God takes great pleasure in having helpless people come to Him, simply and plainly and intimately. He wants us to come without all that great overloading of theology. He wants us to come as simply and as plainly as a little child. And if the Holy Spirit touches you, you'll come like that. AOG030-031

To be able to look into God's face, and know with the knowledge of faith that there is nothing between the soul and Him, is to experience the fullest peace the soul can know. JAS062

THE TRINITY IS PRESENT

But when the Comforter is come, whom I will send ... even the Spirit of truth ... he shall testify of me.

—John 15:26

$\mathcal{W}$ho is the Spirit? The Spirit is God, existing in another mode of being than ourselves. He exists as a spirit and not as matter, for He is not matter, but He is God.

He is a Person. It was so believed by the whole Church of Christ down through the years. It was so sung by the hymnists back in the days of the first hymn writers. It is so taught in the Book, all through the Old Testament and the New. . . .

Now what follows from all this? Ah, there is an unseen Deity present, a knowing, feeling Personality, and He is indivisible from the Father and the Son, so that if you were to be suddenly transferred to heaven itself you wouldn't be any closer to God than you are now, for God is already here.

Changing your geographical location would not bring you any nearer to God nor God any nearer to you, because the indivisible Trinity is present. HTB019-020

People grow on us, and the Holy Spirit, being a Person, can grow on us. HTB039

> *It is certainly not speculative that God is able to manifest Himself most in the lives of those who passionately love Him.* ROL091

No Fear!

If we live in the Spirit, let us also walk in the Spirit.

—Galatians 5:25

*W*hat will we find [the Holy Spirit] to be like? He will be exactly like Jesus. You have read your New Testament, and you know what Jesus is like, and the Holy Spirit is exactly like Jesus, for Jesus was God and the Spirit is God, and the Father is exactly like the Son; and you can know what Jesus is like by knowing what the Father is like, and you can know what the Spirit is like by knowing what Jesus is like.

If Jesus were to come walking down this aisle there would be no stampede for the door. Nobody would scream and be frightened. We might begin to weep for sheer joy and delight that He had so honored us, but nobody would be afraid of Jesus; no mother with a little crying babe would ever have to be afraid of Jesus; no poor harlot being dragged by the hair of her head had to be afraid of Jesus—nobody!

Nobody ever need to be afraid of Jesus, because He is the epitome of love, kindliness, geniality, warm attractive ness and sweetness. And that is exactly what the Holy Ghost is, for He is the Spirit of the Father and the Son. *Amen.* HTB020-021

> In the indwelling of the Holy Spirit, we have God's fullness. *He has given us the very same Spirit that dwelt in Him.* WS106

THE PROMISE OF THE FATHER

Behold, I send the promise of my Father upon you: but tarry ye in the city of Jerusalem, until ye be endued with power from on high.

—Luke 24:49

"The promise of my Father." This takes us back to Joel 2:28-29:

> And it shall come to pass afterward, that I will pour out my spirit upon all flesh; and your sons and your daughters shall prophesy, your old men shall dream dreams, your young men shall see visions: and also upon the servants and upon the handmaids in those days will I pour out my spirit.

. . . In fulfillment of all this there were three periods discernible in the New Testament: (1) The period of the promise; (2) the period of the preparation; and (3) the period of the realization—all this having to do with the promise of the Father and the intention of the Son toward His people. Now I am going to ask that you reverently ponder this and set aside time and search the Scriptures, pray and yield, obey and believe, and see whether . . . [this] possession of the Church may not be ours in actual fulfillment and realization. HTB023-024, 036

> *The Holy Spirit . . . brings to us the presence of Jesus and enables us to realize our oneness with Him.* WS107

THE PROMISE AND THE PREPARATION

For the promise is unto you, and to your children, and to all that are afar off.

—Acts 2:39

*T*he period of the promise [of the Holy Spirit] extends from John the Baptist, roughly, to the resurrection of our Lord Jesus.

The marks of it are these: that there were disciples, and they were commissioned and instructed, and they exercised their commission and the authority granted them by the Lord. They knew the Lord Jesus; they loved Him. They knew Him living, they knew Him and saw Him dead, and they saw Him risen again from the dead. All the time our Lord was with them *He was busy creating expectation in them*. He was telling His disciples that in spite of all they had and all the blessing that God the Father had given them, they were still to expect the coming of a new and superior kind of life . . . an effusion of outpoured energy which they, at their best, did not yet enjoy.

Then our Lord rose from the dead and we have what we call the period of the preparation. . . . They had stopped their activity at the specific command of the Lord. He said, "Tarry! You are about to receive that which has been promised. . . ." Sometimes you are going farther when you are not going anywhere; you are moving faster when you are not moving at all. HTB024-025

Oh, my heart, be still before Him. QTB112

THE
INNER
EVIDENCE

And ye shall know that I am in the midst . . . and that I am the LORD your God, and none else: and my people shall never be ashamed.

—Joel 2:27

The period of realization came upon [the waiting ones] when the Father fulfilled His promise and sent the Spirit. . . . God took religion from the realm of the external and made it internal. Our trouble is that we are trying to confirm the truth of Christianity by an appeal to external evidence.

We are saying, "Well, look at this fellow. He can throw a baseball farther than anybody else and he is a Christian, therefore Christianity must be true." "Here is a great statesman who believes the Bible. Therefore, the Bible must be true." . . .

We are all the way out on the wrong track, brother! That is not New Testament Christianity at all. That is a pitiful, whimpering, drooling appeal to the flesh. That never was the testimony of the New Testament, never the way God did things—never! . . . . The proof lies in an invisible, unseen but powerful energy that visits the human soul when the gospel is preached—the Holy Ghost! HTB026, 029-030

> *[T]he final flash that introduces your heart to Jesus must be by the illumination of the Holy Spirit Himself, or it isn't done at all.* COU028

THEN THE SPIRIT CAME

And it shall come to pass after-ward, that I will pour out my spirit...before the great and ter-rible day of the LORD come.

—Joel 2:28, 31

There is a great modern error which I want to mention: it is that the coming of the Spirit happened once for all, that the individual Christian is not affected by it. . . . This error asserts that the coming of the Holy Spirit is an historic thing, an advance in the dispensational workings of God; but that it is all settled now and we need give no further thought to it. It is all here and we have it all, and if we believe in Christ that is it, and there isn't anything more. . . .

Listen, brother. Our Lord Jesus Christ advertised that He was going away to the Father and He was going to send back for His people a wonderful gift. . . .

Then the Spirit came. Was He equal to the advertising? Did they say, "Is *this* all He meant! Oh, it is disappointing!" No. The Scripture says they wondered. The word "wonder" is in their mouths and hearts. He gave so much more than He promised, because words were the promise and the Holy Ghost was the fulfillment. HTB032, 035-036

The Holy Spirit is always within reach, if we are in condition to receive and absorb Him. HS504

BEFORE YOU ARE FILLED

If a man love me . . . my Father will love him, and we will come unto him, and make our abode with him.

—John 14:23

*B*efore we deal with the question of how to be filled with the Holy Spirit, there are some matters which first have to be settled. As believers you have to get them out of the way, and right here is where the difficulty arises. I have been afraid that my [readers] might have gotten the idea somewhere that I had a how-to-be-filled-with-the-Spirit-in-five-easy-lessons doctrine, which I could give you. If you have any such vague ideas as that I can only . . . say, "I am sorry"; because it isn't true; I can't give you such a course.

There are some things, I say, that you have to get out of the way, settled. One of them is: Before you are filled with the Holy Spirit you must *be sure that you* can *be filled.* . . .

So you have to be sure that it is for you. You must be sure that it is God's will for you; that is, that it is part of the total plan, that it [the gift—the Holy Spirit] is included and embraced within the work of Christ in redemption. HTB037-038

> *The Savior in His Sermon on the Mount said: "Blessed are the pure in heart" (Matthew 5:8). Can anyone believe that Christ would bless a class of people who do not or cannot exist?* SAN005

PART OF THE TOTAL PLAN

*They that are after the Spirit
[mind] the things of the Spirit.*

—Romans 8:5

$\mathcal{T}$he Spirit-filled life is not a special, deluxe edition of Christianity. It is part and parcel of the total plan of God for His people.

You must be satisfied that it is not abnormal. I admit that it is unusual, because there are so few people who walk in the light of it or enjoy it, but it is not abnormal. . . . This is unusual only because our spiritual lives are so wretchedly sick and so far down from where they should be.

You must be satisfied, again, that there is nothing about the Holy Spirit queer or strange or eerie.

I believe it has been the work of the devil to surround the person of the Holy Spirit with an aura of queerness, or strangeness, so that the people of God feel that this Spirit-filled life is a life of being odd and peculiar, of being a bit uncanny. That is not true, my friend! The devil manufactured that. HTB039

> *The Holy Spirit is pure, for He is the Holy Spirit.*
> *He is wise, for He is the Spirit of wisdom.*
> *He is true, for He is the Spirit of truth.* COU075

No Persuasion Necessary

They . . . sought him with their whole desire; and he was found of them: and the LORD gave them rest round about.

—2 Chronicles 15:15

There is nothing eerie, nothing queer, nothing contrary to the normal operations of the human heart about the Holy Ghost. He is only the essence of Jesus imparted to believers. You read the four Gospels and see for yourself how wonderfully calm, pure, sane, simple, sweet, natural and lovable Jesus was. Even philosophers who don't believe in His deity have to admit the lovableness of His character.

You must be sure of all this to the point of conviction. That is, you must be convinced to a point where you won't try to persuade God.

You don't have to persuade God at all. There is no persuasion necessary. Dr. Simpson used to say, "Being filled with the Spirit is as easy as breathing; you can simply breathe out and breathe in." HTB039-040

Jesus, breathe Thy spirit on me,
Teach me how to breathe Thee in,
Help me pour into Thy bosom
All my life of self and sin. HCL251

THE LORD OF YOUR LIFE?

No man can serve two masters: for either he will hate the one, and love the other; or else he will hold to the one, and despise the other.

—Matthew 6:24

$\mathcal{B}$efore you can be filled with the Spirit you must desire to be filled. . . . [A]re you sure that you want to be possessed by a spirit other than your own? even though that spirit be the pure Spirit of God? even though He be the very gentle essence of the gentle Jesus? even though He be sane and pure and free? even though He be wisdom personified, wisdom Himself, even though He have a healing, precious ointment to distill? even though He be loving as the heart of God?

That Spirit, if He ever possesses you, will be the Lord of your Life!

I ask you, Do you want Him to be Lord of your life? That you want His benefits, I know. I take that for granted. But do you want to be possessed by Him? Do you want to hand the keys of your soul over to the Holy Spirit? . . . Are you willing to give the office of your business establishment, your soul, over to the Lord? . . . Are you sure you want this? HTB042-043

> *One thing is plain: Christians cannot be worldlings. They cannot be lovers of pleasure more than lovers of God.* DTC179

ARE YOU SURE?

For he that is dead is freed from sin. Now if we be dead with Christ, we believe that we shall also live with him.

—Romans 6:7-8

re you sure that you want your personality to be taken over by One who will expect obedience to the written and living Word? Are you sure that you want your personality to be taken over by One who will not tolerate the self sins?

For instance, self-love. You can no more have the Holy Ghost and have self-love than you can have purity and impurity at the same moment in the same place. . . .

Self-love, self-confidence, self-righteousness, self-admiration, self-aggrandizement, and self-pity are under the interdiction of God Almighty, and He cannot send His mighty Spirit to possess the heart where these things are. . . .

[Do] you desire to have your personality taken over by One who stands in sharp opposition to the world's easy ways? . . . The Spirit of God, if He takes over, will bring you into opposition to the world. . . . Are you sure, brother? HTB044-045

As the spirit of self-advancement is the root of all sin, so the spirit of self-denial is the root of all holiness. DTC139

A PRELIMINARY TO DAYBREAK

*The Spirit and the bride say,
Come. . . . Whosoever will, let him
take the water of life freely.*
—Revelation 22:17

Maybe you feel in your heart that you just can't go on as you are, that the level of spirituality to which you know yourself called is way beyond you. If you feel that there is something that you must have or your heart will never be satisfied, that there are levels of spirituality, mystic deeps and heights of spiritual communion, purity and power that you have never known, that there is fruit which you know you should bear and do not, victory which you know you should have and have not—I would say, "Come on," because God has something for you. . . .

There is a spiritual loneliness, an inner aloneness, an inner place where God brings the seeker, where he is as lonely as if there were not another member of the Church anywhere in the world.

Ah, when you come there, there is a darkness of mind, an emptiness of heart, a loneliness of soul, but it is preliminary to the daybreak. *O God, bring us, somehow, to the daybreak!* HTB046

> *[W]hen the renewal of the Spirit of God comes to
> your life . . . there may be only one term to de-
> scribe it—exploding love.* ROL089

HOW TO RECEIVE THE HOLY SPIRIT

How much more shall your heavenly Father give the Holy Spirit to them that ask him?

—Luke 11:13

*H*ere is how to receive [the Holy Spirit]. First, present your body to Him (Romans 12:1-2). God can't fill what He can't have.... Are you ready to present ... your mind, your personality, your spirit, your love, your ambitions, your all? That is the first thing. ...

Now the second thing is to *ask* (Luke 11:9-11).... He could give [the Holy Spirit] without our asking, but He chooses to have us ask. "Ask of me, and I will give thee" is always God's order; so why not ask?

Acts 5:32 tells us the third thing to do. God gives His Holy Spirit to them that obey Him. Are you ready to ... do what you are asked to do ... to live by the Scriptures as you understand them? Simple, but revolutionary.

The next thing is, have faith (Galatians 3:2). We receive Him by faith as we receive the Lord in salvation by faith. He comes as a gift of God to us in power. HTB047-048

The power to sin is one thing, the proneness to do so is another. Sanctification takes out the latter, but leaves the former, which is an attribute or necessity in a free moral agent. SAN041

HOW TO CULTIVATE THE SPIRIT'S COMPANIONSHIP

Can two walk together, except they be agreed?

—Amos 3:3

Now this is what is known as a rhetorical question; it is equivalent to a positive declaration that two cannot walk together except they be agreed, and for two to walk together they must be in some sense one.

They also have to agree that they *want* to walk together, and they have to agree that it is to their advantage to travel together. I think you will see that it all adds up to this: *For two to walk together voluntarily they must be, in some sense, one.*

I am talking now about how we can cultivate the Spirit's fellowship, how we can walk with Him day by day and hour by hour. . . . I am going to give you [a] few little pointers to help you into a better life.

Point one is that the Holy Spirit is a living Person. He is the third Person of the Trinity. He is Himself God, and as a Person, He can be cultivated; He can be wooed and cultivated the same as any person can be. HTB049, 053

> *No true Christian can be habitually more engaged in the service of the world and of sin, than in the service of God. His obedience, though not perfect, is habitual.* DTC204

JESUS MUST BE GLORIFIED

That ye manyy with one mind and one mouth glorify God, even the Father of our Lord Jesus Christ.

—Romans 15:6

𝒯he second point is: Be engrossed with Jesus Christ. Honor Him. John said: "But this spake he of the Spirit, which they that believe on him should receive: for the Holy Ghost was not yet given; because that Jesus was not yet glorified" (John 7:39).

I ask you to note that the Spirit was given when Jesus was glorified. Now that is a principle. Remember . . . He came and spread Himself out as a flood upon the people because Jesus was glorified. He established a principle, and He will never, never flood the life of any man except the man in whom Jesus is glorified.

Therefore, if you dedicate yourself to the glory of Jesus, the Holy Ghost will become the aggressor and will seek to know you and raise you and illumine you and fill you and bless you. . . .

To glorify Jesus is the business of the Church, and to glorify Jesus is the work of the Holy Ghost. HTB053-054

> *It is no task to the Christian to obey the commandments of God. . . . The glory of God is the great end of his being.* DTC200

HOLY SPIRIT—
HOLY WAY

All the paths of the LORD are mercy and truth unto such as keep his covenant and his testimonies.

—Psalm 25:10

*T*he third point is: Let's walk in righteousness. The grace of God that bringeth salvation also teaches the heart that we should deny ungodliness and worldly lusts and live soberly and righteously and godly in this present world.

There you have the three dimensions of life. Soberly—that is me. Righteously—that is my fellowman. Godly—that is God.

Let us not make the mistake of thinking we can be spiritual and not be good. Let's not make the mistake of thinking we can walk with the Holy Ghost and go a wrong or a dirty or an unrighteous way, for how can two walk together except they be agreed?

He is the *Holy* Spirit, and if I walk an unholy way, how can I fellowship with Him? HTB054-055

> *No matter how men deny and resist, the Bible teaches that the purification of the heart is the work of God. . . . John states that it is while "we walk in the light," "[having] fellowship one with another," that then "the blood of Jesus Christ . . . cleanseth us from all sin" (1 John 1:7).* SAN020

DECORATIONS IN THE SANCTUARY

Search me, O God, and know my heart: try me, and know my thoughts: and see if there be any wicked way in me.

—Psalm 139:23-24

$\mathcal{T}$he fourth is: Make your thoughts a clean sanctuary. To God, our thoughts are things. Our thoughts are the decorations inside the sanctuary where we live. If our thoughts are purified by the blood of Christ, we are living in a clean room no matter if we are wearing overalls covered with grease.

Your thoughts pretty much decide the mood and weather and climate inside your heart, and God considers your thoughts as part of you.

Thoughts of peace, thoughts of pity, thoughts of mercy, thoughts of kindness, thoughts of charity, thoughts of God, thoughts of the Son of God—these are pure things, good things, and high things.

Therefore, if you would cultivate the Spirit's acquaintance, you must get hold of your thoughts and not allow your mind to be a wilderness in which every kind of unclean beast roams and bird flies. You must have a clean heart. HTB055-056

> *The evil thought is the forerunner of the devil; for Satan knows that if a Christian will allow the evil thought he will in time allow the originator of the temptation to come in.* SAN240

THE HOLY SPIRIT IS IN THE WORD

How sweet are thy words unto my taste! ... Through thy precepts I get understanding: therefore I hate every false way.

—Psalm 119:103-104

*P*oint five: Let us seek to know Him in the Word. It is in the Word we will find the Holy Spirit . . . for the Holy Ghost wrote this Book. He inspired it, and He will be revealed in its pages.

What is the word when we come to the Bible? It is *meditate*. We are to come to the Bible and meditate. . . . Let's open our Bible, spread it out on the chair, and meditate on it. It will open itself to us, and the Spirit of God will come and brood over it.

So be a Bible meditator. I challenge you: Try it for a month and see how it works. Put away questions and answers and the filling in of blank lines. . . . Take a Bible, open it, get on your knees and say, "Father, here I am. Begin to teach me."

He will begin to teach you, and He will teach you about Himself and about Jesus and about God and about the Word and about life and death and heaven and hell, and about His own Presence. HTB056-057

> *After getting the heart filled with the Holy Ghost, it is well to get the head filled with the very facts and truth that should be there. The Bible speaks of grace and knowledge. They go well together.*
> SAN168

CULTIVATE HIS PRESENCE

> *Be strong and of a good cour-
> age; be not afraid, neither be
> thou dismayed: for the LORD
> thy God is with thee.*
>
> —Joshua 1:9

*P*oint six: Cultivate the art of recognizing the presence of the Spirit everywhere. Get acquainted with the Holy Ghost and then begin to cultivate His presence. When you wake in the morning, in place of burying your head behind the *Tribune*, couldn't you get in just a few thoughts of God while you eat your grapefruit?

Remember, cultivating the Holy Ghost's acquaintance is a job. It is something you do, and yet it is so easy and delightful. . . . Is this for ministers? This is for ministers, certainly. Is it for house-wives? Yes, housewives, and clerks . . . and students. If you will thus see it and thus believe it and thus surrender to it, there won't be a secular stone in the pavement. There won't be a common, profane deed that you will ever do.

The most menial task can become a priestly ministration when the Holy Ghost takes over and Christ becomes your all in all. HTB057-058

> *The sanctified life [is] God-centered. . . . Ennui is
> impossible with a soul full of the Holy Ghost. . . .
> God is seen and felt in everything.* SAN089

WHERE LIFE
AND LIPS
JOIN

Not unto [me], O LORD, not unto [me], but unto thy name give glory . . . our God is in the heavens.

—Psalm 115:1, 3

"*Be* thou exalted" (Psalm 21:13) is the language of victorious spiritual experience. It is a little key to unlock the door to great treasures of grace. It is central in the life of God in the soul. Let the seeking man reach a place where life and lips join to say continually "Be thou exalted," and a thousand minor problems will be solved at once.

His Christian life ceases to be the complicated thing it had been before and becomes the very essence of simplicity. By the exercise of his will he has set his course, and on that course he will stay as if guided by an automatic pilot. If blown off course for a moment by some adverse wind, he will surely return again as by a secret bent of the soul.

The hidden motions of the Spirit are working in his favor, and "the stars in their courses" (Judges 5:20) fight for him. He has met his life problem at its center, and everything else must follow along. POG095

> *The spirit of self-denial. It is the result of a calm, deliberate, invincible attachment to the highest good . . . a voluntary renunciation that is consistent with the glory of God and good of our fellowmen.* DTC114

ETERNITY MADE FLESH

*W*hat is it you have always really wanted? It is not religion. You can trace that back—it is recent. It is not philosophy. It is not civilization. . . . They are recent and temporary.

We have been betrayed by every prospect that man creates. But when we know that we are perishing, ready to perish, God's Holy Spirit is faithful, and He whispers, "In the beginning was the Word, and the Word was with God, and the Word was God" (John 1:1).

There is eternity, and eternity was made flesh and walked among us. . . . If you had seen eternity walking around on baby, rubbery legs, tumbling and falling flat among the shavings, you would have run and picked Him up and dusted Him off, whispering, "It doesn't hurt. Be a big boy!"

He would have smiled, shaking away a tear, and toddled off for another tumble. That was eternity walking in flesh. It was God Almighty come to live among us to redeem us and to save us from the recent and the temporal and the transient—and to give us eternity! CES063-064

> *Oh, come to my heart, Lord Jesus:*
> *There is room in my heart for Thee!.* HCL073

GOD IN THE FLESH

And they came with haste, and found Mary, and Joseph, and the babe lying in a manger.

—Luke 2:16

$\mathcal{T}$he mystery and miracle of the Incarnation—God coming to take our humanity and our flesh, yet without sin. Luke quotes the message of the angel Gabriel to Mary:

> Thou hast found favour with God. And, behold, thou shalt conceive in thy womb, and bring forth a son, and shalt call his name JESUS. He shall be great, and shall be called the Son of the Highest. . . . The Holy Ghost shall . . . overshadow thee: therefore also that holy thing which shall be born of thee shall be called the Son of God. (Luke 1:30-32, 35)

The overshadowing of the Most High, the Father; the energy of the Holy Spirit; the enfleshment of the eternal Son—here were the Persons of the Godhead cooperating in a gracious act on behalf of lost men and women. JAF129-130

> *Lord Jesus, reign in us, we pray,*
> *And make us Thine alone,*
> *Who with the Father ever art,*
> *And Holy Spirit, one.* HCL066

> *[The Holy Spirit] is indivisible from the Father and the Son, and He is all God and exercises all the rights of God and He merits all worship and all love and all obedience.* TTPI, Book2/046

CULTIVATING SIMPLICITY AND SOLITUDE

Thou desirest truth in the inward parts: and in the hidden part thou shalt make me to know wisdom.... Wash me, and I shall be whiter than snow.

—Psalm 51:6-7

"The thoughtful soul to solitude retires," said the poet of other and quieter times; but where is the solitude to which we can retire today? . . .

Our "vastly improved methods of communication," of which the shortsighted boast so loudly, now enable a few men in strategic centers to feed into millions of minds alien thought stuff, ready-made and predigested. A little effortless assimilation of these borrowed ideas and the average man has done all the thinking he will or can do.

This subtle brainwashing goes on day after day and year after year to the eternal injury of the populace. . . . There was a time, not too long ago, when a man's home was his castle, a sure retreat to which he might return for quietness and solitude. . . . I cannot refrain from remarking that the most ominous sign of the coming destruction of our country is the passing of the American home. Americans live no longer in homes, but in theaters. . . . Let no one smile. Rather should we weep at the portent. OGM125-127

The mansions of the heart will become larger when their doors are thrown open to Christ and closed against the world and sin. Try it. SIZ025

A PRIVATE PLACE

And my people shall dwell in a peaceable habitation, and in sure dwellings, and in quiet resting places.

—Isaiah 32:18

$\mathcal{F}$or those who want to relearn the ways of solitude and simplicity and gain the infinite riches of the interior life . . . I offer a brief paragraph of counsel.

Retire form the world each day to some private spot. . . . Stay in the secret place till the surrounding noises begin to fade out of your heart and a sense of God's presence envelops you. Deliberately tune out the unpleasant sounds and come out of your closet determined not to hear them. Listen for the inward Voice till you learn to recognize it. Stop trying to compete with others. Give yourself to God, and then be what and who you are without regard to what others think. Reduce your interests to a few. . . .

Learn to pray inwardly every moment. After a while you can do this even while you work. Practice candor, childlike honesty, humility. Pray for a single eye. Read less, but read more of what is important to your inner life. . . . Call home your roving thoughts. Gaze on Christ with the eyes of your soul. Practice spiritual concentration. OGM128-129

> *God is bound to give himself to a heart that is detached. . . . God would sooner be in a solitary heart than any other.* BME089, 096

YESTERDAY, TODAY AND FOREVER

Because ye are sons, God hath sent forth the Spirit of his Son into your hearts, crying, Abba, Father.

—Galatians 4:6

The Scriptures are open and plain. Jesus Christ is our Savior and Lord. He is our great High Priest, alive and ministering for us today. His person, His power and His grace are the same, without change, yesterday, today and forever!

He is the same Lord because He is the same God. He is the same, never having changed in substance, in power, in wisdom, in love, in mercy. In His divine person, Jesus Christ has never known correction or change. He feels now as He has always felt about everyone and everything.

Jesus will not yield to those who charge that He is an absentee, that He is far away and unavailable. Our faith tells us that Jesus Christ is close at hand, that He is a living force in our lives today. He is the Holy Spirit of God fulfilling His promises moment by moment.

We . . . must stand together in our faith. Our Lord is as powerful now, as real now, as near to us now, as loving now as He ever was when He walked among the men and women on the shores of Galilee. JAF142-143

> *God always fills in all hearts all the room which is left Him there.* JAS112

GOD'S
TRUTH IS
ETERNAL

Stand ye in the ways, and see,
and ask for the old paths, where is
the good way, and walk therein.

—Jeremiah 6:16

$\mathcal{T}$here are two errors that are pretty current with regard to old things. The first is that everything old is good, and everything new is bad.

That idea, of course, . . . harms progress and discourages all thought. It also petrifies the imagination and digs a grave for all expectation. I am afraid that . . . when it comes to theology and spiritual thought, we have adopted the notion that the old is good and that everything new is bad. . . . We have to go back . . . yonder to discover a man who has spiritual imagination enough even to state things differently from that which is current in his time.

I will tell you what I would like to see for this critical age . . . a number of persons committed to the everlastingness of the truth as it is given from heaven, manifested in the inspiration of Scripture and the faith of our fathers . . . so that it is impossible to go back theologically. . . . The result would be truth related in an imaginative way for our time. TSS162-163

> *[T]he truths of God are not timely (that is,*
> *geared into time). The truths of God are eternal.*
> *They rise above time.* TSS164-165

GOD IS ENOUGH

*T*he error that everything new is good and everything old is bad takes place in the realm of practice and worship and religious activity generally. This is a view . . . [that] can lead, of course, to great rebellion against the truth. . . .

We will never be where we ought to be until we go back to those old paths and learn to find God. [Then] we will cease to be bored with God. . . . [W]e will center our affections upon God and Christ . . . and become specialists and experts in the realm of the spiritual life.

It is amazing how little outside stimulus we need if we have that inward stimulus. It is amazing how much God will meet our needs. It will not be God *and* something else. It will be God *everything*.

And then, wisely, we will gear into our times . . . and in a moment we will become . . . alert to the needs of the world around us. . . . [A]t the same time, our great anchor will be God above. . . . God [will] be enough. TSS164-166

May God give us the courage to be obedient to His truths in this tragic, critical and dangerous hour in which we live. TSS166

IF WORSE COMES TO WORST

The mercy of the LORD is from everlasting to everlasting upon them that fear him, and his righteousness unto children's children.

—Psalm 103:17

*I*f the world's foundations crumble we still have God, and in Him we have everything essential to our ransomed beings forever.

We [also] have Christ, who . . . died for us and who now sits at the right hand of the Majesty in the heavens making constant and effective intercession for us.

We have the Scriptures, which can never fail.

We have the Holy Spirit to interpret the Scriptures to our inner lives and to be to us a Guide and a Comforter.

We have prayer and we have faith, and these bring heaven to earth and turn even bitter Marah sweet.

And if worse comes to worst here below, we have our Father's house and our Father's welcome. TWP025

> *"The man of the year" cannot impress those men and women who are making their plans for that long eternity when days and years have passed away and time is no more.* NCA009

Reference Codes & Credits

REFERENCE CODES FOR BOOKS
AND BOOKLETS BY A.W. TOZER

AOG ....*The Attributes of God*
BAM ....*Born after Midnight*
CES...*Christ the Eternal Son*
COU ....*The Counselor*
EFE...*Echoes from Eden*
FBR ....*Faith Beyond Reason*
GTM ....*God Tells the Man Who Cares*
HTB ....*How to Be Filled with the Holy Spirit*
ICH ....*I Call It Heresy*
ITB ....*I Talk Back to the Devil*
JAF...*Jesus, Author of Our Faith*
JIV ....*Jesus Is Victor*
JMI ....*Jesus, Our Man in Glory*
KDL ....*Keys to the Deeper Life*
MDP...*Man: The Dwelling Place of God*
MMG..*Men Who Met God*
NCA ....*The Next Chapter after the Last*
OCN...*The Old Cross and the New*
OGM ....*Of God and Men*
POG..*The Pursuit of God*
POM ....*The Pursuit of Man*
PON ....*The Price of Neglect*
PTP..*Paths to Power*
QTB...*The Quotable Tozer, Volume 2*
RDA ....*Renewed Day by Day, Volume 1*
RDB ....*Renewed Day by Day, Volume 2*
ROR ....*The Root of the Righteous*

RRR ....*Rut, Rot or Revival*

SAT ....*Success and the Christian*

SIZ ....*The Size of the Soul*

SOS ....*The Set of the Sail*

TAM..*Those Amazing Methodists*

TCC ....*Total Commitment to Christ*

TET ....*The Early Tozer: A Word in Season*

TIC..*That Incredible Christian*

TTPI ....*The Tozer Pulpit, Volume 1*

TTPII..*The Tozer Pulpit, Volume 2*

TRA ....*Tragedy in the Church*

TSS..*Tozer Speaks to Students*

TWE ....*Tozer on Worship and Entertainment*

TWP ....*This World: Playground or Battleground?*

WHT ....*Whatever Happened to Worship?*

WMJ ....*Worship: the Missing Jewel*

WOS ....*The Warfare of the Spirit*

WPJ..*Who Put Jesus on the Cross?*

WTA ....*We Travel an Appointed Way*

REFERENCE CODES FOR
BOOKS BY A.B. SIMPSON

CC ....*The Cross of Christ*

CFD ....*The Christ of the Forty Days*

CTAB ....*Christ in the Tabernacle*

CTBC..............*The Christ in the Bible Commentary, Volumes 1 - 6*

DHE ....*Days of Heaven on Earth*

HS..*The Holy Spirit*

ISS ....*In Step with the Spirit*
LCL ....*A Larger Christian Life*
MM ....*Missionary Messages*
NJ ....*The Names of Jesus*
PC ....*Practical Christianity*
PSP ....*Portraits of the Spirit-filled Personality*
SI ....*Seeing the Invisible*
SK ....*Serving the King*
TFG ....*The Fourfold Gospel*
WCC ....*When the Comforter Came*
WL ....*Walking in Love*
WS ....*Wholly Sanctified*

REFERENCE CODES FOR
BOOKS BY OTHER AUTHORS

BME ....*The Best of Meister Eckhart*
CDL ....*The Crisis of the Deeper Life*
DTC ....*Distinguishing Traits of Christian Character*
HCL ....*Hymns of the Christian Life*
JAS ....*Joy and Strength*
JJJ ....*John*
PRL ....*Powerlines*
ROL ....*The Revolution of Love*
SAN ....*The Sanctified Life*

Backhouse, Halcyon, editor. *The Best of Meister Eckhart*. New York, NY: Crossroad Publishing, 1992. Used by permission.

Carrandine, B. *The Sanctified Life*. Cincinnati, OH: Office of the Revivalist, 1897.

Choy, Leona Frances. *Powerlines*. Camp Hill, PA: Christian Publications, Inc., 1990.

Foster, K. Neill. *The Revolution of Love*. Camp Hill: Christian Publications Inc./Horizon Books, 1973, 1997.

Hymns of the Christian Life. Camp Hill, PA: Christian Publications Inc., 1992.

Pardington, George P. *The Crisis of the Deeper Life*. Camp Hill, PA: Christian Publications, Inc., 1991.

Spring, Gardiner. *Distinguishing Traits of Christian Character*. New York, NY: American Tract Society, no date).

Tileston, Mary Wilder, editor. *Joy and Strength*. Minneapolis, MN: World Wide Publications, 1901, 1929.

Willoughby, Robert. *John*. Camp Hill, PA: Christian Publications, Inc., 1999.

OLD TESTAMENT

GENESIS
1:26...February 27
3:9 ....September 30
5:24..May 27
17:1, 3...October 21

EXODUS
3:14 ....January 31
15:2 ....July 16
29:46 ....September 29
33:14...May 7
34:29...May 3

LEVITICUS
20:7 ....April 28

DEUTERONOMY
13:4 ....June 6
30:6..May 2

JOSHUA
1:8...May 11
1:9...December 22
24:15..May 19
24:15-16..July 20

JUDGES
5:20..December 23

FIRST SAMUEL
15:22 ....April 18

SECOND SAMUEL
22:50 ....September 16

FIRST CHRONICLES

16:29 ....April 21
28:9..August 1
29:11 ....September 27

SECOND CHRONICLES

6:14..February 26
15:15..December 12
19:9, 11..November 1

JOB

22:21 ....March 29
22:29..May 18
27:6 ....July 6
34:32..February 20
36:10, 22..September 19

PSALMS

1:6 ....June 16
4:4 ....November 5
5:3 ....October 12
5:12 ....October 13
16:8 ....January 19
16:11 ....September 11
18:1..August 2
21:13..December 23
22:22 ....November 21
22:4-5 ....November 28
25:5 ....October 27
25:10..December 19
25:11 ....October 14
27:8 ....January 13
27:14..February 22
29:2 ....April 10

31:19 ....June 15

34:3 ....July 24

37:4 ....April 11

40:8..February 5

42:1..February 24

45:7 ....April 6

45:7-8 ....July 1

47:7-8 ....October 16

51:2, 10 ....January 25

51:6-7 ....December 26

51:10...May 23

62:11 ....November 4

63:1-2 ....September 25

63:5-6..June 25

63:8 ....July 10

75:6-7..January 22

83:1 ....September 9

84:2 ....April 18

85:6 ....March 15

85:8..February 4

91:1 ....April 16

95:6-7..April 29

96:9 ....April 23

97:10...May 26

99:5 ....September 6

99:9..August 28

100:4 ....October 11

103:17...December 31

104:1 ....July 25

115:1 ....March 13

115:1, 3 ....December 23

119:10 ....June 28
119:103-104 ....December 21
119:130 ....July 29
119:137-138 ....August 26
128:1-2 ....February 16
133:1-3 ....March 27
139:7 ....September 29
139:7, 10 ....March 28
139:8-10 ....September 29
139:23-24 ....December 20
145:1-2 ....September 7
146:5 ....August 24

PROVERBS

2:6-7 ....March 18
3:5 ....May 4
3:6 ....May 25
3:13 ....June 7
8:10 ....March 21
8:13 ....April 6
9:10 ....August 23
12:12 ....August 12
13:15 ....August 14
15:3 ....September 26
21:21 ....July 5
22:4 ....May 5

SONG OF SOLOMON

2:4 ....November 21

ISAIAH

1:16 ....January 5
6:1 ....May 21
6:5 ....August 23

6:6-7...March 8

26:8...September 4

30:15...February 21

32:18...December 27

33:14..October 14

35:8...April 25

49:13...October 3

55:7..October 22

57:15..May 1

63:9-10...October 23

JEREMIAH

1:8-9...September 28

6:16...December 29

7:23...December 30

9:24...April 1

EZEKIEL

33:15...August 21

36:26...January 8

36:27...January 9

JOEL

2:27..December 8

2:28-29..December 6

2:28, 31...December 9

AMOS

3:3...December 17

5:15..July 4

MICAH

3:8..April 2

5:4...September 18

ZEPHANIAH

3:17 ....November 20

ZECHARIAH

4:6 ....March 31
4:6 ....September 18
8:13 ....September 23

NEW TESTAMENT

MATTHEW

3:11 ....November 7
3:16 ....May 22
3:17 ....July 11
4:10 ....April 8
5:3 ....March 17
5:6 ....May 6
5:6 ....October 9
5:8 ....December 10
5:13 ....April 15
6:24 ....December 13
7:17 ....May 24
7:24 ....April 4
7:24 ....July 23
12:18 ....October 24
12:30 ....February 14
12:33 ....August 30
12:35 ....March 9
16:24 ....October 5
18:20 ....February 28
22:37 ....October 3
25:32,46 ....February 14

26:33-34	May 23
27:22	March 4

MARK

1:11	September 1
9:23	July 8
9:23-24	November 17
12:32-33	May 20
16:15	April 8

LUKE

1:30-32, 35	December 25
1:35	March 11
1:45	March 16
2:14	December 24
2:16	December 25
3:22	March 24
5:8	September 26
9:23	February 29
9:34-35	March 3
10:27	October 19
11:9-11	December 16
11:13	December 16
12:32	November 22
15:6	November 21
15:10	April 3
22:42	July 21
24:32	July 7
24:49	February 22
24:49	April 8
24:49	October 28
24:49	December 6

JOHN

1:1 ....December 24

1:1-2 ....July 11

1:10-11 ....September 5

1:12 ....February 9

1:13 ....February 19

1:32 ....January 16

3:5 ....February 7

3:8 ....November 2

3:16 ....February 1

3:17 ....June 9

3:27 ....July 29

3:36 ....February 14

4:14 ....June 22

4:23 ....January 14

4:23-24 ....October 12

4:24 ....April 9

5:24 ....March 5

6:35 ....October 9

6:63 ....November 4

7:17 ....November 18

7:38 ....November 24

7:38-39 ....March 5

7:39 ....December 18

8:31-32 ....February 15

8:32 ....February 14

8:32 ....February 16

8:34 ....October 1

9:31 ....April 30

10:10 ....April 5

10:27-28 ....October 1

12:3 ....July 2
14:2 ....June 23
14:6, 15 ....January 15
14:15 ....March 25
14:16 ....November 27
14:16-17..January 11
14:21...February 2
14:21..August 9
14:21, 23 ....April 4
14:23 ....January 12
14:23..December 10
14:24 ....April 22
14:26 ....January 7
15:5 ....October 31
15:9...December 3
15:10 ....April 4
15:11 ....October 18
15:26..December 4
16:7 ....January 10
16:8 ....January 27
16:13..December 2
16:13-15..June 30
17:3 ....January 6
19:11 ....October 26
19:30 ....July 12
20:22 ....June 18
21:16 ....March 19
22:12, 14, 17...June 23

ACTS

1:8 ....October 28
2:1 ....March 14

2:2 ....September 13
2:3 ....November 7
2:4 ....July 1
2:4 ....November 27
2:17 ....March 27
2:18 ....September 2
2:22-24..June 26
2:32..June 26
2:38..March 10
2:39..December 7
2:46..October 10
4:12..March 5
4:31..February 10
4:31..July 1
5:13..April 2
5:32..April 4
5:32..December 16
7:55..July 1
9:17-18..November 6
10:38..March 11
10:38..August 4
10:44..January 29
10:44..July 1
17:24..March 1
17:11..November 12

ROMANS

1:5..August 26
1:8..August 25
5:5..August 2
5:5..August 7
6:2..May 16

6:4 ....January 2
6:6 ....September 14
6:7-8 ....December 14
6:13 ....April 19
6:15 ....September 12
6:16 ....January 17
6:17 ....February 12
6:17-18 ....April 4
6:19 ....June 5
6:22 ....May 28
6:23 ....February 3
7:19 ....November 11
8:1 ....January 4
8:2 ....March 2
8:4 ....May 17
8:5 ....December 11
8:7 ....January 21
8:9 ....September 15
8:9 ....November 23
8:10 ....December 1
8:11 ....August 4
8:13 ....August 29
8:16 ....February 11
8:18 ....June 8
8:26 ....February 25
10:38 ....August 4
11:33 ....July 26
12:1 ....February 18
12:1-2 ....December 16
12:2 ....June 14
12:4 ....March 7

14:11-12..July 17
14:19...May 9
15:6..December 18
15:13 ....October 29
16:25, 27 ....August 9

FIRST CORINTHIANS

2:9..February 23
2:10..February 23
2:12..May 8
2:14 ....October 25
2:16..July 28
3:2 ....July 15
3:13 ....March 12
3:16..May 13
3:17, 23..November 8
6:20 ....July 14
10:31 ....March 16
10:31 ....October 2
12:3 ....June 4
12:7 ....November 4
12:12, 14 ....May 29
12:27..August 11
13..August 2
13:1 ....November 13
13:4 ....October 17
13:13..August 8

SECOND CORINTHIANS

3:3 ....January 30
3:17 ....November 15
4:4 ....January 23
4:5 ....July 31

4:7 ....March 26
4:11..August 5
4:18..August 10
5:1..August 27
5:17 ....April 17
5:21 ....July 3
9:8..August 17
10:5 ....January 20
10:12 ....September 3
11:3..February 8
12:9 ....June 10
13:5 ....November 23

GALATIANS

2:20 ....March 20
3:2..December 16
4:6 ....November 23
4:6 ....December 28
5:16, 25..November 30
5:22..August 2
5:22-23 ....August 12
5:24 ....April 7
5:25 ....December 5
6:8..August 15
6:8 ....October 30
6:10 ....June 11
6:14 ....June 1
6:17 ....July 21

EPHESIANS

1:4 ....April 26
2:4-5..October 20
2:6..June 13

2:8-9 ....February 13

3:20-21 ....October 4

4:13 ....June 7

4:22-23 ....January 1

4:24 ....June 19

4:30 ....January 3

4:30 ....October 23

5:1-2 ....October 17

5:8 ....November 25

5:18 ....May 14

PHILIPPIANS

3:3 ....October 15

3:7, 10 ....June 2

3:14 ....August 6

3:20 ....June 11

4:8 ....January 24

4:13 ....June 30

COLOSSIANS

1:17-18 ....September 10

1:18-19 ....August 20

1:21-22 ....January 18

1:27 ....July 13

3:2 ....July 27

3:1, 3 ....November 29

3:16 ....April 12

3:16 ....June 3

3:17 ....September 8

FIRST THESSALONIANS

2:13 ....April 14

3:12-13 ....April 27

5:17-18 ....September 21

5:21 ....August 3

5:24 ....July 9

FIRST TIMOTHY

3:9..August 18

4:8 ....June 29

4:15 ....July 19

SECOND TIMOTHY

1:7 ....March 24

1:9 ....November 9

1:12 ....January 6

3:5 ....May 4

3:16 ....January 26

4:2 ....September 22

TITUS

2:12 ....October 2

3:5 ....June 27

HEBREWS

3:15 ....January 28

4:12..February 6

5:8 ....March 6

8:1 ....September 17

11:1 ....March 23

12:1..May 30

12:2 ....November 21

12:14 ....April 24

12:14..August 23

12:15..August 13

JAMES

1:18..February 17

1:22 ....April 4

1:22-25...April 4

1:27	September 20
2:22	April 4
2:26	April 13
4:3	July 18
4:7	March 21
4:8	July 22
4:8-9	November 10

FIRST PETER

1:5-6	May 15
1:8	June 12
1:13	May 10
1:15-16	April 20
2:2-3	November 26
3:15	October 6
4:10	August 11
4:11	August 19
5:8	May 12

SECOND PETER

1:4	August 16
1:6	August 22
3:18	November 3

FIRST JOHN

1:7	March 22
1:7	December 19
2:1	May 31
2:15	November 16
3:18	November 14
3:18-22	April 4
4:1	August 3
4:7	March 30
4:10	July 30

4:12	November 19
5:4	August 31
5:7	September 24
5:10	October 18

REVELATION

1:13	June 20
2:7	June 21
2:29	June 17
3:5	October 8
12:11	October 7
22:12	June 24
22:12,14,17	June 23
22:17	December 15

Titles by A.W. Tozer available through
your local Christian bookstore:

The Attributes of God
The Attributes of God Journal
The Best of A.W. Tozer
Born after Midnight
The Christian Book of Mystical Verse
Christ the Eternal Son
The Counselor
The Early Tozer: A Word in Season
Echoes from Eden
Faith Beyond Reason
Gems from Tozer
God Tells the Man Who Cares
How to Be Filled with the Holy Spirit
I Call It Heresy!
I Talk Back to the Devil
Jesus, Author of Our Faith
Jesus Is Victor
Jesus, Our Man in Glory
Let My People Go, A biography of Robert A. Jaffray
Man: The Dwelling Place of God
Men Who Met God
The Next Chapter after the Last
Of God and Men
Paths to Power
The Price of Neglect
The Pursuit of God
The Pursuit of God: A 31-Day Experience
*The Pursuit of Man (*formerly *The Divine Conquest)*
The Quotable Tozer
Renewed Day by Day, Vol. 1
Renewed Day by Day, Vol. 2

The Root of the Righteous
Rut, Rot or Revival
The Set of the Sail
The Size of the Soul
Success and the Christian
That Incredible Christian
This World: Playground or Battleground?
The Tozer CD-Rom Library
Tozer on the Holy Spirit
Tozer on Worship and Entertainment
The Tozer Pulpit 1
The Tozer Pulpit 2
Tozer Speaks to Students
Tozer Topical Reader
Tragedy in the Church: The Missing Gifts
A Treasury of A.W. Tozer
The Warfare of the Spirit
We Travel an Appointed Way
Whatever Happened to Worship?
Who Put Jesus on the Cross?
Wingspread, A biography of A.B. Simpson